Reinventing the City?

Reinventing the City?
Liverpool in Comparative Perspective

Edited by

Ronaldo Munck

First published 2003 by
Liverpool University Press
4 Cambridge Street
Liverpool L69 7ZU

British Library Cataloguing-in-Publication data
A British Library CIP record is available

ISBN 0-85323-797-2 cased
ISBN 0-85323-807-3 limp

Typeset by Servis Filmsetting Ltd, Manchester
Printed and bound in the European Union by Antony Rowe Ltd,
Chippenham, Wilts

Contents

Part III: Transformation

Acknowledgements

This book derives from a research project funded by the Joseph Rowntree Foundation, 'Coping and Hoping in Liverpool', which took place between November 1997 and April 1999 and examined perceptions and experiences of regeneration for residents in two areas of Liverpool, the Dingle and Speke. This resulted in the publication of *Neighbourhood Images in Liverpool: 'It's All Down to the People'*, York: Joseph Rowntree Foundation, 1999. Transcripts of the original interviews and focus groups used in this book are held at the Globalisation and Social Exclusion Unit, University of Liverpool.

Notes on the contributors

Gideon Ben-Tovim is Honorary Senior Research Fellow in the Department of Sociology, Social Policy and Social Work Studies at the University of Liverpool.

Karen Evans is a Lecturer in Sociology at the University of Liverpool.

Colette Fagan is Senior Lecturer in Sociology at the University of Manchester.

Barry Goldson is Senior Lecturer in Social Work at the University of Liverpool.

David Hall is Senior Lecturer in Applied Sociology at the University of Liverpool.

Peris Jones is a Research Officer at the Norwegian Institute of Human Rights.

John Lansley is an Honorary Research Fellow in the Department of Sociology, Social Policy and Social Work Studies at the University of Liverpool.

Richard Meegan is Reader at the European Institute for Urban Affairs at Liverpool John Moores University.

Ronaldo Munck is Professor of Political Sociology at the University of Liverpool.

Tony Novak is a Lecturer in Social Policy at the University of Liverpool.

Barney Rooney is an Honorary Research Fellow at the Department of Sociology, Social Policy and Social Work Studies at the University of Liverpool.

Saskia Sassen is the Ralph Lewis Professor of Sociology at the University of Chicago and Centennial Visiting Professor at the London School of Economics.

Ola Uduku is a Lecturer in Architecture at the University of Strathclyde.

Stuart Wilks-Heeg is a Lecturer in Social Policy at the University of Liverpool.

Foreword

Saskia Sassen

The observations of the men and women, young and old, from the two poor neighbourhoods in Liverpool at the centre of this book are both harrowing and enormously illuminating. They remind us, as the editor notes, that they are more than cannon fodder for the community 'participation' exercises of experts. They bring to life the reality of urban poverty as a complex and highly differentiated condition, and of the urban poor as knowing, aware of how they are perceived, aware of the power of mainstream representations of their condition and of who they are. These men and women also tell us that they are proud of some aspects of their communities even as they are aware that these are misrepresented or obscured by more negative overarching images, proud of themselves even as they understand that they may be considered failures by the broader social system and may indeed never live up to their potential given the limitations of their situation. These residents know that they are not simply a 'suitable case for treatment' as experts would have it.

Some of the authors in this book move deeply into the specifics of these two neighbourhoods and do so through a diversity of analytic pathways. Fagan moves in through the optic of gender, Uduku through ethnicity, Goldson and Lansley through age, Hall through visual representations, Rooney through community development, and Ben-Tovim through Liverpool's futures. Others (Evans, Wilks-Heeg, Meegan, Jones and Novak) locate Liverpool and the issue of urban regeneration in a broader spatio-temporal frame without losing a sharp focus on these two neighbourhoods. Collectively they produce a mosaic that begins to approximate to the complex reality captured succinctly in the statements of the residents themselves.

Through their diverse optics these authors make this collective effort into a particular type of multi-sited ethnography. Rather than studying simultaneously several sites to understand a particular dynamic or condition, they transform their single site into multiple sites. The collective work has the effect of unpacking its object of study – too easily represented through the summary image of urban poverty – and allows the reader to do his or her own re-synthesising. In doing this the book also resists the common strategy of comparisons between the urban poor and non-poor as the method to understand urban poverty.

In his introduction, Munck opens up the account to a larger spatio-temporal frame: Liverpool's historical role as a major slavery port, as a major industrial centre, and famously as the site of the poorly housed English working class. All are deeply imbricated with the city's present – in its imaginaries and in its particular articulations with the wider world. It is, perhaps, more difficult to understand Liverpool's current articulations with the wider world. There is a suggestion in some of the chapters that Liverpool today is a location on multiple global circuits.[1] As these traverse the city they become partly endogenised and produce opportunities and devastations.

Because globalisation is a complex, multi-scalar and multi-sited politico-economic system, its study requires a variety of research strategies. One of the organising themes in my research on cities and globalisation is that place is central to the multiple circuits through which economic globalisation is constituted and hence that local specificities assume a whole new importance (Sassen, 1998: ch1). The capabilities for global operation, coordination and control contained in the new information technologies and in the power of transnational corporations *need to be produced, managed, serviced*. Looking at it this way, we recover the material conditions, production sites and place-boundedness that are also part of the globalisation and the information economy.

Introducing cities in an analysis of economic globalisation allows us to reconceptualise processes of economic globalisation not just as cross-border networks but also as concrete economic complexes situated in specific places. A focus on cities decomposes the nation-state into a variety of sub-national components, some profoundly articulated with the global economy and others not (see, for example, Low, 1999). Here the particularities of Liverpool, its economic distance from London and its past role in the world economy, may all gain a new meaning in the current phase of globalisation. These dynamics also signal the declining significance of the national economy as a unitary category in the global economy. And even if in good part this was a unitary category largely constructed in political discourse and policy, it has become even less of a fact since the late 1980s.[2]

In the final section of this brief foreword I would like to pick up on Ben-Tovim's notion of the futures for Liverpool and Munck's questions about globalisation and city politics. The space of the city is a far more concrete space for politics than that of the nation. It becomes a place where non-formal political actors can be part of

---

[1] The new urban spatiality thus produced is partial in a double sense: it accounts for only part of what happens in cities and what cities are about, and it inhabits only part of what we might think of as the space of the city, whether this be understood in terms of a city's administrative boundaries or in the sense of the multiple public imaginaries that may be present in different sectors of a city's residents. Yet, though partial, it becomes part of the city.

[2] Through the Internet, local initiatives become part of a global network of activism without losing the focus on specific local struggles. It enables a new type of cross-border political activism, one centred in multiple localities yet intensely connected digitally. This is in my view one of the key forms of critical politics that the Internet can make possible: a politics of the local with a big difference – these are localities that are connected with one another across a region, a country or the world. The fact that the network is global does not mean that it all has to happen at the global level.

the political scene in a way that is much more difficult at the national level. Nationally politics needs to run through existing formal systems, whether the electoral system or the judiciary (for example when suing agencies). National politics is the realm of formal political actors. Non-formal political actors are rendered invisible in the space of national politics.

The space of the city accommodates a broad range of political activities – squatting, demonstrations against police brutality, neighbourhood activism, fighting for the rights of immigrants and the homeless, the politics of culture and identity, gay and lesbian and queer politics. Much of this becomes visible on the street. Much of urban politics is concrete, enacted by people rather than dependent on massive media technologies. Street-level politics makes possible the formation of new types of political subjects who do not have to go through the formal political system. The large city of today, especially the global city, emerges as a strategic site for these new types of operations. It is a strategic site for global corporate capital, but is also one of the sites where the formation of new claims by non-formal political actors materialises and assumes concrete forms (Isin, 2000). Those who lack power, those who are disadvantaged, outsiders, discriminated minorities, can gain *presence* in cities, presence vis-à-vis power and presence vis-à-vis one another. It is not simply a matter of having or not having power. There are new hybrid bases from which to act.

References

Isin, Engin F. (ed.) (2000), *Democracy, Citizenship and the Global City*, London and New York: Routledge

Low, S. (1999), *Theorising the City: The New Urban Anthropology Reader*, New Brunswick and London: Rutgers University Press

Sassen, Saskia (1998), *Globalization and its Discontents*, New York: New Press

Introduction: The City, Globalisation and Social Transformation

Ronaldo Munck

The city has long been a privileged site for critical social inquiry given its undisputed centrality for human life in the modern era. More recently, there has been a surge of interest in the postmodern city, the exemplar being usually Los Angeles. We also hear much of the 'global city' – the New Yorks, Londons and Tokyos of the world – linked together through the flows of finance. Yet somewhere like Liverpool – arguably neither postmodern nor global – is studied mainly in relation to its social problems and the perennial schemes for urban regeneration it has been subjected to over recent decades. This volume seeks to redress the balance by making Liverpool its focus but with a purpose that is firmly comparative and general. This introductory chapter sets the scene for the various contributions by re-examining the postmodern global city thesis, surveying the various attempts at regenerating cities like Liverpool, exploring the diverse connections between the local and the global in the city, studying various forms of (re)presenting the city discursively, and, last but not least, critically examining attempts and prospects for transforming the city.

The Postmodern Global City

Peter Hall, in his influential study *The World Cities*, argued some time ago that 'there are certain great cities, in which a disproportionate share of the world's most important business is conducted' (Hall, 1966: 7). These world cities are the seats of national government, crucial nodes in the flow of trade and finance and cultural powerhouses. With globalisation – a qualitative advance of economic internationalisation since the mid-1980s – the importance of these global cities has, if anything, increased. In the new dynamic international system we call globalisation, the great cities play a pivotal role in its variable configuration. As Saskia Sassen shows in *The Global City*, 'a combination of spatial dispersion and global integration has created a new strategic role for major cities' (Sassen, 1991: 3). This includes, pre-eminently, being a command point in the organisation and reproduction of the global economic system, a key location for finance, which has now replaced manufacturing as the leading economic sector, and a major site for the production and consumption of the goods, services and innovations being produced by the new capitalism.

In the literature on the city and globalisation we can detect two broad positions, albeit ones that might be complementary. On the one hand, Manuel Castells tends to emphasise how the power of the global city is mobilised *through* the networks of globalisation (Castells, 1996: 410). Emphasis is placed on the global focus more than on the city as a site of globalisation. For Saskia Sassen, on the other hand, 'place is central to many of the circuits through which economic globalisation is constituted' (Sassen, 1999: 171). By placing the city (as place) at the centre of the process of economic globalisation we reconceptualise the city and globalisation debates. What Sassen's analysis leads to are three central propositions:

1. While globalisation leads to dispersal and flows, it is also embedded in the global city where its central functions of management and coordination are organised.
2. Globalisation does not just 'happen', nor does the 'magic hand' of the market just run it; rather the network of global cities designs, manages and services the new global economy.
3. The new global economy as a highly networked system requires a network of global cities which compete but which also create a division of functions to provide the necessary infrastructure and resources. (Sassen, personal communication)

Against the 'globalisers' who argue that place no longer matters, Sassen thus places globalisation firmly within the mega-cities that are one of the crucial spatial and social manifestations of the globalisation processes. For Sassen, 'Global cities become the sites of immense concentrations of economic power, while cities that were once major manufacturing centres suffer inordinate declines' (Sassen, 1994: 210). The winners in this process are able to agglomerate the necessary resources and skills in these central locations (or nodes) that service and reproduce the new globalised economy. So, globalisation is not 'out there' but in the corridors of power (and the mean streets) of New York as a new geography of centres and margins is shaped. For Manuel Castells the emphasis is on the flows he sees as characteristic of what he calls the new 'network society' (Castells, 1996). For Castells,

> The global city is not a place, but a process. A process by which centres of production and consumption of advanced services, and their ancillary local societies, are connected in a global network, while simultaneously downplaying the linkages with their hinterlands on the basis of information flows. (Castells, 1996: 386)

The power of the mega-city is mobilised precisely through the global networks it is part of, and it is the resources flowing through these that empower certain groups in the New Yorks of the world. It does not seem impossible, however, to work with an understanding of the city as part of this 'space of flows' but also with a critical political economy of the city focused on power struggles within its social and spatial boundaries.

At this point I think it may be useful to explain why the city and globalisation debates might be pertinent to somewhere like Liverpool, which is not a London or even a sub-regional urban centre such as Manchester. Castells, to my mind, explains the process clearly:

> The global city phenomenon cannot be reduced to a few urban cores at the top of an hierarchy. It is a *process* that connects advanced services, producer centres, and markets in a global network [. . .] Inside each country, the networking architecture reproduces itself into regional and local centres, so that the *whole system* becomes interconnected at the global level. (Castells, 1996: 380)

The scale and the intensity of connections may vary but all parts of the world system are interconnected. Globalisation has led to a new regionalisation and, for many commentators, a new localism. Being connected does not imply a simple interdependence, because the process is uneven and the 1970s dependency analysis may still have purchase. What are interdependent are the relations between the global, regional and local logics. What I am saying – against any 'out there–in here' analysis of globalisation as counterposed to the local, conceived of as fixed and traditional – is that globalisation takes shape in particular locales.

If we take a broad historic sweep we can also see how Liverpool always already was a global city in a different way or in a different time. In his popular history of Liverpool, Tony Lane refers to its inhabitants' sense of superiority at the turn of the last century: 'The swagger derived from an inherited collage of beliefs celebrating the significance of a complete seaport economy at the heart of the largest global empire of the modern epoch' (Lane, 1997: 131). The 'triangular trade' between Europe, Africa and America (manufactured goods for slaves, slaves for raw materials) that helped build British hegemony had Liverpool as a key player. Liverpool's global connections created its docks, banks and factories but also its identity as an early global city. As Cameron and Crooke put it, 'Liverpool was not just the economic capital of the slave trade, it was also its political capital' (Cameron and Crooke, 1992: 24). Later, Liverpool became a key staging post for Irish emigration to America and a major recipient of Irish emigrants itself. Liverpool was thus always turned outwards to the Irish Sea and beyond to the Atlantic, symbolising its overseas connections and their precedence over any organic connections with the rest of Britain.

But, as with marriages, what led to Liverpool's early success would also lead to its decline from the mid-twentieth century onwards. This is the theme of Chapter 2 below by Stuart Wilks-Heeg. Following the decline of the transatlantic trade after the inter-war heyday, there was a spate of manufacturing activity in Liverpool, but by the time that had come to fruition it was the era of de-industrialisation. Tony Lane refers appositely to 'an inescapable chain of accelerating external economic forces' (Lane, 1997: 134) hitting Liverpool. The social dislocation caused by these external economic factors can be gauged by the decline of the city's inhabitants from 870,000 just before the Second World War to 440,000 by the time of the 2001 Census. If the rise of Liverpool during the eighteenth century was prodigious, its decline since the mid-twentieth century is equally dramatic. While slavery and colonialism helped make Liverpool, it is the global connection that helped unmake it, as Richard Meegan explains: 'Liverpool's recent decline is similarly set within a new global economic and political context and a newly emerging web of global relationships: the evolution of a new international divison of labour [. . .] and the making of a "new Europe"' (Meegan, 1995: 84). In this way, Liverpool can be seen to be a post-colonial city as much as any metropolis of the so-called Third World.

While Liverpool may be a post-industrial city it is not readily associated with postmodernism. For Ed Soja, Los Angeles epitomises the decentred, decentralised metropolis characterised by post-Fordist working relations and a postmodern cultural setting typical of the flexible (even disorganised) capital accumulation regime of the future (Soja, 1989). The urban social structure is a fragmented quilt or mosaic of different social groups and cultures. This postmodern urban landscape is eclectic and celebrates difference and polyvocalism. There is a belief that 'Every single American city that *is* growing, is growing in the fashion of Los Angeles' (Garreau, 1991: 3). While for some, Los Angeles symbolises the American Dream, for others it is the American Nightmare (Davis, 1990), characterised by repression and poor conditions for its 'non-white' majority population. While Jonathan Raban had famously foreseen the postmodern city as a 'soft city' – 'the city goes soft, it awaits the imprint of an identity [. . .] it invites you to remake it, to consolidate it into a shape you can live in' (Raban, 1974: 11) – for Mike Davis, Los Angeles represents, perhaps more realistically, 'the hard edge of postmodernity' (Davis, 1992: 155).

Even if we accept the ideal of a decentralised, pluralist and innovative postmodern society, there are problems in applying the concept to a city such as Liverpool. In what way can a 'dirty old town' in the de-industrialised north of England be described as postmodern? Certainly, Liverpool – in spite of its muchvaunted 'nightlife' – seems hardly a city of fun and pleasure for the majority of its inhabitants. Take, for example, shopping – on which postmodern urban theorists wax lyrical in relation to North American shopping malls – and examine the practices of a citizen in one of the outlying north of England urban estates. Thus one study of Manchester, while not seeking 'to deny the presence in these cities of the kinds of casual and even pleasurable shopping described in so much of the contemporary writing [. . .] on the postmodern city' (Taylor et al., 1996: 156), goes to show the prevalence of a more 'subsistence' bargain-hunting mode of shopping for most. Or, as a resident of Speke (an outlying estate) put it in our Rowntree study of Liverpool, 'If you want to buy shoes for your kids you've got to drag them into town . . . and they start playing up as soon as you get there . . . McDonald's, that's the first thing they say . . . You go into town to get something specific and you end up coming home without what you wanted, and the kids with a "Happy Meal"' (Andersen et al., 1999: 22).

Postmodern urbanism operates with a conception of a radical break with the past. The new globalised postmodern city is seen as a homogeneous intervention that somehow flattens history and culture. The local/social is seen to dissolve under the influence of the global/economic. Ian Taylor, Karen Evans and Penny Fraser, in their study of two 'not-postmodern' cities (Manchester and Sheffield), argue against this interpretation, that 'the current regeneration of old industrial cities (at least in the north of England) actually reworks and re-represents the facts of local identity and difference, and therefore, importantly, preserves and symbolises these identities, albeit in a modified fashion by comparison with the custom and practice of the modernist period' (Taylor et al., 1996: 35). It is local structures of feeling that shape and set the parameters of the post-industrial (but not necessarily postmodern) city. There is no tabula rasa in relation to local history, culture and class struggle. Our study of two neighbourhoods in Liverpool (Andersen et al., 1999) showed how even in the same city its history and community were 'lived' in very different ways and thus the prospects for regeneration and for community development varied considerably. These themes are developed in some of the chapters that follow: in Chapter 1, Karen Evans develops a broad sweep of the contemporary British city, in Chapter 9 Tony Novak discusses critically what 'living in the city' means today, and in Chapter 11 Barney Rooney deconstructs the all-pervasive concept of 'community development' which comes and goes in discourses around the contemporary city.

If Liverpool was in the past 'a complete seaport economy' (Lane, 1997: 131), it could today be seen as a 'decentred' city, and in this sense postmodern. The port and its global role are no longer a unifying focus and neither is manufacturing. The attempt to have a culture-led regeneration has not been as successful as in Glasgow, for example. In short, Liverpool is still characterised by what it was rather than having reinvented itself. We cannot envisage the same totalising gaze Engels developed for Manchester in *The Condition of the Working Class in England* (Engels, 1969) being articulated for Liverpool today. This big modernist picture is no longer possible. What Liverpool is, or might be, is necessarily fluid and even the boundaries of the debate are fuzzy. The language to describe this transition to a new city will also need to be fluid, open and non-necessitarian. The debates on regenerating the city do not generally accept this interpretation and, on the contrary, they seek to impose a unifying logic – regeneration – on a social and spatial world that has become decentred and thus post-structuralist. What this might mean for its citizens I examine in subsequent sections.

The Local in the Global

What the last section has shown, above all else, is the importance of the local in the new global order. Michael Porter, guru of the competitive 'global class' city, recognises that competitive advantage 'is created and sustained through a highly localised process' (Porter, 1999: 19). It is to the complexity of this localised process and world that we now turn. Our knowledge of globalisation has not kept pace with the globalisation of knowledge (Appadurai, 1999) and our categories of analysis tend to be a bit crude. For example, in response to globalisation many critics have argued for reasserting the power of the local (e.g. Cox, 1997). This has a certain attraction in that it is seen to 'bring people back in' to the workerless story or meta-narrative of globalisation. But ultimately, it seems simply to assert a militant place-based particularism against the evils of an abstract 'globalisation as demonisation'. Liverpool has already suffered the consequences in the 1980s, under the Militant administration of the city, of a conception of politics based on 'us against the world', in this case the evils of Thatcherism, which were never going to be defeated by one (declining) city. The local/global connections must be conceived in a more subtle way if they are to serve as a basis for a strategy of social transformation.

It is common now in the globalisation literature to see reference to 'glocalisation', a process supposedly describing the new global–local intermingling or interpenetration. In cultural studies in particular this term has come to denote a new hybrid blend or fusion (for example, in the 'localising' of McDonald's in Korea). Perhaps there is a somewhat too benign flavour to this metaphor when applied to the de-industrialised city in the era of globalisation. Ash Amin has, however, referred interestingly to 'the urban social fragments and hybridity generated by "in here-out there" mingling' (Amin, 1997: 134). If the response hitherto has been to make the city work in the interests of those 'out there', there is no reason why we cannot start from the interests of those 'in here' (i.e. the city). As Amin puts it, 'the challenge is to mobilise diversity as a source of both social cohesion and urban economic competitiveness' (Amin, 1997: 134). The big issue today in debates on the future(s) of capitalism is 'trust' (see Fukuyama, 1995). A shared sense of reciprocity, trust and citizenship can be and is being generated in cities. That is a resource in terms of 'social capital' and political confidence that cannot be neglected.

To be provocative, I think we can now plausibly reverse the feminist and environmental movement slogan of the 1970s which bade us 'Think globally, act locally'. Local politics is not just given or predetermined by global aggregation of interests. The much-vaunted 'death of distance' due to the time-space compression (Harvey, 1989) inherent in globalisation can certainly be exaggerated. A recent study of city politics concludes that 'local politics in a global era are best understood in terms of the ideas, institutions and interests shaping local policy processes' (Clarke and Gaile, 1997: 28). Certainly the new economics of globalisation sets the parameters in which any city operates but so also does the regional and sub-regional level. There is no reason why a Liverpool cannot develop a northwest of England perspective, or a Glasgow a European perspective, and not just sink into the globalisation blues. Globalisation has created a far greater degree of social polarisation at the local level but it has also generated a new localism that can knit together a social and political alliance to meet human needs at a local level. Globalisation is the context but not the sole horizon of possibilities if we consider the benefits of increased international transactions at all levels of human existence.

What we call globalisation has affected cities everywhere, even those we call 'provincial', in making them more permeable to 'outside' factors, be it migration, global consumerism or the global mass media. Michael Pryke refers to cities as 'places of multiple connections' which can no longer be thought of in isolation or as having some mythical 'fixed coherence' (Pryke, 1999: 326). A city is not just a place on the map: it is a site of power, difference and contestation. The city is cut across by multiple economic, social, political and cultural flows and interconnections. This relational perspective is also, necessarily, fluid, since these interconnections are constantly changing as well as intensifying in scope and depth. Amin and Graham usefully conceptualise cities as 'places of intersection between many webs of social, cultural and technological flow, and the superimposition of these relational webs in the physical space of cities' (Amin and Graham, 1999: 9). Another (more chronological) way of seeing the city is as a palimpsest, a manuscript or text in which layers of writing (or meaning?) are superimposed on the original. Except that, rather than effacing the original, the new layers of the city often coexist with the earlier ones.

The global city analysis strengthens these points in a number of ways, even if Liverpool's entry into this category must be open to debate. The new globalised professional classes need to find in a city the residential amenities, the services and the low-paid (often informal) workers to provide these. Much of Liverpool's 'regeneration' seems to be directed to this purpose as much as 'empowering' the poor. Today's urbanisation (as against suburbanisation) is driven largely by the needs of this professional class, which generates a growing demand for central city space and luxury enclaves. Thus the global city can be seen not only as a site in strategic cross-border circuits but also as a set of contested social spaces where the politics of place becomes the main axis of city dynamics (Sassen, pers. comm.).

If cities must necessarily be conceived of as 'open' in the era of globalisation, they must also be understood as diverse and conflictual in essence. In relating to a city such as Liverpool we have two main prejudices to contend with. First, there is a long-standing myth of the classless northern city characterised by tight-knit 'communities'. A casual acquaintance with the TV serial *Coronation Street* will give you the picture. Second, as Logan and Molotch write, there is a certain tradition of Marxism which gives little attention to neighbourhood life, but when it does it has assumed a homogeneity among almost all neighbourhoods, regardless of race, ethnicity or location (Logan and Molotch, 1987: 101). This would derive either from a productivist and economistic perspective that believed the 'class struggle' only occurred between labour and capital in factories, or from the 'Castells school' in its structuralist phase. From that perspective there was a belief that sharing use of the same services would generate a struggle dynamic based on 'collective consumption' issues. We are now more sensitised to differences based on age, gender, ethnicity, sexual orientation and locality among others. Our Rowntree Project on two Liverpool neighbourhoods, indeed, placed these differences at the centre of our research and analysis.

The city is inevitably always a gendered and a racialised space. As one Liverpool woman told us, 'The men put on the suits and try to be helpful but basically the women run the homes . . . they also run all those types of [community] groups' (Andersen et al., 1999). When it came to the spatial definition of a neighbourhood, many residents of a predominantly 'white' area stressed that they were not part of the contiguous well-known 'black' area. Every aspect of social life, street life and political life in the city is cut across by racial and gender differences. Age, too, is a constant feature in social differentiation. Youth has come to symbolise 'social exclusion' and elders have come to signify 'dependency'. Our study cut across widely cherished stereotypes. Many young people were reflective on their 'troublesome' image and had a general vision for their area. Elders seemed well aware of the frustrations of youth in their area and were not keen to scapegoat them. In the chapters following, Colette Fagan (Chapter 5) deals in detail with gender perspectives while Ola Uduku (Chapter 6) focuses on ethnic minority perspectives and Barry Goldson (Chapter 7) and John Lansley (Chapter 8) focus respectively on the particular views of youth and elders.

In a recent reader on the city, Gerry Mooney argues that Britain's deprived council estates are

> all too frequently portrayed as intense, uniform locales of conflict and unrest, housing homogeneous groups of 'socially excluded' people. Little thought is given to their internal social and spatial differentiation and heterogeneity, to the strategies which residents adopt to 'cope', and to residents' day-to-day struggles with public agencies. (Mooney, 1999: 73)

It is important to note, finally, that the Liverpool Rowntree study, while stressing social differentiation and the diverse perspectives, did find that 'in the last instance' (apologies to Marx) there was a shared working-class identity and a local identity of considerable coherence, especially when faced with what were perceived as external threats.

Regenerating the City

Liverpool has been the recipient of almost every urban regeneration initiative in Britain since the 1960s. This is a story recounted in detail by Richard Meegan in Chapter 3 and, from different perspectives, also by Peris Jones in Chapter 4 and Barney Rooney in Chapter 11. Liverpool, along with the north of England generally, has been seen as a prime candidate for regeneration given the consistently higher than average rates of unemployment, homelessness and poverty in the city region. The problem has been seen to lie with the estates, those sites where popular and academic attention (Power, 1998) have focused on crime, poor housing and a supposed general social and moral decline. The culmination of many failed initiatives has been New Labour's New Deal for Communities, which in the course of 1999 began to promulgate the concept of 'joined-up' thinking and action to deal with problems that are, indeed, clearly interrelated. The New Deal for Communities was pledged to 'target money on the most deprived neighbourhoods to: improve job prospects; bring together investment in buildings and investment in people; and, improve neighbourhood management and the delivery of local services' (DETR, 1998: 7). The mechanisms for its delivery would be through local partnerships and there was a commitment to sustain community involvement. While the major focus was, as always, on jobs, housing and health, there was a new emphasis on 'neighbourhood management' and on 'antisocial behaviour'.

What has emerged, in the long trial and error process of urban regeneration initiatives, is an integrated approach to sustainable improvements in urban life. It would seem that national-level initiatives could only achieve their objectives through local-level actions. Indeed, a Joseph Rowntree Foundation review of area-regeneration programmes found that each area was different, with its own distinctive problems and opportunities (Joseph Rowntree Foundation, 1998). Nevertheless, this research did highlight certain general patterns and the need for regeneration initiatives to address certain key issues, including:

- understanding disadvantaged neighbourhoods – including the views of local people and the local assets available;
- bringing residents to the centre of regeneration-building skills and enhancing confidence to undertake projects with professionals;
- transforming mainstream services at the local level – developing a clear neighbourhood focus for services through partnerships;
- targeting economic development services – to create the training, jobs and finance to link growth with local regeneration;
- strengthening communities – to build community capacity so that long-term income is ensured; and
- ensuring a long-term commitment to sustainable neighbourhood regeneration – policy integration and visionary city leadership. (Joseph Rowntree Foundation, 1998)

While this would appear to be a coherent recipe for progressive transformation of deprived communities, we need to examine the broader context of who is actually involved in urban regeneration. Clearly, the communities themselves are interested, but business and government (both local and national) are the key players. In the era of globalisation, cities are becoming major competitive players. These cities are now 'managed', as are businesses, and not 'planned' as in the heyday of modernist urban planning. Michael Porter has codified what the new managed competitive city needs to do to succeed: 'We must stop trying to cure the inner city's problems by perpetually increasing social investment and hoping for economic activity to follow. Instead an economic model must begin with the premise that inner city businesses should be profitable' (Porter, 1999: 313). The cornerstone of this regeneration model is to seek the competitive advantage a modern city may enjoy and help it find a niche that is hard to replicate. This has led to the scramble to package and repackage cities across the world to make them more attractive to business. This model, which first sprang to prominence in Reagan's America, is now the accepted common sense lying behind most inner-city regeneration initiatives. That it is essentially a 'beggar thy neighbour' philosophy does not seem to concern its advocates.

What have emerged in many cities since the early 1980s are 'urban growth coalitions' committed to 'boosterism'. The classic definition is that of Molotch and Logan who refer to the new urban coalitions as 'a set of actors who push for local growth maximisation to increase returns from real estate manipulation and other business activities specifically dependent on local grown – collectively making up the "growth machine"' (Molotch and Logan, 1985: 144). That these policies are often socially regressive and environmentally destructive does not detract from the overall goal. Competition between places seems to take over from competition between businesses, and the city becomes a growth machine committed to boosting its local fortunes against other cities. Logan and Molotch call this 'the battle of the growth machines' (Logan and Molotch, 1987: 35). However, it is not at all clear whether this battle actually benefits the citizens of the places that are supposedly 'winning' or, for that matter, the public good in any generally recognisable way. What is clear is that community organisations can gain resources for redevelopment of their areas through entering these coalitions, in the same way that businesses and local government can gain through obtaining 'community support' for their growth machines when seeking, for example, to access European funding where the discourse of community 'participation' prevails.

The ideologies of the 'growth machines' tell us that a city is a place where 'people learn better and develop faster' (Rossabeth Moss Kanter, cited in Thrift, 1999: 283) if they develop the 'three Cs': concepts (new ideas or technologies), competence (high-quality products) and connections (international trade). If 'world class' status in one of the three Cs is not achieved the city inevitably becomes residualised or marginalised. To some extent this is the fate of Liverpool and other cities in the north of England; it is not exaggerating to see in Engels' descriptions of mid-nineteenth century Manchester a prescient picture of today's run-down housing estates in these northern cities. Taylor, Evans and Fraser refer eloquently to 'the silence or indifference – at least in public, political discussion – as to the lived character of these residualised places and territories' (Taylor et al., 1996: 291). The people living in these places feel forgotten and find regeneration to be somewhat hollow as far as their direct experience is concerned. Their expectations are hardly radical or unrealistic:

> We want to be recognised, to have the same things as other people, to be equal with the others. That's not asking a lot. We want our own shops, we want things to entertain the children rather than make a mess out of everything. We want councillors who will work for us rather than against us. (Andersen et al., 1999: 25)

What is remarkable is that research had to be commissioned in the late 1990s to find out what people wished for in these places.

While cities are now 'managed' to make them competitive in the world market they must also be governed. The issue of governance in the era of globalisation is a troubled one, and nowhere more so than in relation to the city. Governance today has a political but also a social and economic dimension; it involves governmental but also non-governmental institutions. Parts of the global economy are escaping control by direct political governance. National governments can come to office – as with New Labour – claiming that globalisation constrains their governmental choices. Yet cities have to be governed and not just managed because citizens live in them. It is not surprising that cities are not only sites of 'boosterism' and competitive advantage but also for social movements and radical democratic discourses. The city is a site for the powerful in their global quest for hegemony but it is also where the powerless live, dream and struggle. Nigel Thrift refers in this context to how the 'global cities can be seen as strategic sites within which hierarchies of power are most striking *and* most open to challenge' and refers to grassroots economic innovations such as LETS as 'possible economic contributions to the redefinition of citizenship as a more global-local concern' (Thrift, 1999: 305).

We find in regime theory an interesting new perspective on power and governance in the contemporary city (see Stoker, 1999) that helps us understand the complexity and the interdependence of the modern urban system. While it focuses on the role of business and government it does not neglect the role of disadvantaged groups and argues that 'politics matter'. For regime theory the internal politics of coalition building is crucial in determining the mode of governance in the city. While stressing the relationships between business interests and local government it also embraces the knowledge professionals (for example, urban planners and consultants of various kinds) and communities or their 'representatives'. In his model of urban governance, Jon Pierre distinguishes four ideal types:

1. **Managerial**
   Its objective is efficiency, its style pragmatic, its key instrument the contract and its evaluation criterion efficiency;
2. **Corporatist**
   Its objective is distribution, its style ideological, its key instrument deliberations and its evaluation criterion participation;
3. **Pro-growth**
   Its objective is growth, its style pragmatic, its key instrument partnerships, and its evaluation criterion growth;
4. **Welfare**
   Its objective is redistribution, its style ideological, its key instrument networks, and its evaluation criterion equity. (adapted from Pierre, 1999: 388)

For many cities we can recognise some of these models for particular periods, even if, in practice, they may be 'impure' or combined in their application. It is certainly possible to deploy this model, for example, in Liverpool to see how an alliance of pro-growth city councillors and officers, business interests, urban regeneration professionals and community 'representatives' has been created in recent years. We must also understand that this is a contingent political alliance and not necessarily a natural given. Equally, a common situation of de-industrialisation, for example, will not generate the same type of regime as Di Gaetano and Lawless's corporate study of Birmingham, Sheffield and Detroit shows. They found, rather, that 'despite remarkably common economic experiences, the structures and processes of governance developed in the three de-industrialised cities from 1980 to 1997 varied considerably both across cities and over time' (Di Gaetano and Lawless, 1999: 569). While corporatism has been a common international mode, managerialism is a mainly British phenomenon and clientelism more a US mode. It is inevitably local politics, even with a similar broad regime model being applied, that determines the precise contours, modalities and effectiveness of a given mode.

Finally it may be useful to stand back reflexively from the complex issues of regeneration and governance in the contemporary city and begin to think of the actual language of these discourses. For example, if we examine Liverpool First's Action Plan ('New Commitment to Regeneration'), we read at the start that: 'In the last decade, the political landscape of Liverpool has changed beyond recognition. Since the 1990s a spirit of pragmatism and co-operation has been evident' (LPG, 1999: 5). Later we are told that the three key 'drivers' for regeneration will be competitiveness, social justice and environmental sustainability. Not only is competitiveness placed first but its compatibility with the other two 'drivers' might at least be questionable. But we can assume that 'pragmatism' will prevail and cooperation will be secured from the community for the overriding need to build 'competitiveness' (itself a deeply ambiguous term). When later in the document we find a discussion of 'Local Community Empowerment Strategies' we must dig beneath the surface but it would seem that 'empowerment' is essentially about a partnership agreement: 'This will promote ways to engage communities and businesses and help them to become confident and informed partners' (LPG, 1999: 15). Language always reflects the power arrangements in a given society; it is never 'innocent' or transparent, and it gains authority from the discursive terrain it is embedded within.

As Rob Atkinson has pointed out, the competitiveness drive and the partnership model are 'firmly rooted in a discourse which prioritises the provision of a stable environment for business and the control of social protection costs' (Atkinson, 1997: 7). Thus we find that when official discourse refers to a 'partnership' the concept is usually seriously under-defined. It is bathed in a positive glow but its precise contours and nature are not really specified, beyond general aspirations to a form of 'synergy'. A dominant discourse is also well able to absorb and defuse contestatory elements which might challenge it. For example, the notion of 'empowerment' can be seen as quite radical as applied in Third World contexts, but when applied to urban regeneration the terms become even vaguer than those of 'partnership' (see Chapter 4 by Peris Jones). As Atkinson argues,

> If we are to move beyond such a position then it is essential [. . .] that genuine community empowerment requires not merely that the community be allowed to participate but that we rethink the language of participation in order to tackle imbalances in social, economic and political power. (Atkinson, 1997: 9)

In the Rowntree project *Neighbourhood Images in Liverpool* (Andersen et al., 1999) we found, indeed, that at all levels of the community and in local government there was a disputed discursive terrain around such concepts as 'participation' and the whole nature of 'regeneration'.

(Re)Presenting the City

> To put it polemically, there no such *thing* as a city. Rather, *the city* designates the space produced by the interaction of historically and geographically specific institutions, social relations of production and reproduction, practices of government, forms and media of

communication, and so forth [. . .] *The city*, then, is above all a representation. (Donald, 1992: 417)

Reacting against the excesses of the structuralist vision of the 1970s there is now considerable attention paid to 'the city as text'. David Hall relates in Chapter 10 how the 'image' of Liverpool is constructed, based in part on our Rowntree study and on work with young people with photography. Rather than seek a false coherence and unity in today's city we are bid to read it, and that implies that we can read it in different ways. In part, we are dealing with a paradigm shift here in terms of how we interpret the discourse of the city. Anthony King explains how the city was once the privileged territory where white Western male sociologists and urban planners inscribed their pet theories and models, but that it has now become 'the happy-hunting ground of film theorists, poets, art historians, writers, television producers, literary critics, and postmodern connoisseurs of all kinds' (King, 1996: 2). A degree of theoretical diversity and even disagreement may be necessary to move beyond outdated visions of the city and its discontents.

If someone were to arrive in Liverpool from Mars they would definitely have heard of the Beatles and the Albert Dock (the Slavery Museum?). If they were lucky they would have seen Alan Bleasdale's *Boys from the Blackstuff* and if they were unlucky they would have watched *Brookside*. The point is that we have a cultural image of places. That culture and history are also embodied in the buildings of Liverpool through which we can also 'read' the histories of colonialism, Irish emigration and urban decline. It is through these readings that we produce representations of the city. They exist at a discursive level even if they also have material representation. The cultural dimension of the city is vital in a number of ways. The 'cultural turn' in the social sciences and humanities, referred to above, leads to a situation where '[the] city as an object of analysis has been unbound' (Jacobs, 1993: 827). Furthermore, if we examine the recent history of cities such as Glasgow and Dublin, we see to what extent their cultural revival has led to real economic regeneration given the strong cultural element in globalisation.

It is also important to understand what the 'cultural turn' is not. When anthropologists ran out of exotic 'others' to study in the non-Western world (including the west of Ireland), they turned to the cities. In the new urban settings they did ethnography and they engaged in what Fox called an 'undignified scramble to find substitute savages in slums' (cited in Hannerz, 1980: 2). In the new exotic setting we could rediscover 'community' or rail against 'alienation' in the modern city. It is hardly surprising that radical urban sociologists such as Castells (1997) and Harvey (1973) rejected 'culturalism' in the 1970s. Today, it is more an issue of foregrounding language in that loose family of methods known as discourse analysis (see Howarth, 2000). The emphasis is on the interrelationship between language and power over representation. Michèle Barrett summarises Michel Foucault's *The Archaeology of Knowledge* admittedly 'a little polemically' as 'the production of "things" by "words"' (Barrett, 1992: 131). A discourse can thus be seen as a practice that forms the object of which it speaks. Thus 'Liverpool' as we know it, live it and (re)present it, is constructed historically, socially and politically, but also discursively in the films, plays and TV and newspaper reports about the city region.

As with other 'northern cities' Liverpool is often represented in the national media as a symbolic locale for some horrific crime, an example of a worthy urban regeneration initiative, or the site of an inspiring drama about urban unemployment. Yet there is very little basis for constituting 'the north' as a social/spatial site of special significance and we may, just as validly, refer to an east/west split in Britain. Yet the north exists discursively and George Orwell could refer in *The Road to Wigan Pier* to a 'strange country' above a line a little north of Birmingham where the 'real ugliness of industrialisation' began (Orwell, 1959). Certainly, the uneven development of British capitalism did result in a core and a periphery, in both economic and cultural terms. This spatial discourse marked and accentuated social divisions of power reflected in language and customs – in short, in culture. North of Watford lies the land of 'the British working class' as portrayed in films and plays. In these cultural products, the north becomes a real place: 'place becomes a signifier of character, a metaphor for the state of mind of the protagonists, in the well-worn naturalist tradition' (Andrew Higson, cited in Shields, 1991: 216).

The north, as the land of 'the working class', is yet another ethnographic construction of an Other. As Rob Shields puts it, it is 'an invention cast as the foreign "Other" of the socially constructed orderliness of the British nation centred around London' (Shields, 1991: 218). These images are notionally class images rendered spatially, but also gendered images. The 'salt of the earth' northern worker is also male, preferably a docker, a miner or steelworker. As, say, with the north of Ireland, where gender and religion are symbiotic in cultural images (Catholic/female; Protestant/male) so here manliness and northernness go hand in hand. Boss politics and labour politics in Liverpool have always been gendered, as epitomised in the macho-Marxism of the dismal Militant period. Now, it would be wrong to think that these discourses are simply distortions. Rob Shields is perfectly correct to stress 'the fact that the myths were not simple fictions but related in a complex manner with tangible conditions. In many cases, the images accentuated these conditions; in others, the images became self-fulfilling prophecies' (Shields, 1991: 245). This last point is essential to understanding the difficulties a city like Liverpool has in (re)presenting itself anew as an image-place given the long history of myth-making and 'deviance amplification'.

It is always also in the imagination, though, that a city can be reimagined. This is the theme of Gideon Ben-Tovim's Chapter 12 on the 'futures' of Liverpool. Discourse on the city has always been permeated with utopias, images of the 'good city'. Sociological language is somewhat 'cold' in this regard, and in its vain concern for 'scientificity' it often refuses to engage with change. In academic circles, as Taylor and co-authors argue, there has been 'an absence of the kind of engagement shown by the urban regeneration coalitions or from the pessimistic concerns of the urban retreatists' (Taylor et al., 1996: 312). While it is easy to critique and deconstruct some of the millenarian fantasies of the urban planners, alternative urban imaginaries are less easy to find. Yet we need to understand that a city is not just its buildings, it highways, its parks and its housing estates. As Nestor García Canclini writes in relation to Mexico City: 'Cities are also configured through images. These may be the plans that invent and order the city. But also, the sense of urban life is imagined through novels, songs and films, press stories, radio and television. The city becomes dense as it is loaded with heterogeneous fantasies' (García Canclini, 1997: 109). The programmed or managed city is overloaded as it overflows with multiple, individual and collective stories.

We can now go back to the theme of reading the city as a text. When Engels represented the Manchester of the 1840s in *The Condition of the Working Class in England* (Engels, 1969), 'This reading of the city, this perception and construction of it as a signifying structure, may be regarded [. . .] as prototypical for the nine-teenth century, and the first part of the twentieth' (Marcus, 1973: 232). Yet the late twentieth-century/early twenty-first-century city seems literally 'illegible'. It may be simply because the modernist paradigm has been exhausted, along with total-ising illusions that we can 'grasp' the city in its wholeness. Many writers on the city now complain that their language seems inadequate to the tasks of analysis (and change) at hand. The decentred city of today can only be grasped through the crit-ical and pluralist tools of an affirmative or emancipatory postmodernism (see Sousa Santos, 1999). The city of today is but a metaphor for the strange, new, post-modern, globalised world we are entering. Following Sharpe and Wallock I would, finally, note that, as the examples of Engels and Orwell (in his own way) show, 'learning how to read the city is a necessary part of learning how to change it' (Sharpe and Wallock, 1987: 39).

Transforming the City

There is now a widespread acceptance among policy makers and researchers that urban regeneration requires the cooperation of urban residents. A Joseph Rowntree Foundation report by Marilyn Taylor (1995) is entitled *Unleashing the Potential: Bringing Residents to the Centre of Regeneration.* Consultation with the community or its representatives is now mandatory for most national and European regeneration initiatives. Yet there is a widespread feeling in many of these 'disadvantaged' communities that residents are not in fact properly consulted and that, certainly, they have little actual power in relation to regeneration of their areas. In our Liverpool Rowntree study it was common for us to hear comments like the following:

> Consultation is a poor thing . . . Involvement from the beginning is by far preferable.

> People do get involved but, whatever you say, it doesn't make any difference. You spend all that time in a committee discussing and trying to help the area to get better but then it's decided by someone who doesn't even live here . . . (Andersen et al., 1999)

So, while we may all agree in a general sense that 'It's all down to the people' (the subtitle of the Liverpool Rowntree study), we are still not clear on how citizens may be part of the overall project to transform the city in a democratic development direction.

One important response to the perceived ravages of globalisation is communitarianism, which argues that local community solidarity can provide coherence to a given area and create the resources denied or even destroyed by the state. The theory of 'social capital' explicitly charges the state with 'crowding out' the informal networks that could help regenerate communities. This does not stop enlightened state policies (such as those of New Labour) from seeking to co-opt the notion of social capital to state-led regeneration initiatives. This is 'helping people to help themselves'. But whatever the positive features of the new localism in terms of the empowerment of communities, communitarianism must remain a flawed model for social transformation. 'Community' is a political and highly contested concept (see Hoggett, 1997) so it simply cannot be taken innocently or at face value. Furthermore, as David Harvey puts it, '"community" insofar as it exists is an unstable configuration [. . .] insofar as it does acquire permanence it is frequently an exclusionary and oppressive social form that can be as much at the root of urban conflict and urban degeneration as it can be a panacea for political-economic difficulties' (Harvey, 1989: 439). Indeed, our Liverpool Rowntree study found a constant allusion to 'close' communities also being 'closed' communities intolerant of 'difference' (see Chapter 9 below by Tony Novak).

If 'community' or, more precisely, communitarianism is no panacea for urban problems this does not mean that the state is either. For one thing, in the era of globalisation, the nation-state is too 'small' to cope with international pressures and too 'big' to deal with local issues. The urban growth coalition, referred to earlier, has the potential to create a social and political alliance for redevelopment. It is possible to conceive of a 'synergy', as Peter Evans writes in relation to international development strategies, in which 'civic engagement strengthens state institutions and effective state institutions create an environment in which civic engagement is more likely to thrive' (Evans, 1996: 1034). Networks of civic engagement with local state support can create new norms of trust and reciprocity. Bureaucratic local states can be reformed as the current British engagement with a democratising local government agenda demonstrates. Nor do 'communities' and community activists need to be permanently suspicious of the 'suits' as planners are dubbed in the vernacular of Liverpool (and doubtless elsewhere). John Friedmann is probably speaking for many when he declares: 'I see urban planners being passionately engaged in a transformative politics for inclusion, opportunity for self-development and social justice. It is a politics driven by the energies of a civil society that is beginning to reassert itself in all of its diversity' (Friedmann, 1998: 35).

The discourse of civil society is a broader one than that of 'social capital', and has a definite technocratic edge to it. A flourishing civil society means more than community 'representatives' sitting on regeneration boards. Indeed, it may well be the case that the whole 'participation' drive in regeneration politics has actually demobilised civil society (see Chapter 11 by Barney Rooney). Structures that become formalised, relationships of patronage and clientelism, and a 'soft' funding-driven development strategy are not good for the health of civil society. The development of state–civil society synergy would seem to be essential to a democratic transformation strategy that could avoid both the futility of an abstract revolutionism and the co-option of a lukewarm reformism. The sustainable city depends on the emergence and consolidation of such structures and processes. It is certainly the only way that a genuine democratic development plan can replace the current fashion for the 'management' and 'selling' of great cities. In its progressive aspect, planning has always included a social vision as well as the spatial dimension. As Blowers and Pain note, 'Space itself does not determine the sustainability of cities, but the configuration of social relations does' (Blowers and Pain, 1999: 291). The quest for sustainability, though, faces a major challenge from the forces unleashed by globalisation.

It is one of the great myths of the era that globalisation is an all-powerful tidal wave sweeping away locality and nation-state and putting a lock on any form of contestation. Even the relative autonomy of the state is removed by internationalisation and the city can only compete with other cities to court favour with the agents of globalisation. Yet, as Harvey notes, the spatialisation of globalisation is, in reality, part of 'the space-place dialectic [which] is ever a complicated affair, that globalisation and historical (spatio-temporal) development that creates a variegated terrain of anti-capitalist struggle' (Harvey, 1996: 439). For every door that is closed by globalisation another one is opened. From the protests against the World Trade Organisation in Seattle 1999 to international campaigns against child labour, from social movement unionism challenges to the transnational corporations, to inter-city networks in Western Europe, globalisation is being challenged by many social forces. The 'information city' with its networked citizens, the 'post-colonial city' with its socially diverse populations, and even the 'rustbelt' or de-industrialised city striving to reinvent itself, all have a positive role to play in reasserting social control over capital.

A city in transformation will have a mobilised civil society, will be committed to sustainability (social as much as spatial), and will avoid the twin pitfalls of communitarianism and globalism. It will also, by necessity, and arguably by choice, be an 'open' city (see Chapter 12 by Gideon Ben-Tovim). We have already seen the necessary openness of cities in the era of globalisation but 'open' can also denote a new radical democratic space. Michael Pryke writes in this regard on how the open nature of cities makes them 'spaces of instability and contingency' but also 'offer[s] them the potential to become spaces of opportunity and empowerment' (Pryke, 1999: 334–35). While Pryke seems to give priority to the first element there is no reason why we should not explore the second aspect in more detail. It is not just the powerful who live in the great cities but a great mass of people with hopes, aspirations and energies. There is a new cultural politics of the city emerging with contestation at all levels, from the city council to the schools, from court rooms to public spaces, from community organisations to the places of work. There is in the city a new frontier – more complex, nuanced and contradictory than the old capital–labour opposition – where democracy contests the unfettered rule of capital.

This final section began with the theme that 'it's all down to the people'. In current British regeneration discourse this conception would seem populist at best, co-optive in intent at worst. Certainly we have tried to deconstruct this language and develop a more adequate theoretical and political perspective. A city such as Liverpool is more than 'a suitable case for treatment', a laboratory for 'social inclusion' experiments, its people cannon fodder for participation exercises or social capital calculations. This is an argument made powerfully by Saskia Sassen in her Foreword to this volume. There is still a common assumption abroad that 'disorderly places', such as the urban ghetto, the Third World shanty-town, or the inner-city estate in Britain, breed 'disorderly people' (Mooney, 1999: 81). There is a whole underclass industry examining these people through what Edward Said has referred to as the new 'urban orientalism', an exoticising of the Other. In fact, the attitudes of the young people in the Liverpool Rowntree study were remarkably 'ordinary' for people living in an area where one-third of the working population were unemployed:

> They think we are all dead common and rough. They say don't come here because they rob your car . . . If they go to places where they hire stuff they won't let you . . . People think we are all druggies . . .

> I want to get a good job really and just be happy. I don't want to be on the dole.

> If they did up all the houses, yeah, make it look pretty . . . people aren't afraid of pretty things . . .

References

Amin, A. (1997), 'Placing Globalisation', *Theory, Culture and Society*, 14(2): 123–37

Amin, A., and Graham, S. (1999), 'Cities of Connection and Disconnection', in J. Allen, D. Massey and M. Pryke (eds), *Unsettling Cities*, London: Routledge

Andersen, H., Munck, R., et al. (1999), *Neighbourhood Images in Liverpool: 'It's All Down to the People'*, York: Joseph Rowntree Foundation

Appadurai, A. (1999), 'Globalisation and the Research Imagination', *International Social Science Journal*, 160 (June): 229–38

Atkinson, P. (1997), 'Discourses of Empowerment and Partnership in Contemporary Urban Regeneration', paper presented at the conference 'Discourse and Urban Change: Foregrounding language in housing and urban research', Glasgow: University of Glasgow

Barrett, M. (1992), *The Politics of Truth: From Marx to Foucault*, Cambridge: Polity Press

Blowers, A., and Pain, K. (1999), 'The Unsustainable City?', in S. Pile, C. Brook and G. Mooney (eds), *Unruly Cities?*, London: Routledge

Cameron, G., and Crooke, S. (1992), *Liverpool – Capital of the Slave Trade*, Liverpool: Picton Press

Castells, M. (1996), *The Information Age Volume 1: The Rise of the Network Society*, Oxford: Blackwell

Castells, M. (1997), *The Urban Question*, London: Edward Arnold

Clarke, S., and Gaile, G. (1997), 'Local Politics in a Global Era: Thinking Locally, Acting Globally', *Annals AAPSS*, 551 (May): 28–43

Cox, K. (1997), *Spaces of Globalisation: Reasserting the Power of the Local*, New York: The Guildford Press

Davis, M. (1990), *City of Quartz: Excavating the Future in Los Angeles*, New York: Verso

Davis, M. (1992), 'Fortress Los Angeles: The Militarisation of Urban Space', in M. Sorokin (ed.), *Variations on a Theme Park*, New York: Noonday Press

DETR (Department of the Environment, Transport and the Regions) (1998), *New Deal for Communities*, London: DETR

Di Gaetano, A., and Lawless, P. (1999), 'Urban Governance and Urban Decline, Governing Structures and Policy Agenda in Birmingham and Sheffield, England and Detroit, Michigan, 1980–1997', *Urban Affairs Review*, 34(4): 578–95

Donald, J. (1992), 'Metropolis: The City as Text', in R. Bocock and K. Thompson (eds), *Social and Cultural Forms of Modernity*, Oxford: Polity Press, pp. 416–61.

Engels, F. (1969) [1844], *The Condition of the Working Class in England*, London: Panther

Evans, P. (1996), 'Development Strategies across the Public–Private Divide', *World Development*, 24(6): 1119–32

Friedmann, J. (1998), 'The New Political Economy of Planning: The Rise of Civil Society', in M. Douglass and J. Friedmann (eds), *Cities for Citizens. Planning and the Rise of Civil Society in a Global Age*, Chichester: John Wiley & Sons

Fukuyama, F. (1995), *Trust? The Social Virtues and the Creation of Prosperity*, New York: Free Press

García Canclini, N. (1997), *Imaginarios Urbanos*, Buenos Aires: Eudeba

Garreau, J. (1991), *Edge City: Life on the New Frontiers*, New York: Doubleday

Hall, P. (1966), *The World Cities*, New York: McGraw Hill

Hannerz, U. (1980), *Exploring the City: Inquiries Toward an Urban Anthropology*, New York: Columbia University Press

Harvey, D. (1973), *Social Justice in the City*, London: Edward Arnold

Harvey, D. (1989), *The Condition of Postmodernity*, London: Blackwell

Harvey, D. (1996), *Justice, Nature and the Geography of Difference*, London: Blackwell

Hoggett, P. (ed.) (1997), *Contested Communities*, London: Policy Press

Howarth, D. (2000), *Discourse*, Buckingham: Open University Press

Jacobs, J. (1993), 'The City Unbound: Qualitative Approaches to the City', *Urban Studies*, 50(4/5)

Joseph Rowntree Foundation (1998), *Regenerating Neighbourhoods: Creating Integrated and Sustainable Improvements*, York: Joseph Rowntree Foundation

King, A. (1996), 'Introduction: Cities, Texts and Paradigms', in A. King (ed.), *Re-Presenting the City. Ethnicity, Capital and Culture in the Twenty-First Century Metropolis*, London: Macmillan

Lane, T. (1997), *Liverpool, City of the Sea*, Liverpool: Liverpool University Press

Logan, J., and Molotch, H. (1987), *Urban Fortunes: The Political Economy of Place*, Berkeley: University of California Press

LPG (Liverpool Partnership Group) (1999), *Liverpool First. New Commitment to*

Regeneration. Action Plan Phase 1, Liverpool: Liverpool Partnership Group

Marcus, S. (1973), 'Reading the Illegible', in H.J. Dyos and M. Wolff, *The Victorian City: Images and Realities*, London: Routledge

Meegan, R. (1995), 'Local Worlds', in J. Allen and D. Massey (eds), *Geographical Worlds, Vol. 1*, Oxford: Oxford University Press

Molotch, H., and Logan, J. (1985), 'Urban Dependencies: New Forms of Use and Exchange in US Cities', *Urban Affairs Quarterly*, 21(2): 143–70

Mooney, G. (1999), 'Urban "Disorders"', in S. Pile, C. Brook and G. Mooney (eds), *Unruly Cities?*, London: Routledge

Orwell, G. (1959) [1937], *The Road to Wigan Pier*, London: Secker and Warburg

Pierre, J. (1999), 'Models of Urban Governance: The Institutional Dimension of Urban Politics', *Urban Affairs Review*, 34(3): 372–96

Porter, M. (1999), 'The Competitive Advantage of the Inner City', in J. Allen, D. Massey and M. Pryke (eds), *Unsettling Cities*, London: Routledge

Power, A. (1998), *Estates on the Edge: The Social Consequences of Mass Housing in Northern Europe*, Houndmills: Macmillan

Pryke, M. (1999), 'On the Openness of Cities', in J. Allen, D. Massey and M. Pryke (eds), *Unsettling Cities*, London: Routledge

Raban, J. (1974), *Soft City*, New York: Dutton

Sassen, S. (1991), *The Global City: New York, London, Tokyo*, Princeton, NJ: Princeton University Press

Sassen, S. (1994), *Cities in a World Economy*, Thousand Oaks: Pine Forge Press

Sassen, S. (1999), 'Whose City Is It? Globalisation and the Formation of New Claims', in J. Holston (ed.), *Cities and Citizenship*, Durham, NC, and London: Duke University Press

Sharpe, W., and Wallock, L. (1987), 'From "Great Town" to "Nonplace Urban Realm": Reading the Modern City', in W. Sharpe and L. Wallock (eds), *Visions of the Modern City. Essays in History, Art and Culture*, London: Johns Hopkins University Press

Shields, R. (1991), *Places on the Margin: Alternative Geographies of Modernity*, London: Routledge

Soja, E. (1989), *Postmodern Geographies: The Reassertion of Space in Critical Social Theory*, London: Verso

Stoker, G. (1999), 'Regime Theory and Urban Politics', in S. Pile, C. Brook and G. Mooney (eds), *Unruly Cities?*, London: Routledge

Sousa Santos, B. (1999), 'On Oppositional Postmodernism', in R. Munck and D. O'Hearn (eds), *Critical Development Theory: Contributions to a New Paradigm*, London: Zed Books

Taylor, I., Evans, K., and Fraser, P. (1996), *A Tale of Two Cities, Global Change, Local Feeling and Everyday Life in the North of England. A Study in Manchester and Sheffield*, London: Routledge

Taylor, M. (1995), *Unleashing the Potential. Bringing Residents to the Centre of Regeneration*, York: Joseph Rowntree Foundation

Thrift, N. (1999), 'Cities and Economic Change: Global Governance?', in J. Allen, D. Massey and M. Pryke (eds), *Unsettling Cities*, London: Routledge

Part I: Regeneration

1. The Contemporary City: A Critical Perspective

Karen Evans

Only London, of all the cities in the UK, has been termed a global city (Sassen, 1991). At the beginning of the twenty-first century, much of the rest of Britain, especially in the north, is still struggling with the effects of de-industrialisation. Far from building the new, networked and post-industrial cities of the future, it seems that the majority experience in Britain is of continuing to try to manage the legacy left by the industrial age. It is not clear whether the city-use zones, streets and housing patterns that were necessary to that age fit the work and industry patterns of the present or indeed if they can be adapted to future needs. In many ways, the contemporary city could be said to be in crisis. Urban problems are a recurring theme in popular discourse; recorded crime statistics remain higher in urban than in rural areas, many city communities are seen to be under great stress and the decline of city spaces and traditional routes to employment for the urban population continues to be a focus of concern. This chapter looks at the position of the contemporary city in Britain today. It examines three interrelated themes which have been key to the discussion around British cities over the last two decades: regeneration, division and privatisation. It concludes by asking how far we have moved towards addressing the urban problems of the past and embracing the urban possibilities of the future.

Regenerated Cities

Many cities of the industrialised West have witnessed an intensification of urban problems in the last quarter of the twentieth century. Global economic transformations and industrial restructuring have seen former centres of wealth production slip inexorably into economic decline. Subsequent to this decline, and the withdrawal of capital and rising unemployment that have ensued as a consequence, the physical and social infrastructure of these spaces has also started to fail. The old sites of wealth production – the cities – have shown the earliest and most dramatic signs of decay. Dilapidated cityscapes, declining housing markets and rising crime rates have all been features of urban decline, making urban living unattractive to many and fuelling large-scale population movement towards the suburbs and away from city living altogether. Britain has offered no exception to this trend. The flight from British cities is now well

23

documented. London lost over 1 million residents in the thirty years after 1961, and in the same period Glasgow lost 43 per cent of its population, while Manchester and Liverpool lost 40 per cent each (McIntosh, 1997: 14). This movement of population away from the cities has further fuelled decline as local tax bases have been eroded and the more wealthy, professional population have moved out, leaving the less skilled, less educated and less prosperous behind them (McIntosh, 1997: 14).

Increasing urban poverty and the worsening of urban conditions have been the subject of much government concern and numerous interventions. However, with older economies in decline across the globe, the last quarter of the twentieth century has seen national governments increasingly turning to regional and local economic development policies to attempt to reverse economic decline where this is seen to be at its most acute (Bovaird, 1995). Within the British context, the 1980s and 1990s witnessed a plethora of programmes, funded through national and European financing, aimed at halting continued decline and regenerating local economies. Different funding regimes and regeneration initiatives have seen funds targeted at particular regions, cities and local neighbourhoods which have experienced some of the worst decline and loss of traditional manufacturing. However, it is not only the public sector authorities that have been active in attempting to arrest the decline of the urban environment. Faced with competition from hypermarkets and out-of-town shopping, the retail sector has also begun to see the importance of regenerating traditional city shopping areas. Of course the British government of the 1980s embraced this private sector involvement, arguing that private sector dynamism along with private sector financing was an essential part of any regeneration strategy. This argument fitted the free-market Thatcherite ideology which looked to downgrade public sector involvement in many areas of existing provision. This period saw a degree of deregulation in planning activity and in the financial markets which allowed the government to set up the Urban Development Corporations. These emerged as the public/private partnership bodies which opened up city property markets and ensured the release of derelict inner-city and out-of-town sites for industry, retail and residential uses. All this, it was argued, could only be achieved with partnership between the private and public sectors. Across Britain the work of different local authority departments was increasingly superseded by partnership bodies and 'local growth coalitions' (Mellor, 1997; Taylor et al., 1996) made up of representation from both sectors, which took responsibility for overseeing regeneration and attracting private and public finance into regeneration areas.[1]

And so the story goes that cities were 'reinvented' in the 1980s; cityscapes were transformed, regenerated, marketed and re-branded as sites, not primarily of busi-

---

[1] The move to attract private finance has continued apace despite the change in government, with Private Finance Initiatives which have covered school and hospital building and plans for the London Underground. It was further reported in the *Guardian* in January 2000 that the government wants to transfer all council housing and many local government functions to the private sector.

ness and manufacturing, but of sporting achievement,[2] cultural practices,[3] leisure activities and American-style 'loft-living'. As new and existing retail and business were increasingly (re)sited in purpose-built, out-of-town facilities, the urban growth coalitions fought back. The emptying storefronts, banks and warehouses of the city centres became sites of alternative styles of consumption and were colonised by café-bars, gyms, multiplex cinemas and coffee-houses. Cities were also re-designated as sites of tourism with galleries, theatres and museums and the renovation of old buildings, which were seen to have a rediscovered historical significance. The city, then, has become a place of play, especially for the young professionals and the growing student populations who still work and study within the city boundaries. At night, cities continue to attract the pub- and club-goers, despite the development of the out-of-town cinema and shopping complexes, because people are attracted to the continuing vibrancy and excitement of city centre leisure facilities and music scenes. Different cultural forms, it is argued, are underpinning the economic revival of central urban spaces (Zukin, 1997).

It would be foolish to deny that the above policies have had a positive effect on our urban landscapes. The last decade of the twentieth century, in particular, has seen many physical symbols of an industrial past utilised, in a process that is still ongoing, as the raw material in a system of gentrification and renewal of city centre spaces. Liverpool's Albert Dock, Newcastle's Quayside, Manchester's Gay Village, to name but a few examples, have all created symbols that can point towards a possible, very different, future which still involves notions of local wealth creation.[4] Shopping in many a city centre across Britain, while not exactly transformed into a leisure activity as some may claim, has certainly become a more pleasurable experience for many, due to policies to encourage cleaner, brighter buildings, re-laid paving, the use of urban art and the erection of some imaginative and uplifting office and retail buildings. Shopping areas often now have extended opening hours, encouraging use of the city centre in the early evening – previously a 'dead' time for many city spaces in between the closure of offices and the start of the evening rush to theatre, cinema and pub. Shopping areas are generally better and more imaginatively lit at night; lighting is used to pick out and enhance architectural features on some of the more imposing buildings, and all this leads to the impression that a safer environment has also been created. The value of city living has also been well marketed, leading to somewhat of a reversal in population movement, although this currently appears to be limited to the childless professional, and urban populations have not yet returned to their 1960s levels. Many city centre spaces are busy throughout the evening, there is a greater choice of places to drink and to visit and, as licensing laws are

---

[2] For example, Manchester's bid to hold the Olympic Games and hosting of the Commonwealth Games in 2002 and Sheffield's success in attracting the World Student Games to the city in 1994.

[3] For example, Glasgow as 'City of Culture' and Manchester as 'City of Drama' in 1994.

[4] Of course, other cities have been able to trade on their historical legacy for some time – these are centres of tourism such as London, Edinburgh, York and Oxford.

relaxed by many local authorities, these places are also open later into the evening. More people seem to be attracted to these new and rejuvenated venues than ever before and in cities such as Manchester much of the general revelry spills out into the streets, giving a more European and relaxed atmosphere to city centre spaces.

This redevelopment has been much commented on, but, spectacular though it may be, it hardly goes very far in solving the large-scale urban problems by which our cities are plagued. To begin with, this regeneration is limited, both in terms of the extent of its geography and in terms of the social groups that it affects. One does not have to move very far outside the regenerated city centre before the familiar inner-city area, with its multiple problems, is encountered once again. Indeed the contrast between city centre and inner city is all the more acute as the latter continues to decay while the decline of the former is arrested and, in some instances, reversed. The shopping centres, residential units and leisure facilities found in these inner-city areas are far less likely to attract private sector finance to renew their economies and physical fabric. There is far less economic potential in these areas, which are suffering from low incomes and higher than average levels of unemployment and sickness. There is also the question of transport to the city centres. The level of roadside parking in many cities is testament to the fact that many see private transport as their preferred method of travel. Levels of investment in public transport are still problematic so that its use remains low. Even in Manchester, where much has been made of the addition of the futuristic Metrolink Light Rapid Transport System (commonly referred to as 'the tram'), users outside the city centre are, just over five years after its introduction, complaining of a lack of continuing investment in the system. In the early months of 2000, local free newspapers throughout Manchester were carrying stories of badly lit and run-down Metrolink stations with inadequate security systems and increasing levels of fear expressed by passengers.

The inadequacy of much of public transport and the continued patterns of high unemployment in many neighbouring urban areas may also contribute to the skewed patterns of use of city centre facilities. These remain spaces that, outside working hours, are dominated by the young, the salaried, and, to a large degree, by the male.[5] These are not the use patterns of many European cities, which see families dining and drinking together in restaurants and cafés much later into the evening. Added to this air of homogeneity in British cities, the retail and leisure units in city centres are dominated by the larger corporate entities, so much so that the centres of our cities are becoming more similar and in many ways more bland. Street markets are often frowned on for creating too much litter, family-owned shops have all but disappeared from our high streets and traditional British pubs are few and far between in city centre spaces, as those that still remain are renamed by the larger chains and their interiors hollowed out to create large standing areas served by room-length bars – which are certainly much more efficient at serving

---

[5] See Taylor et al. (1996) for a discussion of these use patterns.

large numbers of drinkers, but which lack the intimate and individual atmosphere of the old public house layout.

Despite some of the drawbacks to this model of city centre regeneration, the same formula is applied in different cities, as it is seen to reap benefits for the partners involved. In an ironic twist, these increasingly similar city and town spaces now compete with one another to attract the tourist, shopper and resident. But when every town has the same retail outlets, the same corporate chains supplying nightlife, all can offer a range of cultural spaces, and waterfronts are developed with warehouse accommodation, there will be little to distinguish one city from another, and the old staples of job opportunities and affordable housing may well resurface as the city's attractions.

Divided Cities

Economic decline in the industrialised world in the 1970s has led to a return to the politics and economics of neo-liberalism (Harvey, 1989). Across the West the 'solutions' of deregulation, flexibility in working practices and concessions to the mobility of capital have been implemented, the benefits of which have not been equally shared. Again the differences are found both within and between nation states. At the beginning of the twenty-first century, Britain is reported to be the most impoverished country in the West, beating both its European neighbours and the USA in a league table of deprivation.[6] While argument still rages over whether Britain suffers from a north/south or an east/west divide[7] in terms of poverty and wealth, the fact that Britain is an increasingly divided country with pockets of affluence existing at the same time as extreme deprivation can no longer be denied.[8] The health of the nation also reflects such division; the Black Report of 1980 demonstrated a widening health gap within Britain and this trend was confirmed as continuing by a Bristol University report published in 1999 (Dorling et al., 1999). This report showed, for example, among other health inequalities, a doubling of infant mortality rates in the poorest areas of Britain when compared with the most affluent. Whatever the truth behind the north/south divide debate – and this truth will be somewhat complex – population estimates show the 1990s as having witnessed a relocation of population from the north of England to the south, the true extent and character of which will become more fully known after data have been analysed from the 2001 population census. The population it seems, by 'getting on

---

[6] The *Guardian*, 12 January 2000, reported the results of a report published by the Organisation for Economic Co-operation and Development which stated that between 1991 and 1996 poverty affected 20% of the British population, as compared with 14% of the US population, and that 38% of the UK population (compared with 26% of the US population) spent at least one year below the poverty line during the same period.

[7] See the *Guardian* and G2 insert for 7 December 1999.

[8] Although the increasing pauperisation of a growing proportion of Britain's population was denied in the years of Margaret Thatcher's government, in January 2000 an internal Conservative Party document from 1992 was leaked to the press which outlined precisely this fact.

its bike' in such numbers, has signalled its general agreement with the idea that there are more and better opportunities available in the south of England.[9]

The divisions within British society are not confined to those between the north and the south, nor indeed between areas of wealth creation and of poverty. It is in the nature of cities across the world, and in part what makes urban living special, that they contain *within* their boundaries immense heterogeneity and 'multiple experiences of time and space' (Amin and Graham, 1999: 31). Cities have always been divided spaces with fractures along lines of class, ethnicity and gender. However, it has been widely acknowledged that increased social and economic polarisation in the late twentieth century has led to further spatial segregation (Byrne, 1999: 109) in the cities of Western societies. Of course spatial segregation, in and of itself, can be a positive choice for particular groups in society as people choose to reside near like-minded people, building sustainable communities of interest and of place. The divisions in contemporary British cities, however, often exist not as a function of unfettered personal choices, but as the result of systems of exclusion. The criminologist, Jock Young, has characterised the last thirty years of the twentieth century as a period when society moved from a more inclusive to an exclusive society. He has tracked many of the effects of 'a movement from modernity to late modernity, from a world whose accent was on assimilation and incorporation to one which separates and excludes' (Young, 1999: 1). In his study *The Exclusive Society,* he has charted the move to individualised ways of life, and the fracturing of community and certainty which has been a feature of much of Western society. So in Britain today the spatial division of our cities can be properly understood only by reference to the wider context of social division in which the British experience has been so extreme.

The increasing social and economic divisions that have developed over the last twenty to thirty years in particular have meant that many British cities include pockets of extreme deprivation. This is as true of the southern half of the British Isles as it is of the northern. These areas concentrate economic disadvantage, environmental degradation and crime (Trickett et al., 1992) onto a significant minority of the population. Hutton (1995) introduced the idea of the 40:30:30 society, but Trickett et al. demonstrate that disproportionately high rates of criminal victimisation are found to be concentrated in around 10 per cent of areas. Again, in 1998 a Rowntree report stated that almost 10 per cent of householders in England identified four or more serious problems with their neighbourhood. The same report goes on to highlight further the concentration of neighbourhood problems, arguing that levels of dissatisfaction are 'profoundly and starkly socially and spatially patterned'. This reality has driven Beatrix Campbell to remark that 'Crime was *spatialised* in the Nineties' (Campbell, 1993: 317).

---

[9] Indeed, in 1999 the Governor of the Bank of England, Eddie George, also seemed tacitly to acknowledge the existence of the north/south divide when he admitted publicly that he thought that high levels of unemployment in the north might be the price Britain had to pay for conditions that would allow continuing prosperity in the south.

Common perceptions regarding the positioning of the city's typical 'problem areas' have altered in recent decades; while received wisdom in the 1970s and early 1980s identified the inner city as the source and site of urban disorder, the late 1980s saw equal attention focused on the outlying council estate. In her much-referenced work *Goliath* (1993), Campbell turned her attention to these demonised council estates situated on the outskirts of many British cities. She characterised these places as poor, predominantly white and marginalised areas struggling with a massive loss of employment in general, and male employment opportunities in particular. The marginal nature of such estates was further under-scored when the Joseph Rowntree Foundation commissioned research in the mid-1990s which demonstrated that housing policies implemented in the 1980s had transformed social housing from formerly mixed income, low-cost housing, attractive to a range of social classes, into a housing option available to the poorest sections of society alone. As a result many people have lost their trust in the effi-cacy of social housing. Local authority housing provision, and the council estate in particular, have come to be popularly identified as a last resort for accommodation, rather than as a first port of call. But it is not only the council estate that has suf-fered from a loss of standing in recent decades; in the late 1990s circumstances forced the new Labour government to recognise that a growing number of areas of mixed tenure and owner-occupation had also collapsed or were on the verge of col-lapsing. Both the housing organisation, Shelter, and the government advisory body, the Social Exclusion Unit, reported in late 1999 that some areas of England's northern cities were experiencing nil demand for housing, and that while pressure on housing remained intense in parts of the southeast, where the housing market remained buoyant, perfectly adequate housing was being abandoned unsold and unwanted in parts of the north. In one part of the northeast, it was reported, demand for housing was so low that a newly built block of social housing was demolished shortly after its completion, without anyone ever having moved in.

It would be a mistake to see these areas of disadvantage and low demand as uni-versally rejected, however; research has shown that there is a great deal of com-mitment and attachment to these areas that have been labelled 'unpopular'.[10] Time and again the remaining residents of these areas, while acknowledging their deep-seated problems, display a sense of pride in their city and in their neighbourhood (Walklate and Evans, 1999; Foster, 1997). While the multiple problems persisting within these areas mean that their residents are commonly seen to be part of 'the socially excluded', the reality is somewhat more complex. These are often places of marked community and familial bonds which provide important networks and sources of self-help for their established residents. There are indeed tensions present within such neighbourhoods and elaborate patterns of exclusion and inclusion are played out in these areas as different groups vie for space and iden-tity within them. However, these high-crime, difficult-to-let areas are lived in and

---

[10] See, for example, the reports from Teesside, Nottingham, Liverpool and East London, which make up the Joseph Rowntree Foundation's Area Regeneration Research Programme, published in 1999.

negotiated by their resident population and meaningful relationships and networks are forged which allow the individual residents to manage their day-to-day
experiences. It would be a mistake to see the similarity in these neighbourhoods'
physical and economic fabric as resulting in correspondingly similar community
structures or local mechanisms of social control. Each of these neighbourhoods
has a history of its own, a diverse social make-up and patterns of victimisation and
possibly of criminality, which are particular to the area and which place it somewhere along a trajectory of either decline or improvement. Social relationships in
these neighbourhoods are not fixed and unchanging; they alter as residents come
and go, and as forces such as employment and the economy, which lie outside the
control of the resident community, change and affect the life patterns of its population.

Just as there is an unevenness (Lash and Urry, 1994) to the experience of different localities, which are responding in various ways to the challenges of global economic culture, so too can smaller neighbourhoods contain different strengths and
capabilities and find themselves responding and reacting to change in distinct
ways. Areas can 'tip' into social disorganisation and despair, as many have done in
recent years, but this movement will not always be one-way and there are also
examples of renewal of community and social ties, although these are fewer. Yet
there is a marked tendency to treat 'problem' areas with a range of 'off-the-shelf'
solutions without consideration of their social and cultural differences.
Regeneration agencies and local and national government policy-makers need to
be aware that what may be a reasonable, considered response to a set of problems
in one area may be inappropriate in dealing with similar concerns in another.

Privatised Cities

The effects of deregulation of economies and of markets, and the subsequent celebration of the consumer and enterprise culture that was thereby unleashed, dominated a great deal of writing on the city in the 1980s and 1990s. The emerging
postmodern city or metropole, situated within the expanding economies of the
USA and the fast developing tiger economies of the East, was also much explored.
Allied to the discovery of novel architectural styles and spatial formations in the
post-industrial city was a recognition that new technology was playing an increasing part in the development of new and existing city spaces. New technologies are
a feature of many aspects of contemporary urban environments, contributing to
their physical forms as well as shaping their local economies. With the demise of
much traditional manufacturing industry there has been a rush to embrace the
service economy as a source of wealth creation. Much of this transformation has
been driven through at a local level. Various national governments and local urban
growth coalitions have emphasised the importance of pushing their cities forward
to occupy space at the cutting edge of technological advances; the USA has its
Silicon Valley and has championed the development of the 'information super-
highway', Malaysia has its 'multi-media super-corridor' and many cities have

developed their science parks and telematics capabilities in order to equip their local enterprises and labour markets with the technology and skills that they will need in order to compete successfully and to sustain their local economies in the twenty-first century.

Cities, it is suggested, are taking their position as hubs or nodal points in a 'network society' (Castells, 1996) through which information will flow and connections will be made. Their heterogeneity, dynamic social structures and location as sites encompassing a variety of skills, knowledge and capitals – social, economic and cultural – mean that they are ideally situated to play an important part in an age of information and service provision. It has been argued that the development of information and communication technologies could mean that the city could actually be bypassed and that offices and teleworkers could be as easily, and perhaps more economically, situated outside city spaces; however, as Amin and Graham argue, city environments remain key locations precisely because 'of their large and diverse labour markets, and property, infrastructure and telecommunications advantages' (Amin and Graham, 1999: 12). Far from new technology overcoming the need for travel and mobility across and within cities, Amin and Graham argue that the new connections, and the asynchronous and speedy communications that this technology makes possible, are contributing to an ever greater need to travel to secure new markets and consumers.

However, as contemporary society adopts the tools that allow it to become more connected and open to dialogue with wider networks of people, forms of new technology that separate and protect the individual from other city dwellers are also increasingly utilised. Transport is a prime example, with an unprecedented use of private motor cars as the currently preferred mode of travel for many people. The flexibility that accelerated working patterns demand can best be gained through the use of private means of transport rather than having to rely on pre-arranged and necessarily inflexible timetables. Throughout Britain especially, criticism of the public transport system, which is seen as expensive to use, increasingly unsafe and suffering from decades of low investment, militates against its use. However, with some of the longest working hours in Europe, the demand for flexible and speedy transport solutions that can be tailored to individual requirements will work to deter use of public transport, even without the problems of unreliability and limited running times of Britain's deregulated and privatised bus and train systems. In addition, greater use of the private car has also been linked to fear of crime on public transport and on the street, especially during the evening hours and at night.

Another use of technology that British cities have taken up in unprecedented numbers is the closed-circuit television (CCTV) camera. Armstrong, Norris and Moran from the University of Hull have charted the dramatic proliferation of the CCTV system throughout Britain. By the end of 1999, all major cities in Britain could boast a city centre scheme at least and some cities had seen systems operating in 'problem' residential areas. In addition, many shops, retail centres, business parks and areas of car-parking have included their own, privately monitored

CCTV schemes. In addition, cameras have been situated in transport interchanges and along roads, motorways and railways at increasingly regular intervals. These surveillance systems are used both to monitor and to control the presence of undesirable 'others' on the streets and in public and semi-public spaces. The overall cost of these CCTV schemes is immense, but appears to be generally justified, even though the efficacy of the systems can be questioned. Speed cameras will only work if they are stocked with film or are advanced enough to automatically process digital images; cameras trained on city centre streets will only be useful in the apprehending of offenders if camera operators can get security personnel to respond quickly enough if they see a crime being committed. The presence of cameras may protect certain spaces from crime, but displace it to outlying, non-monitored places. However, despite the many questions still to be asked about the effectiveness of CCTV systems, they are largely seen by the general public as an important and necessary component in the fight against many forms of crime.

The acceptance of CCTV systems within British cities has been encouraged by television programmes such as *Crimewatch* and *Police, Camera, Action* which routinely marry CCTV camera footage with grave crime prevention messages, and with images that have touched the emotions and insecurities of the entire nation, such as were provided after the abduction of the toddler James Bulger. These terrible images showed how James was calmly led away from a very public shopping centre, a space presumed safe, by his young killers. While fear of crime and reactions to high rates of criminality in the USA have led to the gated and walled communities that are springing up to maintain the security of middle America, Britain has preferred the public eye in the sky. Yet this solution is as likely to exclude as are the brick wall and secure gate. Graham (1996) points to various sources that have highlighted less than favourable reactions to CCTV cameras by particular groups. Young males, and especially black males, feel over-scrutinised and monitored in public spaces, and women, another group likely to be overly watched, but for different reasons, are also more likely to have ambiguous feelings towards CCTV systems.

Concern about levels of crime and subsequent moves to regenerate run-down urban spaces have contributed to the privatisation of many public spaces in our cities in other ways. The image of vandalised and crime-prone residential and retail areas has spurred on regeneration initiatives which have seen private companies take on the ownership and responsibility for the security of previously publicly owned areas both within city centres and in outlying neighbourhoods. Shopping centres have been bought from local authorities and refurbished to provide privatised, secure and covered shopping malls which are closed and gated after opening hours. In the light of local authorities starved of finance to maintain their public housing stock, a solution to the problem of insecure blocks of council accommodation has been to sell them to private companies or social landlords with access to the finances needed to install door entry systems and employ concierges. Even the provision of bus shelters has been contracted out to private

companies in many areas, displacing the problem of renewing repeatedly vandalised bus shelters to the private sector. Crime prevention has been privatised in
other ways too. Individual businesses and householders are held responsible for
preventing crime on their premises and expected to purchase expensive security
systems to try to ensure that they remain free from victimisation. More and more
the public provision of services is being eroded and private solutions sought to
very public urban problems.

Conclusion

So this is the contemporary canvas on which urban activities must be painted.
Despite the problems that still exist within the contemporary city, past economic
and social developments have ensured that the majority of the world's population
is concentrated in and around urban developments. Cities continue to be places
that offer fantastic possibilities for the change and development of humanity.
However, they are equally the sites in which the failures of contemporary society
will be concentrated. The challenge, then, for the regenerators of our cities is to
acknowledge and build on these capacities while recognising the impacts that
wider economic and social processes have on city life.

The contemporary urban environment encompasses the raw materials that
must be utilised if the city is to develop new opportunities and new social and
structural forms. A number of urban growth coalitions have been successful at
tapping into the resources and dynamism of their urban entrepreneurs and private
sector developers, and together with their immediate local authority counterparts
have overseen key transformations within some local economies. However, this
sort of success has been limited and it should be stressed that not all cities have been
equally successful in this task. The benefits accruing from these flourishing local
economies were expected to 'trickle down' to more marginalised and impoverished
areas, yet divisions have persisted and gulfs between those included in such economic success stories and those excluded from them have widened since the 1980s.
More people may be in work but their wages are relatively low; there may be more
choice in the range of cultural practices to consume but the growth in flexible
working means longer hours and less security of employment. In the current political climate in Britain, with its emphasis on 'modernisation' (a term that is often
invoked but rarely explored), those populations that continue to be placed outside
the contemporary global and consumerist cultures – pensioners, those on low
incomes, the sick and refugees, for example – are not generally portrayed as
dynamic, skilled and contributing populations.

And it is not only those without paid employment who are being excluded from
consideration as net contributors to the economy. The emphasis on private
funding and on market forces as saviours of the city has left the public sector and
its officers often portrayed as resistant to change, misguided or workshy in the
dominant discourse of national politicians. In addition, communities in economically disadvantaged areas are considered disordered, fractured and in need of

social organisation,[11] while celebrations of diversity and difference are less often heard.

Urban regeneration policies and practices must look beyond stereotypes. Indeed, many worthwhile interventions are being developed at the local level where agencies and partnerships find themselves closer to the lives of their resident populations and can recognise the skills, creativity and commitment that a great many local people contribute to solutions for their areas. However, the local partnerships that are pushing forward change in these areas are working in the context of difficult economic conditions lying outside their control. With the demise of many small, locally based businesses and their replacement by the international corporations and retail names that dominate our city streets, we are losing the ability to control local economies at the regional level. The global business has little connection with the urban space in which it locates its local operations and thereby less commitment to its civic institutions and close neighbours. This is the template and the challenge for the regeneration task – building inclusion, participation, prosperity and sustainability into the lives of communities whose residents' lives are often fractured and disjointed as they struggle with loss of employment opportunities and increasing social problems while learning how to compete in a global marketplace.

References

Allen, J., Massey, D., and Pryke, M. (eds) (1999), *Unsettling Cities*, London: Routledge

Amin, A. and Graham, S. (1999), 'Cities of Connection and Disconnection', in Allen et al. (eds)

Andersen, H., Munck, R., et al. (1999), *Neighbourhood Images in Liverpool: 'It's All Down to the People'*, York: Joseph Rowntree Foundation

Bovaird, T. (1995), 'Managing Urban Economic Development: Learning to Change or the Marketing of Failure', in Paddison et al. (eds)

Byrne, D. (1999), *Social Exclusion*, Buckingham: Open University Press

Campbell, B. (1993), *Goliath: Britain's Dangerous Places*, London: Methuen

Castells, M. (1989), *The Informational City: Information Technology, Economic Restructuring, and the Urban-Regional Process*, Oxford: Blackwell

Castells, M. (1996), *The Information Age: Economy, Society and Culture. Vol I: The Rise of the Network Society*, London: Blackwell

Cattell, V., and Evans, M. (1999), *Neighbourhood Images in East London: Social Capital and Social Networks on Two East London Estates*, York: Joseph Rowntree Foundation

DETR (Department of the Environment, Transport and the Regions) (1999), *National Strategy for Neighbourhood Renewal: Report of Policy Action Team 7: Unpopular Housing*, London: HMSO

---

[11] See, for example, documents emanating from the Home Office-based Policy Action Teams which reported in April 1999.

Dorling, D. (1999), *The Widening Gap*, Bristol: Bristol University

Fielding, A. J. (1995), 'Industrial Change and Regional Development in Western Europe', in Paddison et al. (eds)

Foster, J. (1997), '"Community" and Neighbourliness on a Difficult-to-Let Housing Estate', in Jewson and MacGregor (eds)

Graham, S. (1996), 'Networking the City: A Comparison of Urban Tele-communications Initiatives in France and Britain', PhD thesis, University of Manchester

Harvey, D. (1989), *The Condition of Postmodernity*, Oxford: Blackwell

Hutton, W. (1995), *The State We're In*, London: Jonathan Cape

Jewson, N., and MacGregor, S. (eds) (1997), *Transforming Cities: Contested Governance and New Spatial Divisions*, London: Routledge

Lash, S., and Urry, J. (1994), *Economies of Signs and Space*, London/Thousand Oaks, CA: Sage

McIntosh, A. (1997), *Towns and Cities Competing for Survival*, London: Chapman and Hall

Mellor, R. (1997), 'Cool Times for a Changing City', in Jewson and MacGregor (eds)

Norris, C., and Armstrong, G. (1999), *The Maximum Surveillance Society: The Rise of CCTV*, Oxford and New York: Berg

Paddison, R., Money J., and Lever, B. (eds) (1995), *International Perspectives in Urban Studies*, London: Jessica Kingsley Publishers Ltd

Policy Studies Institute (1992), *Urban Trends*, Vol. I, London: PSI

Sassen, S. (1991), *The Global City: New York, London, Tokyo*, Princeton, NJ: Princeton University Press

Silburn, R., Lucas, D., Page, R., and Hanna, L. (1999), *Neighbourhood Images in Nottingham: Social Cohesion and Neighbourhood Change*, York: Joseph Rowntree Foundation

Taylor, I., Evans, K, and Fraser, P. (1996), *A Tale of Two Cities: Global Change, Local Feeling and Everyday Life in the North of England*, London: Routledge

Townsend, P. (1992), *The Black Report: Inequalities in Health*, London: Penguin

Trickett, A., Osborn, D., Seymour, J., and Pease, K. (1992), 'What is Different about High Crime Areas?', *British Journal of Criminology*, 32(1): 81–89

Walklate, S., and Evans, K. (1999), *Zero Tolerance or Community Tolerance? Managing Crime in High Crime Areas*, Aldershot: Ashgate

Wood, M., and Vamplew, C. (1999), *Neighbourhood Images in Teesside: Regeneration or Decline?*, York: Joseph Rowntree Foundation

Young, J. (1999), *The Exclusive Society*, London: Sage

Zukin, S. (1997), *The Cultures of Cities*, London: Blackwell

2. From World City to Pariah City? Liverpool and the Global Economy, 1850–2000[1]

Stuart Wilks-Heeg

At the heart of the paradigm shift that has been taking place in urban studies since the early 1970s is the notion that a fundamental restructuring of previous urban hierarchies has taken place as a result of the dynamics of economic globalisation. It is well known that this restructuring has had major implications for the role of cities and that it has given rise to distinct sets of winners and losers. Indeed, a range of studies carried out in the Europe context concur that the world cities of Frankfurt, Paris, London, Brussels and Amsterdam are the key beneficiaries of this process, while the likes of Naples, Duisberg, Le Havre, Liège and Liverpool consistently rank among those cities that have suffered most extensively (Cheshire et al., 1986; Cheshire, 1990; 1999; Lever, 1999; Dematteis, 2000; Brenner, 2000). Yet, if one city epitomises the consequences of economic decline arising from the reordering of urban economic functions, it is Liverpool. As Ronaldo Munck notes in the introduction to this volume, Liverpool's place in the contemporary urban studies literature is as a site of entrenched social problems, a city almost entirely disconnected from the more glamorous study of world city formation. Yet, as Munck notes, Liverpool's claim to 'world city status' in the early twentieth century would have been second to none. Indeed, as this chapter will show, Liverpool was a key node in the global economy that grew up around the British Empire from 1870–1914, vying with London and New York for international significance. Few cities, if any, can match Liverpool's dubious claim to have descended from 'world city' to 'pariah city' during the course of the twentieth century.

With the notable exception of the work of Anthony King (1990a; 1990b), the vast literature on world cities has largely failed to provide us with an understanding of the historical reasons for world city formation. It tells us even less about the reason for world city *decline*. This dearth of historical accounts of world cities is surprising, particularly as there is a clear context for such work. Braudel (1983) has argued that cities have always constituted key nodes in the world economy, with the centre of gravity shifting from Genoa and Venice in the sixteenth century to Antwerp and Amsterdam in the seventeenth and to London in the eighteenth. Much of the explanation for the failure to work through the implications of the

[1] The author wishes to thank Mary Hutchins for her assistance in researching parts of the material used in this chapter.

history of world city formation would appear to rest with the lack of historical perspective in much of the wider literature on globalisation, despite the fact that historical evidence clearly points to the existence of a global economy in the period 1870–1914 (Kenwood and Lougheed, 1992; Foreman-Peck, 1995; Alford, 1996). The significance of this earlier period of globalisation has barely been touched on by world cities research, despite the key questions that it raises. What was the role of cities in this earlier period of globalisation? Which cities constituted the key nodes in this particular phase of international capitalism? Did these cities perform 'command and control' functions similar to today's world cities and how did they shape the structure of the world economy up to 1914? How was the subsequent development of such cities shaped by the long-run restructuring of the international economy from 1914 onwards? To what extent, and in what ways, did local governance in such cities underpin their integration into the pre-1914 world economy and respond subsequently to the progressive unravelling of this system?

This chapter poses these questions in the context of Liverpool. It begins with a brief discussion of the stark similarities between the development of the global economy in the period 1870–1914 and more recent patterns of globalisation. Despite these striking parallels, it is suggested that the key distinction between these two periods of globalisation is provided by significant differences in the international division of labour. Drawing on King (1976; 1990a; 1990b), it highlights the significance of the colonial mode of production to Britain's provincial cities, which effectively formed the second tier in the global urban hierarchy. The second part of the chapter then develops these ideas in the specific context of Liverpool. It shows how Liverpool's central role in the colonial economic system underpinned its development as a key node in the nineteenth-century global economy, again drawing out important parallels with the contemporary role of world cities. The third section looks specifically at issues of governance and argues that Liverpool's position as the 'Gateway to Empire' was fostered by the active participation of the local merchant class in the growth of the colonial system and the governance of the city itself. The fourth and final section of the chapter seeks to show that, as the international division of labour based on the Empire broke down, attempts to reconfigure the political economy of the city proved insufficient, largely because of the failure to recognise the extent to which Liverpool had become dependent on a specifically colonial mode of production.

World Cities in History?

It has been widely noted that many of the developments that are held to be axiomatic to contemporary globalisation dynamics were, in fact, as much features of the international economy from 1870 to 1914 (Hirst and Thompson, 1999; Schwarz, 2000; Kenwood and Lougheed, 1992; Alford, 1996). For instance, the period after 1870 witnessed a rapid growth of international trade (Hirst and Thompson, 1999), high levels of foreign direct investment (Kenwood and Lougheed, 1992) and the development of a global financial system based on 'bills of exchange' and centred on London (Alford, 1996). It also saw the emergence of the precursors of modern-day multinational companies during the late nineteenth century onwards (Dunning, 1983; Hirst and Thompson, 1999). It should also be noted that the scale of international migration in the century after 1815, and particularly after 1880, remains without precedent (Kenwood and Lougheed, 1992; Hirst and Thompson, 1999). Indeed, so strong are the parallels between the late twentieth and late nineteenth centuries that it is tempting to argue that 'the modern world economy [. . .] is becoming much more like the world economy that existed in the late nineteenth century' (Schwartz, 2000: 2). However, there are also important distinctions that need to be drawn between these two periods of internationalisation. In particular, the growth of the international economy from 1870 to 1914 was driven by the British colonial mode of production and, to a lesser extent, by the process of state formation and imperial expansion elsewhere in Western Europe. This form of globalisation was far more state-driven than its modern-day equivalent. While states continue to be central to the dynamics of contemporary globalisation, not least because they set the regulatory frameworks within which international business operates, it is corporate actors such as transnational companies, finance capital and producer services that are generally interpreted as constituting the key drivers.

In this context, it is important to note that world city formation has frequently been placed within the context of the emergence of a new international division of labour (Feagin and Smith, 1989). Whereas the 'take-off phase of globalisation' (cf. Robertson, 1992) from 1870 to 1914 was based on a system of raw material production in the periphery and manufacturing production in the core, the shift to the new international division of labour (NIDL) has seen manufacturing relocate to the periphery and semi-periphery (Fröbel et al., 1980). Transnational corporations (TNCs) have been the key driver in this dispersal of production activity from core to periphery, due to the 'massive expansion in the role of TNCs in the production and exchange of commodities on a world scale' (Brenner, 1998: 5). At the same time, however, TNCs have sought to centralise their higher-order operational and control functions in particular localities. As a result, two of the key consequences of the NIDL, aside from the de-industrialisation of much of the metropolitan core, are 1) the growing concentration of TNC headquarters in a small number of large cities worldwide and 2) the dramatic growth, and again increased concentration, of specialist financial and business services (banking, law, accounting, insurance) which have grown up to serve the TNCs located in these same urban centres. Unsurprisingly, such trends have been most evident in those cities that already boasted well-established financial industries – namely the global banking and stock exchange centres of London, New York, Tokyo and Paris. Such cities thus emerge as 'nodal points to co-ordinate and control [. . .] global economic activity' (Sassen-Koob, 1984: 140) or 'the cotterpins holding the capitalist world economic system together' (Feagin, 1985: 30).

What, though, was the role of cities in the old international division of labour? Here we must turn to the work of Anthony King (1976; 1990a; 1990b), which provides the seminal analysis of urban development under the colonial mode of production that underpinned the emergence of a global economy from 1870 to 1914. King draws direct parallels between contemporary world city formation and the urbanisation process associated with the development of the colonial economy. He argues that the old international division of labour was no different in requiring particular basing points, 'colonial cities', that acted as control and service centres within the context of a particular set of global economic relations. As King notes, the dominance of Great Britain in the nineteenth century world economy meant that its cities also dominated the global urban hierarchy. In 1900 five of the largest 19 cities in the world were in Britain: London, Manchester, Birmingham, Glasgow and Liverpool. By the 1930s London was nearly six times the size of Calcutta, the Empire's next largest city and, relative to their counterparts elsewhere, other cities in the metropolitan core, such as Manchester, Liverpool and Glasgow, were 'equally bloated' (King, 1990b: 35).

As a result, the shift from the colonial economy to a new international economic system had significant implications for those British towns and cities whose form and function were critically shaped by their ties to the colonial mode of production. As King (1990b) notes, by the 1930s, Britain's colonies and dominions accounted for over two-thirds of the value of British exports and almost half of the value of its imports, illustrating the extent to which the metropolitan core had become dependent on the colonial periphery. A key consequence of this was that such cities operated 'within the politically and economically protected circumstances of colonialism' (King, 1990b: 62). As the colonial mode of production broke down over the course of the twentieth century, it was the second-tier cities of the metropolitan core – Liverpool, Glasgow, Birmingham and Manchester – that were most dramatically exposed to the forces of global economic restructuring.

Liverpool: World City?

> London and New York stand in the same rank as Liverpool, as commercial cities, but in some respects, as a place of commerce, it surpasses even the great capitals of the Old and the New World.
>
> Thomas Baines, *Liverpool in 1859*

> [Liverpool] is the New York of Europe, a world city rather than merely British provincial.
>
> *Illustrated London News*, 15 May 1886

Although Liverpool was the smallest of the four cities that King suggests formed the second tier of Britain's colonial urban system, its global reach was undoubtedly greater than that of its immediate rivals. Indeed, Liverpool's integration into world markets had come early, pre-dating the industrial revolution. Soon after becoming an independent port in 1647, Liverpool entered into direct competition with Bristol, Cardiff and London for ascendancy in the lucrative global market in slaves. Following the construction of the world's first enclosed dock in 1715, Liverpool quickly began to gain on its rivals and 'at the end of the eighteenth century [Liverpool] had captured nearly a half of the whole European slave trade, and well over half of the British' (Merseyside Socialist Research Group, 1980: 27). Following the abolition of the transatlantic slave trade in 1808, the city largely built its wealth on the burgeoning Lancashire cotton industry and by 1850 Liverpool handled some 85 per cent of Britain's total annual import of 1.75 million cotton bales (Victorian Society, 1967: 4). As the industrial revolution gathered pace, the port handled an increasing volume of cotton, sugar, grain and tobacco imports and became the principal British port for the export of coal and manufactured goods.

It is no exaggeration to say that by the mid-nineteenth century Liverpool 'with London and New York, was one of the three great maritime commercial centres of the world' (Victorian Society, 1967: 3). By this time, Liverpool had established trading links throughout North and South America, the West Indies, Africa and the Far East (Martin, 1950). Such was the extent of these linkages that Baines (1859: 12) records that in 1857 almost one half of all British exports were shipped from Liverpool and that the total shipping registered in Liverpool in the same year amounted to 936,022 tons, compared with 859,140 tons in London (1859: 10). The city's innovations in dock construction and management, particularly following the creation of the Mersey Docks and Harbour Board in 1857, established Liverpool's global reputation as a model port. Thus, Kirkaldy (1914: 519) reports in his history of British shipping that 'it was Liverpool that first taught the world how a great commercial river and port should be managed'. Moreover, with its leading role as a node for international trade came other forms of integration into the world economy, particularly in the emerging banking, futures and insurance markets. Thus, as Foreman-Peck (1995: xii) reports, when the fall in grain prices in 1857 prompted a crisis among the financial institutions that had lent against the security of high prices, the ensuing 'financial panic and collapse spread from New York to Liverpool, to London and Paris'. Indeed, in the light of such linkages John (1959: 24) claims that the ties between Liverpool and New York in the mid-nineteenth century were 'as close as between Liverpool and London'. Such evidence suggests that Liverpool's global role partly transcended the national urban system in which it was located, thus foreshadowing one of the key hypotheses regarding contemporary world city formation.

During the nineteenth century Liverpool developed key regulatory functions associated with international trade. In particular, the need to regulate aspects of the cotton industry – price, quality, weight – resulted in the formation of the Cotton Brokers' Association in 1841, subsequently reconstituted in 1876 as the Liverpool Cotton Association. Such was the influence of this body that 'the "standards" for various growths of cotton [. . .] established by Liverpool are the universally recognised and accepted standards on which all European cotton transactions are based' (Wilson, 1928: 30). Significantly, the Association's remit included the regulation of the Liverpool futures market which had developed initially as a means of dealing with fluctuations in world cotton prices and had grown dramatically following the laying of the Atlantic cable in 1866. By the late nineteenth century, Liverpool, along with New York and New Orleans, was established as one of the three largest cotton futures markets in the world. Similarly, Liverpool's central importance to futures markets in other commodities was also consolidated in the late nineteenth and early twentieth centuries. Thus, a Stanford University report published in 1936 noted that Liverpool was one of four global centres for trading in grain and suggested that 'for many good reasons, the Liverpool futures prices – more nearly than any other market – represent world price levels' (cited in Martin, 1950: 31).

By the mid-nineteenth century Liverpool had also established itself as the key point of departure for migration from the British Isles. Of the 213,000 emigrants leaving Britain in 1857, some 158,000 (74 per cent) left from Liverpool. Moreover, as the flow of international migration increased, the proportion of British emigrants leaving from Liverpool grew. Of the estimated 5.5 million emigrants who left Britain from 1860 to 1900, all but 750,000 embarked from Liverpool, meaning that the city accounted for 86 per cent of the total (Merseyside Socialist Research Group, 1980: 28). This growth in international migration was, to a significant extent, underpinned by the development of steamship travel, in which the port of Liverpool played a leading role. Although the first transatlantic crossing by steam made from the British Isles sailed from Cork and Bristol, it was the Liverpool-based Cunard Company that won the first British government tender to convey mail by steamship in 1840. As steamship travel grew more popular, there was heightened competition to reduce journey times and improve conditions, thus appealing to a more affluent, and hence more lucrative, market. Competition for the Blue Riband saw the record average speeds for east-bound transatlantic crossings rise progressively from 10.72 knots in 1840, to 15.94 knots in 1876 and 21.09 in 1893 (Chandler, 1960). Boasting some of the world's most renowned shipping lines, such as Cunard and the White Star Line, Liverpool established itself as the principal port for steamship travel between Britain and the United States in the late nineteenth century (Longbottom, 1995).

As in the contemporary world city, the concentration of international business concerns and the market for specialist service functions in nineteenth-century Liverpool prompted the development of perhaps the most extensive office sector outside London. Dominated by international cotton traders and shipping agents Liverpool's office sector grew rapidly, and the city was noted for its collection of tall buildings, many of four and five storeys (Stenhouse, 1984). Key financial functions were attracted to the city as a result of its commercial success: a Liverpool stock exchange was established in 1836 to serve northwest England (Liverpool Stock Exchange, 1936), and a branch of the Bank of England was established with a similar remit during the 1840s. However, it was the insurance industry that constituted the key financial service in nineteenth-century Liverpool. A Liverpool Underwriters Association was formed in 1802, denoting the importance of insurance to the shipping industry (Martin, 1950), though it was not until 1836 that the first Liverpool-based insurance company, the Liverpool Fire and Life Office, was established (*Liverpool Daily Post*, 1927b). Following the creation of the Royal

Insurance Company in 1845, Liverpool rapidly established itself as Britain's principal insurance centre outside London (Hughes, 1999: 54). As a result, at the beginning of the twentieth century Liverpool's office district was highly influential – a 'centre of international authority' (Stenhouse, 1984: 85) – and in 1911, an estimated 32,076 men were employed in specialist commercial jobs, making up 8 per cent of all male employment in the city (Gould, 1982: 4).

Liverpool's reputation as one of a small number of key centres of international commerce lent the city an audacious self-confidence. In 1886, the city hosted the International Exhibition of Navigation, Commerce and Industry, occupying a site in Wavertree 13 acres larger than that used for the Great Exhibition held at South Kensington in 1851 (Belchem, 2000: 5). With the global economy approaching its peak in the early twentieth century, Liverpool's air of assured supremacy became even more evident. Although competition from other ports had seen the city's share of British trade fall steadily since the 1850s, Liverpool remained a comfortable second to London in the value of imports and exports handled and its export trade typically exceeded that of the capital (Kirkaldy, 1914). Thus, a specially commissioned history of the city, published to celebrate its 700th anniversary, underlined its elite global status: 'At the end of her seventh century as a chartered borough, Liverpool finds herself among the greatest three or four ports in the world' (Muir and Platt, 1906: 297). Likewise, in the face of growing competition from Southampton for transatlantic passenger shipping, the Cunard Company introduced two new super-liners, the *Lusitania* and the *Mauretania*, on its Liverpool–New York route, with the two ships retaining the Blue Riband for Cunard for the entire period from 1907 to 1929. As is typical of cities with global articulations, the desire to mark Liverpool's standing in the world economy came to be reflected in the built environment, most evidently in the redevelopment of the pier head. In the early twentieth century the Liverpool waterfront was thus transformed through the completion of new headquarters for three of Liverpool's principal commercial concerns: the Mersey Docks and Harbour Board building (1907), the Royal Liver building (1911) and the Cunard building (1914).

Governing the Gateway to Empire: The Role of the Merchant Class

> Liverpool, thanks to modern science and commercial enterprise, to the spirit and intelligence of the townsmen, and to the administration of the Mersey Docks and Harbour Board, has become a wonder of the world.
>
> *Illustrated London News*, 15 May 1886

Accounts of Liverpool's ascent to 'Gateway to Empire' frequently point to the key roles played by both the Liverpool Corporation and the Mersey Docks and Harbour Board in creating the local conditions for maritime growth (Baines, 1859; Muir and Platt, 1906; Belchem, 2000). The Webbs, for example, suggested that the Liverpool Corporation 'showed itself, generation after generation, markedly superior in energy, dignity, integrity and public spirit to any other Municipal

Corporation' (cited in Belchem, 2000: 9). However, the city's emergence as a key international port was not simply a product of competent local administration. Rather, Liverpool's claim to be the 'second city' of the British Empire appears to have been founded on the active participation of its merchant class in the expansion of British imperial interests and its concomitant influence on aspects of local governance. The political economy of Liverpool's growth thus gave rise to a distinctive set of local–global articulations that increasingly tied the city into a co-dependent relationship with Britain's colonies. Interestingly, it also gave rise to forms of active commercial involvement in wider city governance networks that find significant parallels in contemporary accounts of change in local government (Atkinson and Wilks-Heeg, 2000).

The key means through which Liverpool merchants influenced the development of the Empire was, of course, the extensive trading links they had pioneered, which played a lead role in establishing the context for colonial expansion. As a 1967 conference report makes clear, 'it was Liverpool's business houses which largely created the West African economy by expanding the market for, and supply of, palm oil; who built the docks and stimulated the industries of Hong Kong; and who developed the banana trade with the Canaries' (Victorian Society, 1967: 3). However, the role of the Liverpool merchants in the expansion of the British Empire was often political as well as economic. In several cases, Liverpool's merchants lobbied national government directly to protect their commercial interests through a policy of imperialism and they increasingly organised themselves collectively to pursue such ends. Thus, the African Association, representing merchants with trading interests with the African continent, is proudly cited in a history of the Liverpool Chamber of Commerce 'as a remarkable example of the flag following trade: or, to put it more emphatically, of Government policy being initiated and developed by commerce' (Martin, 1950: 35). Similarly, there were cases where Liverpool merchants pushed for the government to intervene to defend their interests against 'unfair competition'. In the late nineteenth century French and German merchants 'began to enter territory hitherto regarded by British merchants as historically and commercially their own [...] the foreigners claiming that they had as much right to share in the spoils of West Africa as any other country' (Martin, 1950: 36). In response, the Liverpool Chamber of Commerce lobbied the British government directly:

> Memorials were addressed to the British government, therefore, praying that the boundaries of certain British colonies be extended; to proclaim Protectorates so that large areas might be reserved for future trade development; to delimit some of the more recent claims made by other Powers; to press for uniform tariffs within agreed areas; to improve communications and build water works; to assist in the collection and preparation of raw materials; and to introduce money measures and legislation to give effect to all those requests. (Martin, 1950: 6)

In other instances the business community sought, successfully, to mobilise local governance in order to protect and foster the city's role in the colonial economy. The foundation of the Liverpool School of Tropical Medicine is a case in point. During the 1890s, concerned by high death rates from malaria among the British commercial community in West Africa, the Chamber of Commerce initiated discussions with Liverpool's Royal Southern Hospital to investigate the possibilities of furthering the study of tropical diseases. Following agreement that the chair of the Chamber's African section would contribute £350 per annum to running costs, the School of Tropical Medicine was opened in 1899, governed by a committee made up of representatives from the Chamber, University College, Liverpool, the Royal Southern Hospital and the Liverpool Ship and Steamship Owners' Association. By 1912, the new institution had devoted over £100,000 to research expeditions (Martin, 1950). A second example illustrates the same dynamics. In 1902 the Chamber of Commerce organised a petition to the monarch supporting the case for an independent University of Liverpool. The document points to 'continuous cooperation in the cause of commercial education' stating that 'in 1897 a joint committee was formed consisting of representatives of the Chamber, the City Council and the University College' (cited in Martin, 1950: 114). It goes on to note, in particular, this joint committee's development of language classes, citing the need for such provision as one of the key arguments in favour of an independent university:

> The petitioners represent the largest interests of the commerce and shipping of this port. The imports and exports at Liverpool in 1900 amounted to £227,000,000, i.e. more than one-fourth of the combined imports and exports of the United Kingdom. [. . .] The foreign and colonial trade of the port is carried on with every country in the world and especially with the great nations of both hemispheres, their colonies and dependencies. A knowledge of foreign languages is, therefore, a first necessity of many of those engaged in trade at the port, or who are sent abroad to represent the great shipping and commercial houses of the United Kingdom. And consequently, there are needed in this city the greatest possible facilities for the thorough teaching of languages of the West and East. [. . .] A Liverpool University should help supply such wants. (cited in Martin, 1950: 114–15)

Economic Decline: Liverpool's Colonial Legacy?

> They should build a fence around [Liverpool] and charge admission. For sadly, it has become a 'showcase' of everything that has gone wrong in Britain's major cities.
>   *Daily Mirror*, 11 October 1982, cited in Lane, 1987: 11

Liverpool – or at least its merchant class – had prospered exceptionally from Britain's dominance of the world economy and the steady growth of world trade up to 1914. Exporting a higher volume and value of goods than any other British port, Liverpool's wealth was tied directly to the country's manufacturing strength and, in particular, to the importance of the Empire as a market for British manufactured goods. Liverpool's economy was built around the port to an exceptional degree and there had been very limited diversification in the local economy by the

Table 1: Changes in UK trade by volume, 1913–1925 (%)

Year	Imports	Exports
1913	100	100
1914	90.0	82.2
1915	97.5	67.9
1916	83.2	70.4
1917	69.6	58.9
1918	71.7	40.5
1919	87.0	52.2
1920	87.4	69.0
1921	76.1	49.2
1922	87.4	69.0
1923	96.3	77.4
1924	107.8	80.3
1925	111.0	79.6

Source: Alford, 1996: 108.

start of the twentieth century: even more so than London, Liverpool was over-whelmingly a commercial, and not an industrial, centre.

Given this context, the patterns of change in British trade after 1913 were nothing short of catastrophic for Liverpool. Table 1 shows that during the war the volume of British exports declined sharply and by 1925 was at only 80 per cent of the 1913 level. A similar, though less dramatic, pattern is observable in relation to imports, which first returned to their 1913 level in 1923. Moreover, while a modest recovery in British exports took place from 1925 until 1929, decline set in again thereafter and by 1938 the volume of exported goods was 77 per cent of that thirteen years previously (Alford, 1996: 141). These trends did not only reflect an absolute decline in world trade – they were also an indication of Britain's declining importance as an exporter of manufactured goods: whereas Britain's share of world trade in manufactures was 33 per cent in 1990, it was just 9 per cent in 1955 (King, 1990b: 87).

While the volume of British exports was to increase steadily after 1945 in the context of a long-run expansion in world trade, Britain's share of world exports continued to decline. Moreover, the pattern of British trading relations was to change significantly. Table 2 shows that from 1948 to 1983, British trade with the EEC and other West European countries grew at the direct expense of trade with both the so-called 'white dominions' (Australia, Canada, New Zealand, etc.) and with less developed countries. Since the 1950s 'the UK economy has been integrated with that of the (European) Community at the relative expense of links with the USA and ex-colonial Commonwealth countries' (King, 1990b: 87). Thus, while Britain sent 17.9 per cent of its visible exports to the future EEC countries in 1948, by 1983 the EEC accounted for 43.4 per cent of the total. Conversely, exports to the 'white dominions' and less developed countries were 23.7 and 27.1 per cent respectively of UK exports in 1948 and just 5.3 and 7.5 per cent by 1983.

Table 2: UK visible trade by area, selected years, 1948–1983 (%)

a) Imports

	1948	1958	1965	1974	1983
EEC	13.2	20.1	23.6	33.4	45.9
Other W. Europe	8.1	10.1	12.5	14.8	16.2
USA	8.8	9.3	11.7	9.7	11.0
Japan	0.3	0.9	1.4	2.5	5.2
'White dominions'	25.3	20.1	18.6	8.7	5.1
OPEC	6.9	12.1	9.7	16.4	4.3
New industrialised countries	2.5	2.3	2.4	3.2	4.8
Centrally planned economies	2.9	3.2	4.3	3.2	2.4
Other less developed countries	32.1	21.7	15.8	8.2	5.2

b) Exports

	1948	1958	1965	1974	1983
EEC	17.9	19.6	26.4	33.4	43.4
Other W. Europe	12.7	10.5	15.3	17.4	13.1
USA	4.3	8.7	10.6	10.7	14.1
Japan	0.0	0.6	1.1	1.9	1.3
'White dominions'	23.7	22.2	18.0	11.3	5.3
OPEC	7.3	7.9	5.5	7.3	10.1
New industrialised countries	4.6	3.5	3.6	4.2	3.3
Centrally planned economies	2.4	3.2	2.9	3.0	1.9
Other less developed countries	27.1	23.7	16.5	10.7	7.5

Source: Alford, 1996: 230 and 303.

These trends had a direct impact on Liverpool as a port, since the city's wealth had been built on trading links with Africa and North America. The tonnage passing through Liverpool had increased fourfold between 1858 and 1914 and registered tonnage at the port reached 19.0 million by 1914 (Gould, 1982: 3). But Liverpool's overall share of British trade was falling, from a high of 45 per cent to less than 25 per cent in 1914. Liverpool's relative standing among British ports was given a temporary boost by a shift in shipping and trading patterns arising from the First World War. The city's share of total UK trade rose to 36.8 per cent in 1918, remaining above pre-1914 levels until 1921. Thereafter, while there were expansions in some areas, the overall tonnage handled by the port of Liverpool went into decline (Hyde, 1971). In particular, Liverpool's share of British imports fell sharply, from 36 per cent in 1913 to just 20 per cent in 1939, indicating that 'the exceptional importance of Liverpool in the import trade of the United Kingdom had gone' (Corlett, 1946: 21). And while Liverpool remained the most significant UK port for exports during the inter-war years, handling 30 per cent of British exports, there had been a sharp drop in the total exports by value (Lister, 1983: 126).

Table 3: Net registered tons (millions) passing through the Port of Liverpool, 1858–1939, selected years

Year	Tonnage	Year	Tonnage	Year	Tonnage
1858	4.4	1890	9.6	1920	13.4
1860	4.7	1900	12.3	1930	16.2
1870	5.7	1910	16.6	1933	14.2
1880	7.5	1914	15.1	1939	16.6

Source: Hyde, 1971.

As Britain forfeited its dominance of world trade and the old international division of labour centred on the British Empire began to break down, Liverpool's merchants were increasingly exposed in world markets. In the context of growing international competition, they failed to exploit new markets and began to lose ground in established markets to overseas interests. One example is the Brazilian the rubber trade. In 1913 the Liverpool-based Booth Line exported 47 per cent of world's rubber supply from Brazil, but by the late 1920s, competition from Malaysia and the Dutch East Indies saw Brazil's (and the Booth Line's) share of the world rubber trade fall to just 2 per cent (Hyde, 1971: 152). The Harrison Line experienced a similar decline in its cotton piece exports, which, by 1930, had fallen to just 20 per cent of their 1913 levels. This decline was due, in part, to a boycott of British-made cotton goods by the Indian Congress Party, demonstrating the effect of nationalist action against the colonial power.

With Liverpool's fortunes tied to Britain's standing in the international economy, British decline after 1913 also became Liverpool's decline. Employment in Liverpool was dominated by the port, primarily in dock-work, but also in associated commercial services. In 1931 the Board of Trade estimated that more than half of all insured workers on Merseyside were employed in industries associated with shipping, transport and distribution, compared with just 23 per cent in Britain as a whole (cited in Bean, 1983: 95). Decline in port activity between 1918 and 1939 inevitably had a devastating impact on local employment and unemployment rates reached 28 per cent in 1932, compared with a national rate of 22 per cent. Liverpool's unemployment rate has remained above the national average ever since.

Although specific initiatives aimed at combating the decline in port trade were embarked on from the 1920s, they invariably failed to recognise the full implications of changes in the world economy for the city. It is also significant that such economic development focused exclusively on attracting industrial production to the city and made no attempt to build on the city's considerable service sector strengths. In 1923 the Liverpool Organisation was established to advance the interests of Liverpool 'as a leading industrial centre'. The result of direct co-operation between the city council and local businesses, the Liverpool Organisation promoted the city as a site for inward investment both in the UK and abroad. In 1927 the *Liverpool Daily Post*, in association with the Liverpool Organisation, published *The Ambassador of Commerce*, a supplement highlighting the industrial and commercial 'potentialities' of Merseyside (*Liverpool Daily Post*, 1927a). Readers were encouraged to 'advance the interests of the Port by despatching a copy of this issue to some suitable quarter'. A remarkable portent of future forms of governance in the city, most notably the Mersey Partnership established in the 1990s (see Atkinson and Wilks-Heeg, 2000), it was reported in the same publication that 'the Liverpool Organisation [. . .] is influencing what people think about Liverpool the whole world over. It is broadcasting in every language its advantages as an industrial centre and a great seaport' (*Liverpool Daily Post*, 1927a: 35)

National and local government initiatives to strengthen the economic base of Merseyside date from the 1930s. National government's response initially concentrated more on the harder hit areas of the North East and Wales and although Merseyside was included in the 1931 Board of Trade Inquiry, it was omitted from later regional surveys and left outside regional aid measures. However, the Liverpool Corporation Act of 1936 gave the City Council new powers, including authority for land development and industrial promotion, that were 'unprecedented for a British Local Authority and gave the city a unique role in the sponsorship of regional economic adaptation' (Lister, 1983: 154). In 1936 the City Council approved the development of two industrial estates, at Speke and Fazakerley, and by 1938 16 factories had opened at Speke alone. But despite manufacturing expansion across Merseyside, there were almost as many factory closures as openings between 1931 and 1938 and male unemployment remained high – 18 per cent in 1938 (Lister, 1983: 158). Meanwhile, these attempts to diversify the Liverpool economy by attracting manufacturing investment sat alongside promotional material that proudly proclaimed Liverpool's key role in the international economy. The 1930 City of Liverpool Handbook boasted of Liverpool's international significance and, in declaring it to be the 'second seaport of the world', persisted with the increasingly defunct notion of the city's centrality to the colonial mode of production. Similarly, a second supplement to the *Liverpool Daily Post*, published in 1927 to celebrate the opening of the Gladstone system of docks (*Liverpool Daily Post*, 1927b), had portrayed Liverpool in a similar vein, taking every opportunity to highlight the city's international significance: 'the world's fastest ocean service' (15); 'the greatest port authority in the world' (26); 'the world's greatest cotton market' (52).

The post-1945 period was to prove no kinder to Liverpool as a port. The lucrative transatlantic passenger lines inevitably declined as air travel increased. Even more importantly, the growth of British trade with Europe and the concomitant decline in trade with the Commonwealth 'left Liverpool marooned on the wrong side of the country' (Lane, 1987: 45). In the two decades from the mid-1960s trade shifted decisively to the east coast ports with the result that Liverpool slipped from second to sixth in the hierarchy of UK ports (see Table 4). Lane (1987: 46) notes that while Dover and Felixstowe handled just one-ninth of Liverpool's volume of goods *between them* in 1966, they were individually handling 10 per cent more than Liverpool in 1985. Attempts to attract manufacturing investment continued and, from the mid-1960s, the Labour government's regional policies resulted in a number of international companies locating and expanding operations in and

Table 4: Ten largest UK ports, 1966 and 1985

1966	1985
1 London	1 London
2 **Liverpool**	2 Tees and Hartlepool
3 Tees and Hartlepool	3 Grimsby and Immingham
4 Manchester	4 Felixstowe
5 Clyde	5 Dover
6 Hull	6 **Liverpool**
7 Newport	7 Clyde
8 Bristol	8 Medway
9 Port Talbot	9 Port Talbot
10 Grimsby and Immingham	10 Manchester

Source: Lane, 1987: 47.

around Liverpool, including Dunlop, Ford, Lucas Engineering and Kodak. However, Liverpool's long-awaited success in attracting manufacturing investment was to prove short-lived. The city had simply become dependent on a branch-plant economy that was shortly due to collapse as a result of the shift of TNC production from the core to the periphery and semi-periphery. In the mid-1970s it was estimated that a half of Merseyside's workforce were employed in factories with more than 1,000 employees (Merseyside Socialist Research Group, 1980: 19). In the period 1975–78 alone some 50,000 redundancies were announced in the Merseyside Special Development Area, with the result that unemployment in the county rose to 11.7 per cent (Merseyside Socialist Research Group, 1980: 10–11). Liverpool's descent from world city at the centre of the old international division of labour to pariah city in the new international division of labour was thus complete. There can be no more dramatic a case of a city that had been a key driver of globalisation subsequently becoming one of its most significant victims.

Conclusion

The historical analysis presented in this chapter has implications for urban theory as well as urban policy and practice. In arguing that Liverpool's historic rise and decline were closely linked to processes of restructuring in the global economy, this chapter has sought to show that contemporary patterns of global city formation have important parallels in the nineteenth century. While the emergence of a particular group of global cities must, in part, be explained by these earlier patterns of urbanisation, it is equally apparent that the shift to a new international division of labour has implications for cities at all levels of the global urban hierarchy, many of which have yet to be explored. This account has also sought to make clear that the political economy of Liverpool's rise as a global city in the nineteenth-century world economy was based critically on the engagement of its merchant class in aspects of politics and governance at multiple spatial scales. Similarly, the decline of Liverpool from 1914, though linked closely to the demise of the colonial mode of production from which the city's commercial interests had prospered, was not an inevitable process. The way in which the governance of Liverpool related to international economic change was thus as much of a factor in its emergence as a city with global articulations as it was in its steady economic decline.

Such analysis may now be more pertinent that ever. Since the mid-1990s Liverpool has entered a period of sustained growth and there is now a widespread recognition of the city's claims to be spearheading an urban renaissance. Although the Port has continued to restructure, and now employs only a few hundred people, it has also experienced substantial growth in recent years and today handles more cargo than at any time in its history. The city boasts a booming cultural scene, has become an increasingly popular tourist destination and, outside London, is rivalled only by Manchester in its explosion of city centre 'loft living'. However, while there is a powerful, and long overdue sense of optimism about the city's future, Liverpool continues to experience some of the worst poverty of any UK city and doubts remain about the real extent of the city's economic recovery. Based on the arguments advanced in this chapter, it would seem that the key issue for those engaged in shaping Liverpool's current development trajectory is to understand the extent to which the city's future will be shaped by its past. Indeed, history may be as much part of the solution as it is part of the problem. For, as Belchem (2000: 30) notes: 'Packaged as heritage, history has become Liverpool's main "trade" and source of attraction, the last hope for a city blighted by post-industrial collapse and now ill-placed geographically [. . .] for trade with European partners'.

References

Alford, B. W. E. (1996), *Britain in the World Economy Since 1880*, London: Longman

Anderson, B. L., and Stoney, P. J. M. (eds) (1983), *Commerce, Industry and Transport: Studies in Economic Change on Merseyside*, Liverpool: Liverpool University Press

Atkinson, H., and Wilks-Heeg, S. (2000), *Local Government From Thatcher to Blair: The Politics of Creative Autonomy*, Cambridge: Polity Press

Baines, T. (1859), *Liverpool in 1859*, London: Longman and Co.

Bean, R. (1983), 'The Port of Liverpool: Employers and Industrial Relations, 1919–1939', in Anderson and Stoney (eds)

Belchem, J. (2000), *Merseypride: Essays in Liverpool Exceptionalism*, Liverpool: Liverpool University Press

Braudel, F. (1983), *The Perspective of the World*, New York: Collins

Brenner, N. (1998), 'Global Cities, Glocal States: Global City Formation and State Territorial Restructuring in Contemporary Europe', *Review of International Political Economy*, 5(1): 1–37

Brenner, N. (1999), 'Globalisation as Reterritorialisation: The Re-scaling of Urban Governance in the European Union', *Urban Studies*, 36(3): 431–51

Brenner, N. (2000), *Entrepreneurial Cities, 'Glocalizing' States and the New Politics of Scale: Rethinking the Political Geographies of Urban Governance in Western Europe*, Working Paper #76a and #76b, Centre for European Studies, Harvard University

Chandler, G. (1960), *Liverpool Shipping: A Short History*, London: Phoenix House

Cheshire, P. C. (1990), 'Explaining the Recent Performance of the European Community's Major Urban Regions', *Urban Studies*, 27: 311–34

Cheshire, P. C. (1999), 'Cities in Competition: Articulating the Gains from Integration', *Urban Studies*, 36(5–6): 843–64

Cheshire, P. C., Carbanaro, G., and Hay, D. G. (1986), 'Problems of Decline and Growth in EEC Countries', *Urban Studies*, 23(2): 131–49

Corlett, W. J. (1946), *The Import Trade of the Port of Liverpool: Future Prospects*, Liverpool: The University Press of Liverpool

Dematteis, G. (2000), 'Spatial Images of European Urbanisation', in A. Bagnasco and P. Le Gales (eds), *Cities in Contemporary Europe*, Cambridge: Cambridge University Press

Dunning, J. H. (1983), 'Changes in the Level and Structure of International Economic Production: The Last One Hundred Years', in M. Casson (ed.), *The Growth of International Business*, London: George Allen and Unwin

Feagin, J. R. (1985), 'The Global Context of Metropolitan Growth: Houston and the Oil Industry', *American Journal of Sociology*, 90(6): 1204–30

Feagin, J. R., and Smith, M. P. (1989), 'Cities and the New International Division of Labour: An Overview', in M. P. Smith and J. Feagin (eds), *The Capitalist City*, Cambridge, MA: Basil Blackwell

Foreman-Peck, J. (1995), *A History of the World Economy: International Economic Relations Since 1850*, Hemel Hempstead: Harvester Wheatsheaf, 2nd edn

Fröbel, F., Heinrichs, J., and Kreye, O. (1980), *The New International Division of Labour*, Cambridge: Cambridge University Press

Gould, W. T. S. (1982), *The Resources of Merseyside*, Liverpool: Liverpool University Press

Hirst, P., and Thompson, G. (1999), *Globalisation in Question*, Cambridge: Polity Press

Hughes, Q. (1993), *Seaport: Architecture and Townscape in Liverpool*, Liverpool: Bluecoat Press

Hughes, Q. (1999), *Liverpool: City of Architecture*, Liverpool: Bluecoat Press

Hyde, F. E. (1971), *Liverpool and the Mersey: The Development of a Port, 1700–1970*, Newton Abbot: David & Charles

John, A. H. (1959), *Liverpool Merchant House: The History of Alfred Booth and Company*, London: George Allen and Unwin

Kenwood, A. G., and Lougheed, A. (1992), *The Growth of the International Economy, 1820–1990*, London: Routledge

King, A. D. (1976), *Colonial Urban Development: Culture, Social Power and Environment*, London: Routledge & Kegan Paul

King, A. D. (1990a), *Urbanism, Colonialism and the World Economy*, London: Routledge & Kegan Paul

King, A. D. (1990b), *Global Cities: Post-Imperialism and the Internationalisation of London*, London: Routledge & Kegan Paul

Kirkaldy, A. W. (1914), *British Shipping: its History, Organisation and Importance*, London

Lane, T. (1987), *Liverpool: Gateway of Empire*, London: Lawrence and Wishart

Lever, W. F. (1999), 'Competitive Cities in Europe', *Urban Studies*, 35(5–6): 1029–44

Lister, P. H. (1983), 'Regional Policies and Industrial Development on Merseyside, 1930–60', in Anderson and Stoney (eds)

Liverpool Daily Post (1927a), *The Ambassador of Commerce: Merseyside's Industrial and Commercial Potentialities*, Supplement to the *Liverpool Daily Post*, 21 February

Liverpool Daily Post (1927b), *The Foundations of Liverpool's Greatness: Docks and Shipping*, Supplement to the *Liverpool Daily Post*, 18 July

Liverpool Stock Exchange (1936), *The Centenary Book of the Liverpool Stock Exchange 1830–1936*

Longbottom, K. (1995), *Liverpool and the Mersey. Volume 1: Gladstone Docks and the Great Liners*, Peterborough: Silver Link

Mariner, S. (1982), *The Economic and Social Development of Merseyside*, London: Croom Helm

Martin, W. A. G. (1950), *A Century of Liverpool's Commerce*, Liverpool: Liverpool Chamber of Commerce

Merseyside Socialist Research Group (1980), *Merseyside in Crisis*, Manchester: Manchester Free Press

Muir, J. R. B., and Platt, E. M. (1906), *A History of Municipal Government in Liverpool, from earliest times to the Municipal Reform Act of 1835*, London: Williams and Norgate

Robertson, R. (1992), *Globalization: Social Theory and Global Culture*, London: Sage

Sassen-Koob, S. (1984), 'The New Labour Demand in Global Cities', in M.P. Smith (ed.), *Cities in Transformation*, London: Sage

Schwartz, H. E. (2000), *States versus Markets: The Emergence of the Global Economy*, London: Macmillan

Stenhouse, D. K. (1984), 'Liverpool's Office District 1875–1905', *Historic Society of Lancashire and Cheshire*, Volume 133: 77–85

Victorian Society (1967), *Victorian Seaport: 5th Annual Conference Report*, London: Victorian Society

Wilson, S. (1928), 'Liverpool as a Market', in *The Book of Liverpool*, Liverpool: The Liverpool Organisation

3. Urban Regeneration, Politics and Social Cohesion: The Liverpool Case

Richard Meegan

Peter Hall concludes his authoritative history of urban planning, *Cities of Tomorrow*, with a despairing discussion of the persistence of poverty and disadvantage in the city, of what he reluctantly describes as the 'city of the permanent underclass' (Hall, 2002). Although he does not use Liverpool to support his argument, there is no question that he could have done so. At the height of its global economic and political power, the city had a marked social geography. In the south were the mansions of the wealthy (Liverpool housed the largest number of millionaires of any city in the country at the time) while in the north end of the city were the overcrowded and unsanitary cellars and courts whose inhabitants experienced a poverty that, unlike that of today, was both relative *and* absolute. Contemporary press reports referred to these areas in a language of social pathology that was to be echoed, albeit less bluntly, in some of the early debates about the 'urban problem' in Britain in the 1960s:

> Here resides a population which is a people in itself, ceaselessly ravaged by fever, plagued by the blankest, most appalling poverty, cut off from every grace and comfort of life, born, living, and dying amid squalid surroundings, of which those who have not seen them can form a very inadequate conception. (extracted from an article investigating 'Squalid Liverpool' in the *Liverpool Daily Post*, November 1883)

Flash forward 120 years and we see the city introducing a Neighbourhood Renewal Strategy (Liverpool Partnership Group, 2002a) aimed at tackling a geography of social exclusion that takes in not only the areas in the 'north end' of the city that had so concerned Victorian commentators but also inner-city and outlying social housing areas in the south (including Speke as discussed in a number of chapters below).

As Stuart Wilks-Heeg argued in the previous chapter, the city has experienced a profound economic and social restructuring as it has gone from playing a leading role in the 'old international division of labour', based around colonial and imperial trading connections, to the urban core of a city-region officially designated as a 'lagging region' in the European segment of the triadic structure of the global economy (USA–Europe–Japan and the Pacific Rim). Figure 1 shows how this transformation has been reflected in the city's population. The population grew from 5,000 at the beginning of the eighteenth century to just over 700,000 at the start of the twentieth century; and it continued to grow thereafter, to a peak of

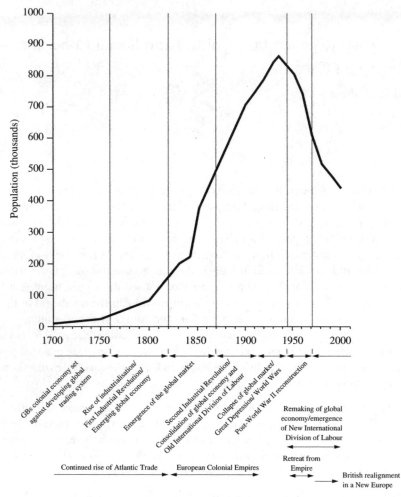

Sources:
(i) Population figures: Brabner, n.d.; Cook and Stevenson, 1978; Lawton and Pooley, 1992; 1991 Census of Population Preliminary Report for England and Wales 2001 Census of Population.

(ii) Periodisation: Hobsbawm, 1989; Barraclough, 1986; Knox and Agnew, 1989; Marshall, 1987; Taylor, 1989; Pollard, 1992, 1997.

Figure 1. Liverpool's population in global economic and geopolitical context

around 870,000 just before the start of the Second World War. The decline there-after has been relentless, only slowing down in the 1990s. The 2001 Census shows that there were some 440,000 people living in the city, very nearly half of the peak in the late 1930s. And this contraction, as already indicated, has been the context for the development within the city of a mosaic of social advantage/disadvantage.

Liverpool is, of course, not alone in experiencing increasing social exclusion and polarisation. Cities across Europe and the USA are also displaying, in varying degrees, similar patterns and processes, as Peter Hall (2002) acknowledges. These patterns and processes appear to be the outcome of what can best be described as 'disjointed structural change' (Allen and Cars, 2002). Structural economic change impacting on aggregate employment patterns through broad sectoral and occupational shifts produces new demands (in terms of the provision of education, housing and social insurance) on welfare states that are limited in their capacity to adjust by financial constraints operating on them as part of the political adjustment to the changing role of the state in increasingly global economic management. The loss of (manual) employment and long-term increase in unemployment, accompanied by the growth of flexible labour in service sectors demanding particular accredited and personal skills, have detached from the labour market groups and individuals who are also suffering the effects of a welfare state that is struggling to cope (in terms of education, income support and housing). In metropolitan areas, these macro-structural processes interact with micro-local factors in the form of labour, land and property markets to produce geographical concentrations of disadvantaged groups (Byrne, 1999; Glennerster et al., 1999; Madanipour, 1998; Musterd and Ostendorf, 1998). This socio-spatial polarisation, as Liverpool also amply demonstrates, has proved to be highly resistant, if not impervious, to remedial state intervention, both national and local.

In this chapter, I want to trace Liverpool's recent history, charting some of the key attempts at 'regeneration' in five periods: the decentralisation of population and employment in the 1950s and 1960s; the inner-city focus of the 1970s; the radical politics of the 1980s; the 'governance by partnership' of the 1990s; and the city's current position at the start of the third millennium.

'Liverpool Turned Inside-out': The 1950s and 1960s

Liverpool was probably at the peak of its economic power at the turn of the twentieth century, a power symbolised in the bricks and mortar of the three world-famous waterfront buildings at the Pier Head, which were started in 1906 and finished in 1917. But while these buildings were being erected, the world was changing, the international division of labour was changing and with it Liverpool's role. In the inter-war years, as global trade (and the old international division of labour) closed down, the city was pushed into recession as its trading links both globally and domestically were severed. Developments in the national spatial division of labour, pulling the locus of economic activity away from the north and north-west towards the midlands and south-east, were working inexorably against the city.[1]

---

[1] The threats were disguised to a degree, however, by the onset of the Second World War when the western-facing port fulfilled one of its greatest roles, handling the materials and food that helped to sustain the country in the war against Fascism.

Both the national and local state were aware of these trends. The city was the first local authority in Britain to seek legal power to undertake local economic development – in the shape of the Liverpool Corporation Act (1936). The Act gave the council the necessary powers to buy up land on the city's outskirts for industrial development and was partly inspired by the city failing to qualify for designation for assistance from central government's first attempts at regional policy (with the Special Areas Act of 1934). The aim was to try to create new employment opportunities to compensate for the already apparent decline of port and port-related activity. 'Urban entrepreneurialism' got off to an early start in Liverpool.[2]

The council's efforts in this direction were overtaken by preparation for what became the Second World War, which steered development towards military-related production. The Merseyside Plan, drawn up just before the end of the war, confirmed the move to base future development (it was not then referred to as 'regeneration') of the city on the decentralisation of both population and industry from the core of the city-region (effectively north Liverpool) to the outskirts. The problems of overcrowding and slum housing, exacerbated by wartime bomb damage, had put housing firmly on the local political agenda, where it has remained, albeit with differing emphases, pretty resolutely ever since. Shifting people to new homes in municipal housing estates on the city's outskirts and in nearby New Towns was seen as a key remedy to the housing problem, although it is now clear that it produced new problems of geograph-ical and social dislocation for the 'decanted' families living in social housing perceived by them (particularly in its high-rise form) as soulless and 'anti-social'.

A key element of this decentralisation of people and economic activity was central state regional policy that helped the city-region to receive more than its share of so-called 'mobile industry'. In the six years after the war, for example, regional policy helped to steer to Liverpool some two-thirds of the employment generated by relocating industry (about 24,000 jobs). More came in a second wave in the 1960s (Meegan, 1989). These waves of investment represented a new form of external orientation for the city-region and saw it being assimilated in a new way into the newly evolving international division of labour that underpinned the 'Golden Age' of development in the advanced capitalist countries in the 1950s and 1960s (Knox and Agnew, 1998). The city's dwindling colonial role in the global economy was being replaced by integration through the operations of national and overseas-owned multinational corporations. Some features of the previous localised social structure were reinforced (the semi-skilled nature of the labour processes) while others were changed (with provision, for the first time, of substantial numbers of full-time jobs for women in the new food processing plants). But it was a fairly tenuous connection, as was revealed in the restructuring

---

[2] If Liverpool is anything to go by, then 'urban entrepreneurialism' (Harvey, 1989b) is not simply a 'post-Fordist' phenomenon.

that followed the abrupt ending of the 'Golden Age' in the early 1970s and the transformation became apparent from what has been characterised as 'Fordism' and/or 'organised capitalism' to, respectively, 'post-Fordism' and 'disorganised capitalism' (Harvey, 1989a; Lash and Urry, 1987). While Britain's economic growth had been historically relatively strong during the 1960s and early 1970s, it was markedly lower than that of other 'late starters'. And just as Liverpool had both contributed to and benefited from Britain's (and previously England's) cycles of world leadership in the international economy, so it suffered as Britain lost its economic and political power.

With hindsight, it is also possible to see how the turning of the city 'inside out' in the 1950s and 1960s helped to contribute to problems in the city core through depopulation and de-industrialisation (with, for example, small firms in the inner city finding themselves unable to compete in the labour market with the multinational newcomers). And as the processes of circular and cumulative decline settled in, these problems became magnified, alongside the newly emerging social and economic problems experienced in the outer estates.

This local social geography was reflected in political concern at the national level over the perceived concentration of economic and social problems in Britain's cities. The 'regional problem' was gradually overshadowed by the 'urban problem'. Liverpool has not only been on the receiving end of virtually all of the subsequent urban policy initiatives, it has also often operated as a kind of experimental test-bed for a significant number of them.

The 'Inner-city Problems' of the 1970s

The first phase of urban policy development reflected a degree of political consensus between the two Labour governments of 1966–1970 and 1974–1979 and the intervening Conservative administration of 1970–1974. Indeed it is arguable that the Conservative administration, with its Inner Area Studies of 1972, was perhaps even more committed to intervention in the cities than its Labour counterparts. The political consensus was initially informed by a belief that the inhabitants of inner cities needed direct help to be better able to participate in their local housing and labour markets. This social pathology philosophy, emphasising the social and economic characteristics of disadvantaged inner-city residents, was only challenged towards the end of the period as a more structural approach developed, shifting emphasis away from the economic and social characteristics of inner-city residents to a political-economy perspective in which the so-called inner-city problem was seen as one produced by global and national structural change. This shift in emphasis was seen in its most radical variant in the Community Development Projects, initiated by the Labour government in 1969 but with most of the projects themselves put in place under the Conservative government of the early 1970s. Liverpool had already provided one of the two neighbourhood projects started by the Urban Programme (in the Brunswick area), and the Vauxhall area of north Liverpool was subsequently selected as one of the first wave of

Community Development Projects.[3] It was this area that had been the focus of concern over poverty a hundred years earlier. As elsewhere, a team was established in the area to analyse the problems and recommend community-based solutions. The analysis emphasised the structural problems faced by inner-city residents in both housing and labour markets and, along with most of the other projects, argued for radical, systemic change. Its critique of 'reformist' intervention found few friends in local or central government, however, and the projects were systematically wound down.[4]

Liverpool also provided one of the three Inner Area Studies (along with Birmingham and Lambeth) set up by the Conservative government in 1972, which reported to its Labour government successor. The study focused on an area to the south-east of the city centre (taking in the Smithdown, Granby and Edge Hill areas). The structural emphasis of the reports was revealed in the emphasis on the role of economic factors in shaping the fortunes of the inner cities and the less radical policy recommendations for a targeted inner-city-based approach with joint working between central and local government. The recommendations were largely taken up in the Labour government's White Paper 'Policy for the Inner Cities' in 1977 and the following 1978 Inner Areas Act. Following the latter, an Inner City partnership was formed in Liverpool (1979–1982) that took in 19 inner-city wards and parts of four adjacent ones, pretty much the whole of inner Liverpool.

Liverpool in the 1980s: City of Conflict

The regional and urban policy initiatives of the 1960s and early 1970s were swamped in their effects by the severity of global economic recession in the late 1970s and its local impact. The 'Golden Age' had seen employment in the city-region peak in the mid-1960s. Apart from the last few years, to which I will return below, there has been relentless decline thereafter and most dramatically in the late 1970s and early 1980s (Figure 2). Between 1966 and 1978, employment in the city fell by some 20 per cent (compared with national, regional and city-regional declines, respectively of 5, 12 and 15 per cent). The acceleration post-1978, however, is particularly marked. In just three years, 1978–1981, employment in the city fell by a further 18 per cent. Over the longer period, 1978–1991, 37 per cent of jobs disappeared (a loss of just under 9,000 jobs per year). The local economy was devastated. Unemployment soared and out-migration accelerated.

---

[3] There were 12 projects in all set up in four phases: Coventry, Upper Afan (Glamorgan), Southwark and Liverpool (1970); Batley, Newham (Canning Town) and Paisley (spring 1971); Cumberland and Newcastle (summer 1971); and Birmingham, Oldham and Tynemouth (North Tyneside) (winter 1971).

[4] In Chapter 11, Barney Rooney uses the initiative to make an important point about the timescale over which regeneration policy needs to be judged, arguing that a longer-term view of the Liverpool Community Development Project would be more favourable than the one attributed to it at the time. He cites the example of the Eldonian Housing Cooperative in Vauxhall. Another example is that of the Vauxhall Neighbourhood Council, whose current staff have direct links back to the Community Development Project.

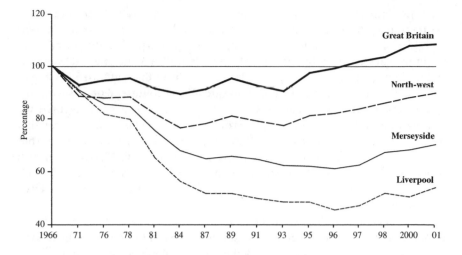

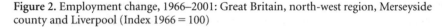

Notes: For continuity over the period, the north-west region excludes Cumbria (which has been included in official definitions of the region since the mid-1990s).

Changes in the method of data collection and industrial classification mean that there are a number of discontinuities in the figures pre-1981 and 1991. These discontinuities have been accommodated where possible. Nevertheless, the lines in the figure should be seen as representing only a reasonably approximate rather than an exact measure of change.

Source: Various local authority (pre-1978) reports, estimates by CRED Research Unit, Department of Geography, University of Liverpool (Liverpool 1966 figure) and Annual Census of Employment/Annual Business Inquiry (re-scaled figures 1995–2001), NOMIS (1978 onwards).

Figure 2. Employment change, 1966–2001: Great Britain, north-west region, Merseyside county and Liverpool (Index 1966 = 100)

While regional policy had helped to attract new industry to the city-region, it had increasingly mixed success in keeping it there as conditions in the global economy worsened. As Stuart Wilks-Heeg points out in the previous chapter, multinationals closed and shifted operations abroad, contributing to the formation of the new international division of labour that characterises the era of 'disorganised capitalism'. Liverpool and its city-region were the losers in this global restructuring of production. To make matters worse for the local workforce, the pressures of restructuring encouraged labour-saving production changes in the factories that remained. Not all of the multinationals left the city-region. Some have remained and continue to invest in their production facilities, but the operations of this remaining 'modern core' of multinational manufacturing (such as Vauxhall and Ford/Jaguar in motor vehicles or the American pharmaceutical companies) have increasingly been characterised by 'jobless growth', and the periodic injection of state regional development funding into this core has increasingly been concerned with job retention rather than job creation.

As the manufacturing branch plants either closed or shed labour to retain competitiveness, the docks began to feel the consequences of the declining relative economic importance of their hinterland (as de-industrialisation cut through the northern manufacturing regions) and the reordering of Britain's trade patterns around new geopolitical interests in Europe, leaving Liverpool on the periphery of the European segment of the 'Triad'.[5] The closure in 1984 of the Tate and Lyle sugar factory in inner Liverpool was particularly symbolic of this shift. Membership of the EEC meant adoption of its policy towards the encouragement of sugar production using sugar beet at the expense of sugar cane. This shift favoured the southern and eastern beet-growing areas of the country and meant, of course, that the industry was not only turning its back on Liverpool as a manufacturing site but also on the West Indies as a materials provider. The closure in 1990 of the British American Tobacco factory (the name says it all) in the same area as Tate and Lyle provided yet another sign, if one was needed by then, of the demise of the city's previous global role.

The implications of this restructuring for civil society and the local social fabric were revealed in the serious inner-city rioting in 1981 in Liverpool 8. The despair and anger underlying the rioting flagged up the extent of deprivation in the inner city and, with similar public disturbances in Bristol and London, once again forced urban policy up the national political agenda. But this agenda was very different from that of the 1970s. The election of Margaret Thatcher as Conservative prime minister in 1979 saw national state policies subject to a neo-liberal overhauling as the New Right obsession with extending private ownership and the market system, rolling back the state and cutting public expenditure permeated all areas of government policy. Urban policy was overhauled accordingly. The central priority was to give a more prominent role to the private sector through deregulation (the removal of planning regulations and relief from rates through the creation of Enterprise Zones) and subsidy (through such grants as the Urban Development Grant, later subsumed under the City Grant). Mirroring this promotion of the private sector was the relative downgrading of local government influence on inner-city policy through a combined strengthening of the arms of central government departments operating in inner-city areas (with the introduction of Task Forces and City Action Teams in inner-city areas), the establishment of quangos with specific urban regeneration remits (the Urban Development Corporations) and the removal of a whole tier of metropolitan local government (the so-called 'Streamlining [of] the Cities').

Again, Liverpool featured in these initiatives. It had one of the first Enterprise Zones (in Speke in 1981), the first Task Force (the Merseyside Task Force), one of the first City Action Teams (in Granby and Toxteth), one of the two first-generation Urban Development Corporations (the Merseyside Development Corporation, 1981–1998) and the first National Garden Festival Site (1984). 'Streamlining the Cities' meant that it lost its city-regional tier of government, the

---

[5] There is an interesting historical coincidence in the dating of Britain's entry into the European Economic Community (in 1973) and that of the 'turning point' that most commentators identify in terms of the shift from 'Fordism' to 'post-Fordism' or 'organised' to 'disorganised' capitalism.

Merseyside County Council, in 1986. Regeneration of the city was to be based principally on property-led development (and its hypothesised social 'trickle-down' effects) and the local state was to play a subordinate role in it.

This national state intervention interacted with and conditioned the local state. In the years when economic restructuring really began to bite – the late 1970s and early 1980s – the city council was led by an unstable Conservative–Liberal coalition with the largest single party, Labour, refusing to take a lead. This situation changed dramatically in 1983 when the local elections returned a Labour council led by a left-wing ('Militant') faction (Parkinson, 1985; 1989). Tracing its growth locally to the 'collapse of British capitalism [. . .] expressed in a particularly extreme fashion in the early 1980s on Merseyside' (Taafe and Mulhearn, 1988: 9), it was resolutely against civic boosterism (it closed the council promotional agency) and traditional local economic development (it refused, for example, to fill the seat set aside on the Board of the Merseyside Development Council for a city council politician). It focused instead on municipal employment and particularly housing in the shape of its 'Urban Regeneration Strategy', which focused resources on the renovation and rebuilding of the municipal housing stock in identified priority areas. This particular variant of municipal socialism (it was very different, for example, from that pursued at the time by other Labour-controlled metropolitan authorities and particularly that of the Greater London Council) and its funding implications – and Militant's national political ambitions – inevitably brought the council into conflict with a Conservative central government seeking to restrain local spending and encourage a less interventionist role for local government.

The political odds were not favourable for the council. Continuing population decline and a shrinking local rate base increased its dependence on central government support. Indeed, to sustain its strategy, it had to take up a number of loans from overseas banks and sell off sizeable chunks of municipal real estate. Its political stance also brought it under attack from a national Labour Party attempting to rid itself of Militant influence as part of its national electoral ambitions and produced opposition from sections of the local polity (inner-city black groups, a large working-class housing cooperative and outer-estate community groups; Meegan, 1989). As the conflict heightened it also lost the support of local trades unions. A combination, then, of national political opposition and local civil society undermined the council's strategy, which ended in the law courts with the disqualification from office and surcharging of a majority of city councillors in 1987 for 'wilful misconduct' (in delaying the setting of a local rate).[6]

Meanwhile jobs and people continued to be lost to the city. Over the 1980s (1981–1991), employment and population fell by 23 and 12 per cent respectively (some 59,000 fewer jobs and 60,000 fewer people). And the city's geography of disadvantage extended from the inner city to include the outer council estates.

---

[6] For two opposing political interpretations of Militant in Liverpool see Taafe and Mulhearn, 1988, and Kilroy, 2000. There is also a website commemorating the disqualified councillors and their political stance, www.Liverpool47.com

Liverpool in the 1990s: From City of Conflict to City of Partnership?

As the 1980s drew to a close, urban policy, along with the extreme neo-liberal experiment in government of which it was a part, was being exposed to a sustained critique (Lawless, 1996; Moore, 1992; Robson et al., 1994). It was seen to lack strategic vision, comprising a hodge-podge of policies and agencies with imple-mentation handicapped, and local democracy undermined, by centralisation and the intrusion of centrally accountable Development Corporations and privatised Training and Enterprise Councils. The policies seemed incapable of coping with rapid social and environmental change in an innovative way, and were failing both to tackle social and economic disadvantage in the inner cities and to reduce the gap between conditions in them and in other areas. In effect, there was a recognition of the failure of increasingly property-led development both on its own terms and on its ability to secure 'trickle-down' benefits to especially disadvantaged areas and groups (Imrie and Thomas, 1999).

The 1990s thus saw yet another raft of new urban policy initiatives and institu-tional change. Coordination of programme spending became the leitmotif of the new urban policy. Some 20 spending programmes formerly managed by five sep-arate government departments were consolidated into one Single Regeneration Budget. English Partnerships was established to oversee physical regeneration pro-jects across England and government departments and their spending pro-grammes were brought together at regional level into Integrated Regional Offices.

City Challenge provided the first indication of the shift in policy emphasis. While it still bore the mark of the 'competitiveness' ethic of Conservative govern-ment thinking (with local authorities having to compete with one another to secure funding from the programme for the regeneration of specified areas), it also introduced a new emphasis on, and definition of, partnership. Local authorities were recognised as being the most appropriate bodies for coordinating the project bids but were expected to involve a range of private, public and, importantly, vol-untary and community bodies in both the design and the implementation of the regeneration programme. An implementation agency, independent of the local authority and based on a partnership between the latter, other public agencies and the private sector, was responsible for delivering the five-year programme.

This new wave of urban policy was introduced into a very different local politi-cal context. The dismissal of the Labour councillors in 1987 was followed by a decade of Labour rule heavily conditioned by the political fallout of the Militant period. Elected with an increased majority but riven with internal splits over poll tax payment, budget setting and staffing cuts, the council experienced difficulties in the first years. When City Challenge was introduced in 1991, there were effec-tively two Labour parties in the council chamber: 'Official Labour' (with 43 of the total 99 seats) and 'Liverpool Labour' (with 25 seats). While the former was the largest group in the council its position was compromised on a number of occa-sions by a voting coalition of Liverpool Labour and the other main group in the council, the Liberal Democrats. It was in this context of relative political inertia that a new era of governance in the city started to take shape, an era of 'partner-ship'. Urban policy was important in structuring this, in the shape of the city's suc-cessful bid for City Challenge funding for the regeneration of the eastern fringes of the city centre. There were 37 signatories to the Liverpool City Challenge bid, a mix of representatives of the public, private and voluntary sectors operating in the area.[7]

Significantly, there were also other pressures on the need for partnership and these emanated from what was becoming an increasingly important dimension of political intervention – Europe. While Liverpool was clearly experiencing eco-nomic difficulties as a result of the country's geopolitical turn towards Europe, these difficulties were themselves making the city eligible for intervention by the European Commission's Structural Funds programmes. The city-region had received support from the European Regional Development Funds in the early 1980s and this was increased between 1989 and 1993 in the shape of 'Objective Two' funding and the so-called 'Merseyside Integrated Development Operation'. The latter was an important initial experiment in European intervention and had considerable impact on the partnership working that was developing in the city-region.[8] This impact was cemented by the granting of Objective One status to Merseyside in 1993.

An informal relationship between the five Merseyside local authorities had been established, bringing together the chief officers – and, through them, the political leaders – to discuss strategic issues and to fill the administrative and political vacuum created by the abolition of the county council. Europe and European funding had given more impetus and rationale for this 'shadow' city-regional gov-ernance. In conjunction with local MEPs and MPs, a campaign was launched to secure Objective One funds assisted by the Merseyside European Liaison Unit, based in Liverpool City Council offices (and eventually with an office in Brussels) but funded by all of the five local authorities. As the name suggests, the unit's role was to act as an intermediary between the local authorities and the European Commission.

Designation was not entirely straightforward because the key statistical indica-tor for Objective One designation (namely levels of GDP per capita at or below 75 per cent of the European Union average) had not yet been reached. The fact that the trend was very clearly in that direction (as figures have subsequently con-firmed) sealed the political argument that greater levels of 'aid intensity' from the Structural Funds were justifiable. Merseyside moved, in July 1993, from Objective Two to Objective One designation, the first major conurbation in an old industrial

---

[7] One of the signatories was the former Beatle, Paul McCartney, who had a particular interest in the establishment of what became the Liverpool Institute for Performing Arts on the site of his former, and by then derelict, secondary school. This building became one of the showpieces of City Challenge.

[8] It required a Directing Committee comprising the major central government departments and agen-cies, the five local authorities in Merseyside County, the Merseyside Development Corporation, the Merseyside Chamber of Commerce, the Merseyside Tourism Board, Merseytravel, the North West Water Authority, voluntary sector representatives and European Commission representatives.

region to be so defined. At its core was Liverpool, a city that was now having to recognise its status as a European city not least because it was now embroiled in the 'multi-level social governance' that intervention by the European Commission was creating (Geddes and Bennington, 2001).

Governance of the Objective One programme was the responsibility of a Monitoring Committee made up of representatives of the agencies that were now the local partnership constituency for regeneration activity. Significantly, the European Commission, in an attempt to push subsidiarity in the delivery of the programme below city-regional level, negotiated a priority in the finally agreed plan, or more accurately Single Programming document, called 'Action for the People for Merseyside'. This priority was based on the premise that one of the key 'drivers for change' in the economic and social conversion of the area had to be the people of Merseyside themselves, including, of necessity, groups and individuals hitherto excluded from or in danger of being excluded from mainstream economy and society. The priority included measures for career development and training, equal opportunities in the labour market, training targeted at people 'at risk of permanent exclusion from the labour market', improved education, training and employment services, increased access to work through improved public transport and environmental improvement and the treatment of derelict land. These measures applied across the city-region. People living in areas with particularly pronounced economic and social problems were also to be eligible for a raft of measures (subsumed under 'Driver 5.1') aimed at providing 'pathways' to education, skills, training, jobs, a better quality of life and assistance to secure community involvement in designing, implementing and monitoring the initiatives funded in their areas. They were to be given something extra from the programme and this extra resource was to be delivered with the involvement of people living in the designated areas in Area Partnerships. In the event 38 areas were designated across Merseyside (11 of them in Liverpool), predominantly on the basis of census indicators of disadvantage. In each of these, local partnerships involving representatives of public, private, voluntary and, notably, community sectors were created (Meegan, forthcoming).

By the early 1990s, then, partnership had become the main mechanism for regeneration in the city and city-region. In the city, this development was crowned by the formation in 1995 of the Liverpool Partnership Group, which brought together the chief executives or head officers of 18 public, private and voluntary bodies including, for example, the city council, the Government Office for Merseyside, the police, English Partnerships, the Housing Corporation, the Liverpool Housing Association Trust, the Employment Service, the Benefits Agency and the local universities.

The city's developing partnership structure and ethos were reinforced by changes in both national and local government. The election of 'New Labour' nationally in 1997 saw urban policy overhauled, with an emphasis on social inclusion and neighbourhood-based regeneration, promoted through the Social Exclusion Unit (1998), the Regional Development Agencies for the English regions

(1999, with responsibility for administration regionally of the Single Regeneration Budget), the New Deal for Communities (1998), the Urban Task Force (1999), the second Urban White Paper (2000) and the National Strategy for Neighbourhood Renewal (2001). Partnership was central to the new urban policy and 'modernised local government' was expected to take a lead role in it.

The election of 'New Labour' nationally was followed by Liverpool demonstrating once again its exceptional local politics. After what appeared to be a stabilisation of Labour control in the mid-1990s (the Labour leadership changed hands five times in the period 1987–1997), there was a dramatic turnaround in 1998. The massive national swing towards 'New Labour' was followed by the election locally of a Liberal Democrat administration that currently has just over two-thirds of the seats in the council, leaving Labour with its lowest level of representation since the early 1950s.[9] In the event, the new Liberal Democrat-controlled city council has proved itself almost more 'New Labour' than 'New Labour' itself. It has enthusiastically pursued the agenda of modernisation of local government, opting for the leader and cabinet model of government (but rejecting an elected mayor). The council had become a 'pathfinder authority' for the 'New Commitment to Regeneration' and this has been extended to engage with all the urban policy initiatives of national government. The city thus has a major New Deal for Communities initiative (in Kensington, north of the city centre) and the council leader chairs what was the country's first Urban Regeneration Company, Liverpool Vision, which is responsible for the redevelopment of Liverpool city centre (assisted by Single Regeneration Budget funding), and also the board of Liverpool First, the strategic arm of the local community strategy, to which I will return below. The council sponsored the successful bid for European Capital of Culture in 2008, a year after the city's official 800th birthday. The success of the bid can be seen as recognition of the Liverpool First vision of Liverpool as a European renaissance city.

By giving local authorities the power 'to do anything' to promote or improve the economic, social and environmental well-being of their areas, the Local Government Act of 2000 marked a significant milestone in the evolving relationship between central and local government in the UK. The Act introduced a counterweight to the growing central control of local government activities that had marked the previous two decades. It also reinforced the shift towards partnership in urban governance. Local authorities are required to produce 'community strategies' in partnership with other organisations and agencies working in the locality and with the involvement of local communities. The Act thus not only gives local authorities new powers to intervene but also imposes on them the duty to work in partnership with other agencies and local communities – through 'Local Strategic Partnerships' – to exercise those powers.

---

[9] In the period since the mid-1960s there have only been two full years when political control of Liverpool City Council has coincided with that of central government, and only another three when there has been some overlap as control shifted.

Liverpool's community strategy is set out in *Liverpool First*, a document produced by the city's Local Strategic Partnership, the aforementioned Liverpool Partnership Group (Liverpool Partnership Group, 2002b). It is a remarkable document, not just for the context in which it was produced – through partnership in a city that, on the basis of recent political history, might be expected to be one of the last to embrace the notion – but also for what it says:

Our Vision

For Liverpool to become a premier European City. Achieved by building a more competitive economy, developing healthier, safer and more inclusive communities and enhancing individual life chances.

Our Aspirations

To create an inclusive European Renaissance City by 2010.

To be the most 'business friendly' city in the country by 2006.

To meet and exceed national targets for schools, qualifications and employment by 2005.

To reduce levels of poor health, preventable death, impairment and disability so that Liverpool is better than the national average by 2010.

To stabilize the population by the year 2010. (Liverpool Partnership Group, 2002b, inside cover)

Liverpool in the Twenty-first Century: A European Renaissance City?

The city has certainly witnessed a major physical transformation in recent years and this transformation has been heavily reliant on public sector policy. Thus, the Merseyside Development Corporation's reclamation of derelict land literally provided the ground for the resuscitation of both housing and office markets in its territory (Meegan, 1999). There are now housing developments and offices on riverside land that was disused and with zero market value 20 years ago. City Challenge helped to transform dramatically the built environment of the eastern wedge of the city centre, with the Liverpool Institute for Performing Arts and Blackburne House (the home of a pioneering women's technology training centre) acting as the anchors for the development of the area around the Anglican cathedral (Russell, 1997). Funding from Objective One and English Partnerships has transformed parts of the city centre, with new hotels, bars, shops and public transport facilities. Between 1995 and 2000, average retail rents in the city almost doubled from £150 to £250 per square metre (for A-grade retail property; *Estates Gazette*, 2000).

This physical regeneration has helped to set the stage for private sector developers such as Urban Splash and the Beetham Organisation to invest in the conversion of warehouses, lofts and old office buildings into residential apartments. This promotion of 'urban living' saw the population of the city centre grow to 9,000 in 2000, nearly four times the figure from a decade earlier (Liverpool City Council, 2000). While a substantial proportion of this early development was in student accommodation, the balance has shifted towards young managerial and professional workers. This 'urban living' has created a niche housing market reflected in a free glossy magazine, *Homes*, which markets the 'new property' and its associated lifestyle and which would have been unviable five years ago. In the year to mid-June 2000, house prices in the city centre increased more quickly than the national rate, at an average of 30 per cent, with capital values ranging from £14 to £18 per square metre (*Estates Gazette*, 2000). And there are now signs that this city centre gentrification is beginning to ripple outwards to immediately adjacent areas.

In these circumstances, it has been hard for the writers of the city's promotional literature to contain their enthusiasm:

> Visitors to the new Liverpool are amazed at the transformation of the city. Once derelict docklands are now home to award-winning retail and leisure amenities, waterfront apartments, family housing, marinas, hotels, offices and restaurants.

> The magnificent city centre architecture – testament to the city's heritage – has been retained and is being creatively restored and converted to create modern city living and office space. Developer interest in the city's at its highest for over a century. Liverpool's world famous waterfront is one of the most outstanding in Europe and is in line to become a World Heritage Site.

> With a masterplan for the city centre co-ordinated by Liverpool Vision . . . creative developers are restoring the best of the past to meet the needs of the future. Stunning new developments include the Paradise Street Development Area with 1 million sq ft (93,000 sq m) of prime retail development and state of the art, multi-purpose arena and conference facility at Kings Dock.

> Liverpool will soon have a retail, office and leisure offer which rivals anything in the UK.

> Renaissance is not just confined to the city centre. The Speke Garston Development Company have created superb business space at Estuary Commerce Park and Boulevard Industry Park, adjacent to Liverpool John Lennon Airport and the stunning new Marriott South Liverpool Hotel . . .

> £3 billion (4.8 billion euro) of construction projects are planned throughout the city region over the next 5 years – in retail, office, leisure, schools and hospitals . . .

> Liverpool is one of the most competitive locations in the UK for businesses seeking an investment location, with prime office rents in Liverpool up to a third less than other UK cities . . .

> *Rental and capital values for retail, office and residential space are on the increase, creating a healthy growth environment for investors.* (Liverpool Business Centre, 2002; emphasis in original)

While parts of the city have been transformed, there has also been a recent increase in employment and a slowing-down of population loss (see Figures 1 and 2). Indeed, between the mid-1990s and the start of the third millennium, Liverpool saw a faster growth of jobs than did comparable 'core cities' nationally (Hutchins, 2001).[10]

So where are the new jobs being generated? Certainly not by the port, in any significant number. 'Jobless growth' still applies. The port now handles more traffic (in tonnage) than it did in the mid-1960s but this recovery has not had anything like the local impact generated by previous dock activity. The operational docks are now much smaller in size, having predominantly retreated to the mouth of the estuary into the adjacent local authority district of Sefton (albeit in Bootle, the 'Liverpool-speaking' part). This relocation was marked by the sale by the Mersey Docks and Harbour Company of its Port of Liverpool building at the Pier Head in 2001. Indeed, the development of its former land ownings has given the company a significant source of profit, most notably in its development activities in the Princes Dock in the city centre.

The port's direct employment impact has withered. In the early 1980s what is now the Mersey Docks and Harbour Company alone employed around 10,000 people. It now employs 800 in its Liverpool operations – a reflection predominantly of the shift in transport technology towards containerisation of cargoes. Its imports have also done little to encourage the local secondary import processing industries which were so important in the past. The main imports still reflect the old links with the Americas (particularly for grain and timber) and Ireland, but the port is now operating much more as a 'hub' operation for trans-shipment on to Ireland and parts of Europe (especially Portugal and Spain) and Israel. A factor in this reduced local impact must also be the designation of part of the port's operations as a Freeport. The Freeport offers traders freedom from import duties, VAT, European Commission levies, taxes and quotas as long as the affected cargoes are retained within its confines. This, of course, further encourages 'hub' operation and constrains potential leakage of economic activity outside the zone boundaries. In terms of exports, manufacturing goods have now been replaced in importance (symbolically?) by scrap metal. Liverpool is now second only to Rotterdam in the export of scrap metal. While the port thus retains an international space of economic activity, its equivalent local space is much constrained. Estimates of the size of the maritime sector suggest that something like 400 companies together provide 7,000 jobs (Liverpool Business Centre, 2002).[11] Indeed, as Table 1 shows, the transport sector as a whole (road, rail, air and sea) now accounts for only around 24,000 jobs in the Liverpool travel-to-work area as a whole and represents about the same share of total employment as nationally (around 6 per cent).

---

[10] Established in 1997, the 'Core Cities Group' brings together the local authorities of the seven largest cities outside London – Birmingham, Bristol, Leeds, Liverpool, Manchester, Newcastle-upon-Tyne and Sheffield – to represent their interests in policy debates.

[11] The Mersey Docks and Harbour Company has adjusted to the country's geopolitical and economic shift towards Europe with its acquisition of the Medway Ports. While Liverpool's geography places it on the Atlantic Arc periphery of Europe, the company has made sure that its operations are more centrally placed.

Table 1: Employment change, Liverpool travel-to-work area (TTWA) and Great Britain, 1995–2001

	Employees by sector, Liverpool TTWA		Change 1995–2001 Liverpool TTWA		Change 1995–2001 GB	Employment share (%)	
	1995	2001	No.	%	%	L'pool	GB
Agriculture and fishing	155	356	201	**129.7**	(12.4)	0.09	0.97
Energy and water	1,426	1,218	(208)	(14.6)	(9.9)	0.31	0.82
Manufacturing	50,622	44,047	(6,575)	(13.0)	(9.8)	11.17	14.15
Construction	10,308	13,254	2,946	**28.6**	27.5	3.36	4.51
Distribution, hotels and restaurants	73,245	97,064	23,819	**32.5**	15.3	**24.62**	24.26
Transport and communications	22,994	23,555	561	2.4	15.9	5.98	6.12
Banking, finance and insurance, etc.	53,261	59,755	6,494	12.2	23.8	15.16	19.63
Public administration, education and health	110,116	133,869	23,753	**21.6**	12.1	**33.96**	24.31
Other services	20,321	21,104	783	3.9	25.2	5.35	5.23
TOTAL	342,449	394,222	51,773	15.1	12.0	100.00	100.00

Notes:
Numbers in bold indicate: (i) where percentage employment change is more favourable in the Liverpool TTWA than nationally (faster growth than national rate or growth set against national decline); (ii) where the sectoral share of total employment in the Liverpool TTWA is greater than the national share.
The Liverpool TTWA encompasses all of the local authority districts of Liverpool, Knowsley and Sefton, the bulk of wards in West Lancashire and one ward each from Halton and St Helens.
Source: NOMIS.

It is against this background of restructuring and job loss that the recent protracted strike by Liverpool dockers needs to be placed. Lasting nearly two and a half years between 1995 and 1998, it was played out at national and global levels as well as locally (see, for example, Castree, 2000; Lavalette and Kennedy, 1996). It raised all kinds of issues about the scale and nature of industrial struggle but what it also underscored was the 'depoliticisation' of the local polity. A weakened and divided Labour city council, struggling to position itself in the new terrain of governance through partnership, was unable to come out in unequivocal support of the dockers, something that would have been a political given just ten years earlier. The distancing of promotional bodies such as the Mersey Partnership from the dispute was understandable, but the issue made it clear that the whole ethos of partnership actively conditions the politics of local government. Here was a dispute that put on the agenda problematic issues not only of city image but also of balancing competitiveness with social cohesion. And the 'city of partnership' found it difficult to respond.

Table 1 gives a breakdown of employment change by broad sector in the period between 1995 and 2001, with national comparisons of percentage growth rates. It also shows the sectoral distribution of employment in the Liverpool travel-to-work area and Great Britain in 2001. A number of factors stand out, particularly the continuing decline of manufacturing both locally and nationally. Manufacturing employment in the Liverpool travel-to-work area actually fell faster than it did nationally (by 13 per cent compared with a national decline of just under 10 per cent), reinforcing just how tenuous the city-region's grip on manufacturing had been in the 1960s and 1970s. Within manufacturing, there were some gains (in telecommunications equipment and motor vehicle parts) but these were more than outweighed by losses (in food and drink, clothing and printing). Altogether, a further 6,600 manufacturing jobs were lost in the travel-to-work area in the five-year period. And the sector still looks vulnerable. Since the census date for the 2001 employment figures, the telecommunications company Marconi has cut back employment as part of its global retrenchment. The specialist sports car manufacturer Jensen Motors and the computer games software firm Rage have both gone into receivership, and the pharmaceutical multinational Glaxo Smith Kline has confirmed the closure of its Liverpool factory in 2004.[12] Of some concern for local planners is the fact that three of these companies were in the knowledge-based industries that policy is seeking to encourage (Marconi and Rage in information communication technologies and Glaxo Smith Kline in the biosciences sector).

The recent growth in jobs has come from services and very noticeably in the distribution, hotel and restaurant sector, which grew by a third over the six years, more than double the national rate of growth, and provided in total nearly 50,000 jobs (just over 12,500 jobs in Liverpool itself). In Liverpool, these jobs were mainly in retailing (nearly 7,000 jobs) and in bars, cafés, restaurants and hotels (together about 5,500 jobs). The retailing growth suggests that the city might well be recapturing its city-regional and sub-regional shopping centre role, which has been eroded by, for example, Chester and Greater Manchester in recent years. And this growth will be reinforced by the recently commissioned redevelopment of the core of the city centre shopping area. Costing nearly £1 billion and scheduled for completion in 2007, the redevelopment will include over 100 shops alongside offices, apartments, a cinema and public squares. All of this reflects and reinforces the city centre property development already referred to. The city is becoming more and more a city of consumption.[13]

---

[12] All four of these companies feature in the listings of leading firms in the promotional brochure produced by Liverpool Business Centre (2002).

[13] One major cloud on the retail horizon, however, has been the recent sale of the Littlewoods mail-order business. Since Littlewoods is one of the few remaining large locally controlled businesses, there is reason to be concerned about the impact of the sale on the existing relatively well-paid and high-status jobs associated with its headquarters functions. There is also every reason to be concerned about what the sale might mean for the firm's hitherto exceptional levels of local philanthropy.

As du Noyer (2002) argues, Liverpool has always been renowned as a place of entertainment and especially of music. The adjective 'lively' certainly does not do the city full justice. A key element of both the city's image and reality has been its media, entertainment, arts and cultural activities. It has its indigenous television company (Phil Redmond's Mersey TV), but it has also seen recent employment cutbacks by the Manchester-based Granada Television company, with the loss of its national morning programme previously filmed at the Albert Dock (and crucially important in giving a public image to that development) and the failure of the company's joint venture with Littlewoods into television shopping (also based in the Albert Dock). What remains of its presence is the relatively small newsroom. Music recording studios, nightclubs, the Philharmonic Hall and Orchestra and a nascent film sector all contribute to the cultural heartbeat of the city but still, as yet, do not provide a substantial amount of (regular, full-time) employment.

Much more important in terms of employment has been the banking, finance and insurance sector. This has grown in the last few years but only at about half the national rate, and there are signs that an evolving regional spatial division of labour in the sector heavily conditions the nature of this growth. Thus, for example, the paucity of large locally owned companies has seen the concentration of corporate accountancy and related services in Manchester, while Liverpool concentrates more on life and maritime insurance, general banking support centres and call-centre banking.

One area in which the city and city-region have disproportionately attracted new investment is that of call centres (in banking and finance and mail-order retailing): Liverpool now claims to be the 'number one contact centre' in the UK and the only UK location to figure in the European top ten. Labour availability (including graduates from the local universities), low-cost sites and financial assistance have been important in the development of what has become a significant infrastructure for the activity. The transnational ownership of these facilities (with companies such as 7C, Bertelsmann, Swiss Life and US Airways all having operations in the city) illustrates the new global connections that are developing. What remains to be seen is how strong these connections prove to be, given the intense global competition for such activities. Competition for these centres is not only between UK cities and city-regions but also, increasingly, with overseas locations, most notably (in the case of British banking operations) locations in countries with old imperial connections such as India.

Despite recent cutbacks in employment in the city council (which employs around 2,000 fewer people than it did in 1998), public sector jobs remain important in the city, with public administration and health accounting for a third of its workforce (compared with a national figure of 24 per cent). It is noticeable, however, that the sector as a whole did not grow in employment terms as quickly as the national rate, and the fact that some of the jobs are dependent on population levels means that growth is likely to be further constrained to the extent that population continues to decline.

The city's renaissance, then, appears to be being built principally on leisure and entertainment. The decision by a group of the sacked dockers to pool their severance pay to invest in a bar in the city centre is surely a poignant testament to this re-making of the city. But the local economy remains weak. The awarding of a second round of Objective One funding (2000–2006) was a recognition of the fact that gross domestic product per head had actually fallen over the period of the first programme, reflecting the deep-seated structural problems it faces. A first attempt at measuring the productivity and competitiveness of UK cities – the so-called UK Urban Competitiveness Index 2002 – was produced by a firm of consultants, Robert Huggins Associates (2002). This index attempts to combine measures of gross domestic product per head of population, economic activity, business density, proportions of 'knowledge-based businesses', unemployment rates and average earnings. On this index, Liverpool comes out nationally as the least productive city. And some of the basic contours of the prevailing spatial division of labour are indicated by the fact that only three of the top 20 cities (Aberdeen, Edinburgh and Bristol) in the index are outside what the report calls the 'South East England arc'.

Recent employment growth has seen unemployment fall, but more slowly than nationally, and its current rate remains over double the national average. The Indices of Deprivation (2000) rank Liverpool as the second worst local authority district in terms of 'employment deprivation' in England (out of 354 local authority areas). The state of the local labour market is also reflected in the fact that the Indices also place the city second worst in terms of income (with mean income 75 per cent of the national level). Overall, the Indices of Deprivation rank Liverpool as the fifth most deprived local authority in England. Given the state of the local labour market and low levels of income locally, it is no surprise that the housing market is also depressed, despite all the inner-city housing development that features in the promotional literature. This inner-city 'property boom' has to be set against whole areas of the city in which the housing market is not so much depressed as non-existent (Nevin et al., 1999). The housing stock is massively biased towards low-cost council and social housing, with all the implications for council tax revenue for the council (Figure 3).

The Indices of Deprivation also give a measure of the degree to which deprivation is spread across local authority areas (the Rank of Extent). Liverpool is ranked seventh on this measure, showing relatively widespread deprivation: 26 of the city's 33 wards are in the worst 10 per cent in England. The Neighbourhood Renewal Strategy referred to in the introduction (Liverpool Partnership Group, 2002c) maps this geography of disadvantage that takes in both inner-city and outer housing estate areas, as Figure 4 shows.

The Neighbourhood Renewal Strategy clinically documents relative disadvantage and social exclusion within the city. Overall, the city has a 'real unemployment rate' over twice the national figure and this rises to six times the national rate in the worst affected ward, Granby, which is also the ward with the highest proportions

Council Tax Band	England (%)	Liverpool (%)	Key to Council Tax Bands
A	26.12	66.86	Up to £40,000
B	19.30	13.95	£40,001 to £52,000
C	21.53	9.99	£52,001 to £68,000
D	14.86	5.38	£68,001 to £88,000
E	9.24	2.08	£88,001 to £120,000
F	4.87	0.93	£120,001 to £160,000
G	3.52	0.74	£160,001 to £320,000
H	0.55	0.06	£320,001 and above
Unallocated	0.01	0.06	

Relates to dwellings which are expected to become available for occupation in the near future but have not yet been verified or allocated to a band by the Valuation Office Agency.

Total	100.00	100.05

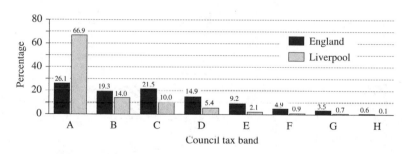

Figure 3. Council tax: percentage of properties in tax bands, England and Liverpool, 2001

of black and ethnic minority groups. No Liverpool ward has a rate lower than the national figure.[14]

The implications of these rates of unemployment for the local income base are clear, as Table 2 shows. The table gives income estimates for the 21 wards that have been designated as Neighbourhood Renewal Areas in the Neighbourhood Renewal Strategy. Columns 5 and 6 show the differences between the ward averages and those for Liverpool and the UK. The average household income in Liverpool is just 79 per cent of the national figure. To match the national figure, average household incomes would need to be increased by, at best, 8 per cent (Canning) and, at worst, 126 per cent

---

[14] The measure of the 'real rate of unemployment' includes groups who are not officially registered as unemployed but who have been effectively forced out of the labour market (such as elderly former coalminers who re-registered as sick).

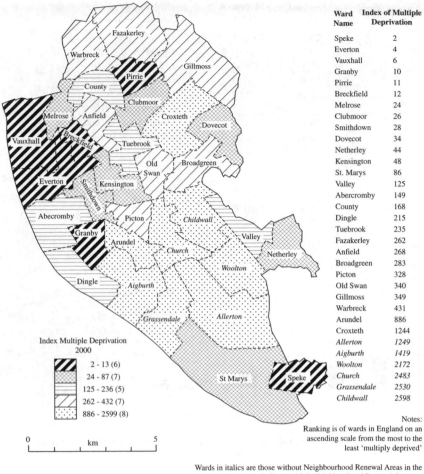

Ward Name	Index of Multiple Deprivation
Speke	2
Everton	4
Vauxhall	6
Granby	10
Pirrie	11
Breckfield	12
Melrose	24
Clubmoor	26
Smithdown	28
Dovecot	34
Netherley	44
Kensington	48
St. Marys	86
Valley	125
Abercromby	149
County	168
Dingle	215
Tuebrook	235
Fazakerley	262
Anfield	268
Broadgreen	283
Picton	328
Old Swan	340
Gillmoss	349
Warbreck	431
Arundel	886
Croxteth	1244
Allerton	*1249*
Aigburth	*1419*
Woolton	*2172*
Church	*2483*
Grassendale	*2530*
Childwall	*2598*

Index Multiple Deprivation 2000

2 - 13 (6)
24 - 87 (7)
125 - 236 (5)
262 - 432 (7)
886 - 2599 (8)

0   km   5

Notes:
Ranking is of wards in England on an ascending scale from the most to the least 'multiply deprived'

Wards in italics are those without Neighbourhood Renewal Areas in the Local Strategic Partnership's Neighbourhood Renewal Strategy.

Source: Liverpool Partnership Group (2002c)

Figure 4. Ranking of Liverpool wards by Index of Multiple Deprivation, 2000

(Chatsworth). For the Neighbourhood Renewal Areas as a whole, the increase would need to be 55 per cent.

The table points to a couple of key characteristics of Liverpool's urban renaissance. First, the relatively depressed levels of household income within the city clearly constrain consumer-based growth. The entertainment and retailing activities on which this renaissance is based will need to draw on commuter and visitor spending (and, of course, the unmeasurable income generated locally by the 'informal economy') to maintain growth. Second, it gives an indication of a new pattern of socio-spatial segregation that 'urban living' appears to be producing, with the

Table 2: Income in Liverpool Neighbourhood Renewal Areas (NRAs), 2001

Neighbourhood Renewal Area	No. of households	Income (£ per annum)	Mean income (£ per annum)	Difference from Liverpool average (%)[1]	Difference from UK average (%)[2]
Anfield/Breckfield	11,723	203,202,100	17,333.62	−19	−51
Canning	2,375	57,609,600	24,256.67	15	−8
Chatsworth	492	5,709,100	11,603.86	−78	−126
Dingle	6,526	105,990,200	16,241.21	−27	−61
Dovecot	9,640	157,109,200	16,297.63	−26	−61
Elm Park	1,706	34,465,000	20,202.22	−2	−30
Fazakerley	2,458	41,961,600	17,071.44	−21	−53
Gillmoss	3,372	60,501,400	17,942.28	−15	−46
Granby/Lodge Lane	7,863	136,160,000	17,316.54	−19	−51
Kensington	5,949	93,314,700	15,685.77	−31	−67
Kirkdale	4,000	65,370,900	16,342.72	−26	−60
L1	1,419	21,996,600	15,501.47	−33	−69
Larkhill/Tuebrook	3,524	71,005,100	20,149.00	−2	−30
Lower Breck	3,142	55,128,100	17,545.54	−17	−49
Molyneux	3,219	52,744,100	16,385.24	−26	−60
Netherley	7,493	129,579,700	17,293.43	−19	−52
Norris Green	11,816	188,104,400	15,919.46	−29	−65
Picton	5,069	86,466,800	17,057.96	−21	−54
Speke/Garston	9,989	166,176,100	16,635.95	−24	−57
Urban Village	6,699	98,252,900	14,666.80	−40	−79
Walton/Florence Melly	8,132	135,095,600	16,612.83	−24	−58
All NRAs	116,606	1,965,943,200	16,859.70	−23	−55

Notes: Based on data provided by CACI
1 Mean Liverpool income = £20,600
2 Mean UK income = £26,200
Source: Liverpool Partnership Group, 2002c.

ward that stands out as having the highest average household incomes in relation to both Liverpool and the UK averages, Canning, being the location of some of the most expensive apartments. These apartments are forming a relatively privileged segment of a ward that overall still needs 'Neighbourhood Renewal'.

Conclusion

Behind Liverpool's current aspirations to be a 'premier European renaissance city' and its bid to be European Capital of Culture in 2008 lies a profound transformation in the city's status in the global urban hierarchy, a transformation that is itself inextricably linked to Britain's changing geoeconomic and geopolitical relationships. It has lost jobs and people on a scale and at rates that are exceptional even among the industrial cities of the north, and it finds itself at the core of one of the most disadvantaged city-regions in Europe. Disadvantage is not new to the city. At the height of its power there were pronounced social divisions between the rich and the poor that also had a marked geography. This geography of poverty has become more extensive, with 26 of the city's 33 wards now featuring in the 10 per cent most disadvantaged wards in England.

The city has been on the receiving end of substantial political and policy intervention at different scales and in different forms. In the 1950s and 1960s, national regional policy and nationally encouraged population dispersal policies sought to create new jobs and better social housing on the city's outskirts. The 1970s saw regional policy overshadowed by urban policy as conditions in inner-city areas and some of the peripheral housing estates deteriorated. The city experienced the whole battery of urban policies thereafter, followed in the 1980s and especially the 1990s by programmes funded by the European Union's Structural Funds. The scale of this intervention testifies to the severity of decline, and policy has clearly struggled to make an impact. That said, Liverpool has shown some signs of renaissance in recent years and this has been due, in no small part, to this public sector intervention. The physical transformation of the city centre has been dramatic and seems set to continue, and there has been some related recovery in both labour and housing markets. But this transformation has not benefited everyone and has not reached all parts of the city; indeed, some of the developments threaten to reinforce established patterns of socio-spatial segregation. The city's aspiration to be an '*inclusive* European renaissance city' still remains a very difficult challenge, a difficulty created by the very power of the processes that combine to create the 'disjointed structural change' discussed in the introduction.

For Liverpool to become such a city requires a politics and policies that operate at the whole range of spatial scales, from neighbourhood to global. The city's first community strategy, 'Liverpool First' (Liverpool Partnership Group, 2002b), does offer the potential for building upwards from neighbourhood-based development plans to a city-wide regeneration framework in which public service spending can be 'joined up' and steered towards areas of need. It also offers the potential for reinforcing central government neighbourhood-based initiatives such as Sure Start (aimed at children at risk of exclusion). The potential is also there for the Neighbourhood Renewal Strategy to link up, at city-regional level, with the second Objective One programme, which retains a strong emphasis on social inclusion (as shown, for example, by attempts to make the jobs generated in so-called 'Strategic Investment Areas' accessible to people in 'Pathways Areas' looking for work). At regional level, the Government Office for the North West offers the potential for better coordination of departmental programmes, and the North West Development Agency offers the potential for developing an evolving Regional Economic Strategy that could promote collaboration rather than competition between the region's two city-regions, Liverpool and Manchester. The next scale is the national, and what seems essential for Liverpool's renaissance (and for that of other similarly positioned cities) is a genuine commitment on the part of national government to balanced regional growth (which, it has to be said, seems to be lacking at the time of writing, with developments such as the Thames Gateway being planned for the south-east). This national regional policy needs to fit within broader European social and economic programmes.

At all levels, there needs to be an openness to alternatives to orthodox policies of economic development – alternatives that can develop broader definitions of 'work' and in which 'social economy' initiatives such as Intermediate Labour Markets, Local Economic Trading Schemes and 'time banking' (what Nathan and Westwood [2001] refer to as 'broad work') are developed. In such an approach, the payment nationally of 'basic income', 'citizen's income' or 'participation income' (Atkinson, 1995; 1998; Desai, 1998; Hines, 2000) makes sense. There do appear to be pieces of this jigsaw falling into place in Liverpool (in the form, for example, of the Neighbourhood Renewal Strategy, Sure Start and the developing social enterprise sector that has recently been boosted by the North West Development Agency's sponsorship of a 'Merseyside Social Enterprise Initiative'), but other pieces (such as a strong national regional policy) still need to be found.

References

Allen, J., and Cars, G. (2002), 'The Tangled Web – Neighbourhood Governance in a Post-Fordist Era', in G. Cars, P. Healey, A. Madanipour and C. De Maghalhães (eds), *Urban Governance, Insititutional Capacity and Social Milieux*, Aldershot: Ashgate, 90–105

Atkinson, A. (1995), *Incomes and the Welfare State*, Cambridge: Cambridge University Press

— (1998), *Poverty in Europe*, Oxford: Blackwell

Baines, T. (1852), *History of the Commerce and Town of Liverpool*, London: Longman

Barraclough, G. (ed.) (1986), *The Times Atlas of World History*, London: Times Books

Bloxham, T. (2001), 'Creating an Urban Splash: Rehabilitation of Central Sites', in M. Echenique and A. Saint (eds), *Cities for the New Millennium*, London and New York: E & FN Spon

Brabner, J. H. F. (ed.) (n.d., c.1900), *The Comprehensive Gazetteer of England and Wales*, London: Will

Byrne, D. (1999), *Social Exclusion*, Buckingham, Open University Press

Castree, N. (2000), 'Geographic Scale and Grass-Roots Internationalism: The Liverpool Dock Dispute, 1995–1998', *Economic Geography*, 76(3): 272–92

Cook, C., and Stevenson, J. (1978), *Longman Atlas of Modern British History: A Visual Guide to British Society and Politics, 1700–1970*, London: Longman

Coyle, D. (1999), 'Britain's Urban Boom: The New Economics of Cities', in *The Richness of Cities: Urban Policy in a New Landscape*, Working Paper 7, London, Comedia and Demos

Desai, M. (1998), 'A Basic Income Proposal', in *The State of the Future*, London: Social Market Foundation du Noyer, P. (2002), *Liverpool: Wondrous Place – Music from Cavern to Cream*, London: Virgin Books

Estates Gazette (2000), 'Focus 2000: Liverpool and Merseyside', *Estates Gazette*, 17 June: 99–199

Falkus, M., and Gillingham, J. (1981), *Historical Atlas of Britain*, London, Granada

Geddes, M., and Bennington, J. (eds) (2001), *Local Partnerships and Social Exclusion in the European Union: New Forms of Local Social Governance?*, London: Routledge

Glennerster, H., Lupton, R., Noden, P., and Power, A. (1999), 'Poverty, Social Exclusion and Neighbourhood: Studying the Area Bases of Social Exclusion', Case Paper 22, London: Centre for Analysis of Social Exclusion, London School of Economics

Hall, P. (2002), *Cities of Tomorrow: An Intellectual History of Urban Planning and Design in the Twentieth Century*, 3rd edn, Oxford, Blackwell

Harvey, D. (1989a), 'From Managerialism to Entrepreneurialism: The Transformation in Urban Governance in Late Capitalism', *Geografiska Annaler*, 71B: 3–17

— (1989b), *The Condition of Postmodernity*, Oxford: Basil Blackwell

Hines, C. (2000), *Localization: A Global Manifesto*, London: Earthscan

Hobsbawm, E. (1989), *The Age of Empire: 1875–1914*, London: Cardinal

Hutchins, M. (2001), *Are Big Cities Getting Better? Socio-Economic Trends in England's Core Cities*, Liverpool: European Institute for Urban Affairs, Liverpool John Moores University

Imrie, R., and Thomas, H. (eds) (1999), *British Urban Policy*, London: Sage

Kilroy, P. (2000), *Left Behind: Lessons from Labour's Heartland*, London: Politico's Publishing

Knox, P. L., and Agnew, J. (1998), *The Geography of the World Economy*, London: Arnold

Lash, S., and Urry, J. (1987), *The End of Organized Capitalism*, London: Polity Press

Lavalette, M., and Kennedy, J. (1996), *Solidarity on the Waterfront: The Liverpool Lockout of 1995/96*, Liverpool: Liver Press

Lawless, P. (1996), 'The Inner Cities: Towards a New Agenda', *Town Planning Review*, 67: 21–43

Lawton, R., and Pooley, C. (1992), *Britain 1740–1950: An Historical Geography*, London: Arnold

Liverpool Business Centre (2002), *Liverpool*, Liverpool: Liverpool Business Centre

Liverpool City Council (2000), *Liverpool City Centre Living*, Liverpool: Liverpool City Council

Liverpool Partnership Group (2002a), *The Liverpool Neighbourhood Renewal Strategy Framework and Action Plan*, Liverpool: Liverpool Partnership Group

Liverpool Partnership Group (2002b), *Liverpool First (2002–2005) Workbook: Our Community Strategy*, Liverpool: Liverpool Partnership Group

Liverpool Partnership Group (2002c), *The Liverpool Neighbourhood Renewal Strategy Baseline Report*, Liverpool: Liverpool Partnership Group

Madanipour, A. (1998), 'Social Exclusion and Space', in A. Madanipour, G. Cars and J. Allen (eds), *Social Exclusion in European Cities*, London: Jessica Kingsley

Marshall, M. (1987), *Long Waves of Regional Development*, Basingstoke: Macmillan

Meegan, R. (1989), 'Paradise Postponed; The Growth and Decline of Merseyside's Outer Estates', in P. Cooke (ed.), *Localities: The Changing Face of Urban Britain*, London: Unwin Hyman

— (1990), 'Merseyside in Crisis and in Conflict', in M. Harloe, C. Pickvance and J. Urry (eds), *Place, Policy and Politics: Do Localities Matter?*, London: Unwin Hyman

— (1999), 'Urban Development Corporations, Urban Entrepreneurialism and Locality', in R. Imrie and H. Thomas (eds), *British Urban Policy*, London: Sage

— (forthcoming), 'Pathways to Integration: Tackling Social Exclusion on Merseyside', in M. Parkinson and M. Boddy (eds), *Changing Cities: Lessons from Research*, Bristol: Policy Press

Moore, B. (1992), 'Taking on the Inner Cities', in J. Mitchie (ed.), *The Economic Legacy 1979–1992*, London: Academic Press

Musterd, S., and Ostendorf, W. (1998), *Urban Segregation and the Welfare State: Inequality and Exclusion in Western Cities*, London: Routledge

Nathan, M., and Westwood, A. (2001), *Broad Work: Fast Futures*, London: Industrial Society

Nevin, B., Lee, P., and Phillimore, J., with Burfitt, A., and Goodson, L. (1999), *Measuring the Sustainability of Neighbourhoods in Liverpool*, Liverpool, Liverpool Partnership Group and Liverpool City Council

Parkinson, M. (1985), *Liverpool on the Brink: One City's Struggles Against Government Cuts*, Hermitage, Berks.: Policy Journals

— (1989), 'Liverpool's Fiscal Crisis: An Anatomy of Failure', in M. Parkinson, B. Foley and D. R. Judd (eds), *Regenerating the Cities: The UK Crisis and the US Experience*, Glenview, IL: Scott, Foresman and Company

Pollard, S. (1992), *The Development of the British Economy, 1914–1990*, London: Arnold

— (1997), *The International Economy since 1945*, London: Routledge

Robert Huggins Associates (2002), *The State of Urban Britain*, Cardiff: Robert Huggins Associates

Robson, B., Parkinson, M., Bradford, M., Deas, I., Evans, R., Garside, P., Hall, E., Harding, A., Harrison, E., and Robinson, F. (1994), *Assessing the Impact of Urban Policy*, London: HMSO

Russell, H. (1997), *Liverpool City Challenge: Final Evaluation Report*, Liverpool: European Institute for Urban Affairs, Liverpool John Moores University

Taafe, P., and Mulhearn, T. (1988), *Liverpool: A City that Dared to Fight*, London: Fortress Books

Taylor, P. (1989), *Political Geography: World-economy, Nation-state and Locality*, 2nd edn, London: Longman

4. Enhancing Spaces of Inclusion? Power, Participation in Governance and the Urban Regeneration Litany

Peris S. Jones

The contemporary struggle for social inclusion in cities is infused with a range of seemingly common-sense terms such as 'participation', 'area partnership', 'downscaling', even 'inclusion' itself. This policy discourse, or, more appropriately, given its self-reverential tone, urban regeneration litany, is accompanied by a more spatially aware and contextualised urban policy apparently legitimised in terms of its retreat from inappropriate 'top-down' strategies. When no longer at arm's length – in other words, when decentralised – claims are made that 'downscaled' localised policy induces 'relevance' and therefore 'efficiency', 'sustainability' and 'accountability' at the local scale (Social Exclusion Unit, 2001; Department of Social Security, 1999). The changing forms and functions of the national state, on the one hand, involves a re-scaling of state functions and strategies upwards to a supranational level. However, this chapter focuses upon the implications of 'downscaling' – that is, the shift in functions downwards – for governance and local policy interventions which purport to enhance spaces of inclusion in our cities.

The urban imprint of socio-economic and political restructuring under advanced capitalism is therefore particularly noticeable in the efforts of national and local governments to reconfigure policy and offload functions in certain areas of policy design to state or non-state coalitions. Systems of local govern*ment* apparently give way to wider processes of local govern*ance* beyond, but importantly not necessarily dis-embedded from, existing methods of working (Imrie and Raco, 1999; Ward, 2000), involving partnerships comprising 'complex sets of organisations from the public, private and voluntary sectors' (Stoker and King, 1996: 1). These 'complex sets' involved in governance also include the community sector, in which there was a resurgence of interest in the UK in the 1980s, and particularly the 1990s (Atkinson and Cope, 1997). Since 1997, successive Labour government mapping of the landscape of socially cohesive 'stakeholder' capitalism increasingly reifies the role of active citizenship and places 'community' *participation* at the centre of local regeneration initiatives. Participation is closely associated with social exclusion because the latter is often represented as a condition or process resulting from a lack of participation (Musterd and Ostendorf, 1998; De Haas, 1998; Madanipour et al., 1998). Social inclusion through *participation* is now a policy objective entrenched within the urban regeneration litany. It remains to be seen, however, whether predominant interpretations and practices of participation and its preferred institutional vehicle, partnerships, are democratising governance in our cities. Gauging the potential for participation is inevitably influenced by debates raging concerning interpretations of the 'transition' from local government to local governance. Should this 'transition' be regarded as democratising or de-democratising: new, profound, universal, or, alternatively, exaggerated, not so new, less linear and less dichotomous and more hybrid (Imrie and Raco, 1999; Ward, 2000; Hall and Hubbard, 1996)? In cities such as Liverpool, claims of the demise of local government might be considered premature. As Ward, argues, however, 'in fact there has been both a quantitative and qualitative shift in local government apparatus but this does not mean there are not continuities through time' (Ward, 2000: 171).

Some interpretations of 'downscaling' therefore remain overly pessimistic and cite the 'instability and inadequacy of neo-liberal programmes for resolving its [post-Fordist systemic] contradictions' (Tickell and Peck, 1996: 595; Peck, 1995; 2000). And, while an appreciation that spatial awareness incorporates contingencies and variations across space is characteristic of contemporary regeneration policy (and indeed of poststructuralist and postmodern academic approaches – which is particularly intriguing for human geographers), claims that oppressive centralising structures located at the 'centre' can be simply reversed through downscaling to the 'local' scale should be treated with the caution reserved for spatial fetishism. Rather than reflecting any real transfer of power to communities, these regeneration policy techniques can reproduce existing dominant rationalities of both central and local government due to the co-optive powers of this fast-growing 'institutional supply' (Murdoch, 2000; Gonzales, 2000). Yet, while the chapter recognises and, indeed, looks at some of these pitfalls, nonetheless it also resonates with more upbeat accounts which at least offer the possibility that communities, and individuals within them, under certain conditions, can *act* to democratise governance of urban regeneration policy by manipulating and manoeuvring within these new spaces of inclusion and the struggle over the sphere of 'collective consumption' of services (Mollenkopf, 1996; Mayer, 1994).

Participation involves mechanisms that delegate and channel power, and that prescribe subject positions for participants which bind actors and organisations into goals or objectives of governing authorities. Participation can therefore be considered as a form of governance (Cooke and Kothari, 2001). If power is therefore interpreted discursively as multi-directional and fluid, downscaling can potentially expose the vulnerabilities of the 'system' portrayed in neo-structuralist critiques. In other words, thinking about governance as discourse can enable more flexible analysis, focusing not on power as rooted in a particular institution in a particular place, but on power and authority as more fluid and dispersed through networks. These networks extend beyond the state and, according to Murdoch (2000), only 'work' if they recruit non-state actors and agencies. Ironically, these networks are therefore 'always susceptible to disruption by external political forces' (Murdoch, 2000: 504). It is recognised here that this potential for exposure is, ultimately, contingent upon central–local configurations of power and the political struggle over spaces of inclusion. Spaces of inclusion are not therefore created through government intervention in an unproblematic way. Rather, the potential for including the excluded also depends on both the organisational and political experiences of the different social groups and the strategic use of political and social discourses which construct the rules of the game (see Webster, 2000). With these factors in mind, a more constructive and pragmatic approach can reflect on these shifts in governance as opportunities to be exploited (Jones, 2003; Taylor, 2000; Mayer, 1994; Mollenkopf, 1996), and, in particular, on the ways in which 'marginalised groups may be able to profit from temporary or long-term changes and gain leverage in various areas of social life' (Webster, 2000: 4).

The 1980s and 1990s might well have witnessed the creation of institutionalised spaces of participation and partnerships, but this mainstreaming has been associated with softening the radical transformative edge of participatory practices (Gaventa, 1998). Some authors even highlight participation as an 'unjust exercise of power' and as having a real capacity for tyranny (Cooke and Kothari, 2001). Naïve perspectives on power, based on simplistic binary oppositions of poor and powerless local 'have-nots' pitted against powerful central 'haves', have profound implications for policy interventions based on representations of local communities as in need of the tutelage provided through 'top-down' initiatives, or in need of acquiring more responsibility. Participation has therefore become increasingly entwined with the vigorous re-scaling of policy towards a focus on *locality*, supposedly in order to encourage participation (whether that of the voluntary sector, the community, or, significantly, business) but arguably to legitimise policy interventions (Social Exclusion Unit, 2001). Participation is often portrayed as 'common-sense', relevant, sustainable, taken-for-granted technical project or programme input, either into special targeted initiatives or into 'bending' mainstream spending, funding and targets to create a more 'joined-up' policy framework, and is therefore seen as efficient, even 'empowering' (Social Exclusion Unit, 2001). But what does participation actually mean at the local level? There is a real danger that the intricate problems of many communities remain framed in terms of a *lack* of participation and as *localised* problems of inequality. Participation thus becomes a 'portmanteau concept' meaning all things to all people (Nelson and Wright, 1995).

This chapter argues that claims made for participation as enabling individuals and communities to 'take control of their own situation' (Department of Social Security, 1999) conceal far more than they reveal because of fundamental problems in conceptualising the relationship between governance, power and participation. First, I locate the move towards downscaling within the context of the emergence of the so-called 'entrepreneurial' or post-Fordist city. Second, I discuss urban governance and the ways in which competing interpretations relate to different conceptualisations of power. Third, I examine the concept and practice of 'participation' and the problems associated with the politics of inclusion in governance. I shall look briefly at the appropriateness of 'consensual' deliberative models or more 'radical' models of democracy. The chapter ends by asking whether the limits of participation in urban regeneration have already been reached and,

crucially, whether participants themselves see it this way; or whether, for all the 'roadblocks' and frustrations, the taste of governance has whetted people's appetite for more involvement.

Downscaling and the 'Entrepreneurial' City

The discourse of downscaling has become part of an emerging neo-liberal hegemony which, ironically, resonates with a more critical and radical envisioning of governance involving 'action from below' through participation of civil society. Indeed, even in mainstream accounts, 'downscaling discourse' is supposedly closely related to the enhancement of societal bonds through the fostering of community participation, which in turn is cited as creating more effective governance and economic development (World Bank, 1997; Putnam, 1992). Power relations are seen as embedded in different geographical scales; poststructuralist and postmodernist perspectives in particular have embraced a spatial framework. Human 'reality', as interpreted by Foucault (1980), is socially constructed, culturally and – crucially – *locally* specific, struggling against the single totalising truth and metaphysics of modernity. It is therefore interesting to note how the current shift towards downscaling policy is legitimised, somewhat simplistically, through reification of the alleged qualities of the 'local' scale and the local community in public policy, as if the 'centre' is all-powerful and distant from a more efficient and knowledgeable 'local' sphere. However, in the UK, area-based policies have been implemented since the 1960s, aimed at ameliorating the social and physical problems associated with post-war slum clearance and redevelopment (Taylor, 2000). Taking a longer perspective therefore provides an important vantage point in revealing what are, for Taylor, the 'persistent tensions' regarding 'joined-up' policy, community empowerment and the transition from government to governance. Some of these tensions will be addressed in the section on participation in governance, below, but first, some explanation is offered as to the recent proliferation of local community involvement in contemporary regeneration policy.

Mayer (1996) identifies three major trends emerging from post-Fordist restructuring in cities. First, there is a revalorisation of local politics, with cities mobilising local resources aimed at promoting economic growth. Second, while proactive economic growth coalitions have emerged in cities, there has been a reversal of social provision and a reorganisation of public services. The advent of the 'entrepreneurial city' supposedly revolves around how well local political coalitions tailor and package the particular set of local conditions of production and mobilise local resources and potential. This move towards a more outwardly oriented stance, typically in alliance with private capital, and concerned with creating prosperity for local economies, affects the whole terrain of urban politics. Urban politicians and governors increasingly argue that cities benefit less from 'conventional' welfare measures than from the mobilisation of local resources in the scramble for rewards in an increasingly competitive free-market system. Hall and Hubbard (1996: 153) cautiously describe this as a transition 'to a more

outward-orientated stance designed to foster and encourage local growth and economic development', with 'the public sector taking over the characteristics once distinctive to the private sector – risk-taking, inventiveness, promotion and profit motivation – leading many commentators to term such modes of governance as entrepreneurial'. These factors are undoubtedly important (leaving aside closer scrutiny of how new these pro-growth strategies actually are). But Mayer identifies a third element as the imprint of restructuring on urban governance. The different bargaining systems emerging from the restructuring of the city are therefore seen by some authors as a potentially beneficial outcome of post-Fordist transformation, 'address[ing] the limits of the centralized, hierarchical, bureaucratic-corporative structures that were characteristic of the Fordist state and that ended up producing huge costs, inefficiency and waste, as well as protest by social movements' (Mayer, 1996: 237). Local governments have supposedly seen their dominant role as the 'big players' in development and delivery of policy changed to that of strategic enablers, concerned with a broader range of activities.[1] Apparently recognising the limitations of central governance, Tony Blair pointed to the role that the 'Third Sector' (broadly, those organisations neither solely commercial nor part of government) can play in partnership, as an adhesive binding individualism to broader societal responsibilities:

> In the first half of this century we learnt that the community cannot achieve its aims without the help of government providing essential services and a backdrop of security. In the second half of the century we learnt that government cannot achieve its aims without the energy and commitment of others – voluntary organisations, business and crucially, the wider public. That is why the Third Sector is such an important part of the Third Way. (Blair, 1998)

This development does not mean, however, that the concept of 'local governance' should be used to read off the roles for actors and institutions (Ward, 2000: 173). Rather, 'researching local governance requires a greater sensitivity to geographical variations in and of the roles of government', which, for Ward, in tune with Mayer (1996), are the product of socially constructed political imperatives and political realities 'introduced through the spatially and temporally uneven shift to some form of more complex (and arguably unmanageable/ungovernable) multi-agency governance' (Ward, 2000: 170). This is the context for the interplay between wider changes in political economy and local politics, within which different interests are now being 'included', coexisting (or competing?) through processes of participation in governance.

One has only to look at Liverpool, for example, to see the extent of the change in governance. With over 60 partnerships, Liverpool is often called *the* city of partnerships. Eleven of these partnerships have been set up in conjunction with European Objective One funding as area-specific local partnerships reflecting the

---

[1] Although Imrie and Raco (1999) suggest that local government was always more hybrid than standard governance accounts portray.

multi-layered nature of governance in the city and the growing influence of the European Union on local policy making. Other partnership arrangements, such as the Rope Walks Partnership and Liverpool First, cover redevelopment of the city centre. Government initiatives such as the Single Regeneration Budget, New Deal for Communities, health action zones, national health trusts, education zones, primary care groups, 'best practice' zones and cross-sectoral housing action trusts and housing associations all produce additional players on the governance scene. Similarly, the local authority is now also pioneering joint public–private companies, hoping to emulate the results achieved in the redevelopment of Manchester's city centre. Take all of these more recent partnerships, and add them to the unaccountable quangos created under previous Conservative governments, such as the former urban development corporations and training and enterprise councils, and the contracting out of local services and this adds up to a complex picture. It would thus appear quite in order to ask, 'Who governs our cities?' There has been a real blurring between the public and private sectors, with some of these examples showing that public policy is reliant on private funding (and vice versa). This increase in unelected players is all the more striking given that in Liverpool, as in other cities, in less than two decades the number of people voting in local elections more than halved, with the average turn-out around 20 per cent and under 10 per cent in many wards.[2] Furthermore, local hearings throughout the city, involving the Liverpool Democracy Commission, had also uncovered, according to the commission's secretary, a 'profound loss of faith' in party politics and cynicism towards local government, which was perceived as not accommodating of 'real' people.[3] This led the commission to suggest that although the problem was not considered to be unique to Liverpool, 'local democracy is failing at its point of delivery . . . the problem is clearly more acute in cities where deprivation and the failure of governance have left many feeling that democracy has little to offer' (Liverpool Democracy Commission, 1999a: 16). The commission, however, also cited an overreliance on partnerships, whether multi-agency or community-based. These concerns echo those of other more critical commentators, who link the shift to governance with

[2] In December 1996, Liverpool recorded the lowest ever turn-out on mainland Britain, with 6 per cent in an inner-city ward. According to Gerry Stoker, who was invited to give evidence to the Liverpool Democracy Commission (1999a), such figures compare with European turn-outs of between 60 and 80 per cent.

[3] Jon Egan, secretary to the Liverpool Democracy Commission, personal communication, 14 December 1999. The creation of the Liverpool Democracy Commission was a response to widespread concerns about apathy and cynicism towards the local democratic process. It was formed primarily in response to central government's initial plans to revive local democracy and explore alternative routes for this revitalisation. An initial two-hour discussion arranged by the local newspaper and radio proved inadequate to deal with the issue. These same bodies, in conjunction with academics at local institutions and both public and private sponsorship, established an independent commission which conducted a six-month survey of over 400 residents and received extensive evidence from citizen juries composed of 'experts' and community figures. The commission also arranged meetings with a number of community-based forums throughout Liverpool.

a de-democratisation of new institutional structures. Yet, arguably, as will be discussed in later sections, it is precisely these new arenas or 'spaces' that are enabling citizen involvement and that do represent an exciting resurgence of local politics to which both local authorities and citizens alike are responding.

Yet the question of governance and citizen involvement is often subsumed in polarising accounts of the effects of the shift in Western cities. Some accounts depict the involuntary (or, on the part of agencies, intentional), co-option of communities. Alternatively, radical resistance and a politics of conflict are deemed by more critical observers to characterise city politics. Somewhere between these two viewpoints is the actual impact that shifts in governance and service delivery are having on emerging spaces of participation which communities can harness in order to combat their social exclusion. Given that there has been a paucity of research on these 'spaces' it is unsurprising that academics have tended to see local residents as either 'co-opted and conforming' or 'resistant'. But communities are not simply resisting or co-opted and powerless in the face of unaccountable partnerships. Instead, we should be asking whether there are any successes – and, moreover, any unforeseen consequences – stemming from even limited, contrived spaces of participation. Although there have been numerous intermittent claims for a locally sensitive and progressive urban regime, it is certainly hard to envision, according to Hall and Hubbard (1996), how such an inclusionary regime may come about, particularly given the rhetoric about 'accountability' and 'democracy'.

There are therefore very different political readings of the current celebration and promotion of civil society-centred community involvement in delivering inclusive governance. These different readings apparently reflect a high level of convergence among agendas associated with the 'new' Left and the 'new' Right, with the common ground now apparently based on the micro-level and the reification of the 'local' (Mohan and Stokke, 2000) as the terrain of 'area'-based urban regeneration intervention. So, on one level, there are convergences as regards new attitudes to social and urban (re)development, which involve reconceptualisation of the relations between state, civil society and markets. Ironically, the version of civil society-led 'empowerment' now proposed by institutions such as the World Bank and the United Nations – 'capitalism with a human face' – resonates with some aspects of post-Marxist conceptualisations of empowerment and radical democracy (Stokke, 1998). Yet key differences concern the direction in which change is initiated. Post-Marxist emphasis is placed on the collective mobilisation of the marginalised and dispossessed from the bottom up, rather than on the top-down directives of neo-liberal perspectives, with fundamentally different perspectives with regard to power and conflict. The 'rediscovery' of civil society is indicative of a more general theoretical and policy transition, away from traditional, modernist, top-down approaches and towards the promotion of active citizenship, which is supposedly shifting responsibility from the planners and bureaucrats, technocentrism and the state to 'communities', 'pluralism' and 'voluntarism'. A new language is being invented which centres on 'communal action' and implicitly recognises the capabilities of others, of the 'excluded' (Bell and Franceys, 1995: 1174). Changes in welfare state provision, and the depth of deprivation and exclusion of neighbourhoods, have increased the involvement of non-governmental groups and organisations, with a shift towards self-help and also community participation in governance. For all the rhetoric, local people are now regarded as at least knowledgeable, with their involvement seen as a potentially countervailing force to dominant elite groups, and as a means towards more efficient allocation of resources. Before we look at the potential for democratising governance we need a fuller discussion of the context within which cities are governed and what constitutes power in the city.

The Form of Urban Politics and Power

There is a common notion that urban politics is dominated by monolithic interest groups who gain leverage only by virtue of their electoral power. According to Harding (2001) many abstract accounts of urban politics tend to anthropomorphise cities – that is, they treat cities as individuals, with a single brain, with a unity of purpose. Journalists and lay people also do this. For example, Harding asks us to take the claim that 'Berlin tried for the 2000 Olympic Games'. While it may be accurate to say that there was a coalition of Berliners attempting to attract the games, there was also a substantial opposing coalition who might therefore say that 'Berlin did not want the Olympics'. For Harding, this anthropomorphisation is therefore a lazy shorthand description of complex processes. Cities are much more complex than individual decision-making entities; they do not act like an individual, a household or even an organisation or firm. 'Berlin' does not do anything – things are done by decision-making units and while the shorthand simplifies, it also distorts. Overall it is important to take issue with the notion that the city is the decision-making unit, and to focus instead on 'the actions, intentions and understandings of individuals and groups who in various ways are involved in decision-making decisions for cities' (Harding, 2001: 50). With this in mind, attempts to balance the opportunities associated with new bargaining structures and shifting governance (Mayer, 1996) with exclusionary constraints and pressures need to recognise the politically structured, fragmented and shifting nature of networks of power and exclusion involving groups, individuals, spatial arrangements, cultural, gender, class and ethnic struggles and tensions which underpin governance in the city (Watson, 1999). Why, then, as Taylor (2000) reminds us, is there a consensus of successive studies of community participation that communities, by and large, remain on the margins of power in most partnership programmes to date, 'even when they are relatively well organised'? Why do participants remain as 'peripheral insiders' (Maloney et al., in Taylor, 2000: 1022) in these participatory processes, 'at the table but unable to influence central issues'? City politics is inseparable from insights into how power operates and is embedded in complex networks of power. The potential for participation is therefore very dependent on how we view and interpret power. Before discussing power in more detail, it is useful to foreground the three key ways proposed by Watson (1999) in which power can be understood. First, who has the power to define what are 'urban problems'? Second, who has the power to intervene in an urban conflict situation? Lastly, who can maximise their advantages, such as access to resources and amenities, at the expense of the weaker, excluded groups and individuals?

Lukes (1974) provides an influential treatise which summarises three particularly important interpretations of power. The first is termed 'one-dimensional' and is broadly labelled 'pluralist' because it concerns the relative bargaining power of a multiplicity of groups. A range of approaches focus on the observed behaviour involved in decision making which defines the boundaries of politics. Policy-area issues are therefore regarded as set by the political system and concern the way in which 'power shows up' within coalitions addressing the specific issue(s). The locus of power can therefore be determined by seeing who prevails in cases of decision making where there is observable conflict – and whoever prevails has 'more power'. Pluralist analysis tends, therefore, to focus on the exercise of power rather than on potential power. Power can only be analysed after careful examination of a series of concrete decisions involving direct (i.e. actual and observable) conflict and policy preferences emerging from this conflict. Observation of people's behaviour and interests as reflected in policy preferences opposes the idea that 'interests might be unarticulated, and above all, [that] the ideas people have might actually be mistaken or they may be unaware of their own interests' (Lukes, 1974: 14). Pluralists denied that this observable exercise of power in the political arena conceals, and is overlapped by and reinforces, wider social and economic inequalities (Mollenkopf, 1996). The urban protests that erupted in the late 1960s in New York City and elsewhere, according to Mollenkopf (1996: 221), made the pluralists' 'relatively tranquil picture of urban politics as a kind of market equilibrium-reaching mechanism seem anachronistic'. However, these approaches did show that economic and political elites do not control urban politics in any unified or direct way.

Cities do not comprise one single set of 'interests'. The process of negotiation between competing interest groups is understood in neo-pluralist accounts of urban politics through 'urban regime' theory. As depicted by Harding (2001), the stress is on the need to put politics back into the analytical picture. The central point is that actors do not need to hold total power over the city's population to act but instead merely need the power to act. While structuralist political economy accounts overlap with public choice (micro-economics) views, emphasising the necessity of the 'developmental' role cities must adopt in order to survive (in other words, cities compete to attract better-off residents and private investment), the ability of local government to shape urban futures must be put in the context of the social reproduction of governance, with struggles and bargaining, which rewards some groups ahead of others. Because of the complexity of politics, Stoker (1995) suggests that we focus on what he calls 'limited segments or domains of command power' and the ways in which they combine both forces and resources for a publicly significant result. They derive this ability through coalitions and the partnership principle, and the process through which a broadly shared political agenda may be constructed. According to Cochrane (1999), the strength of regime theory therefore lies in its recognition of the importance of existing power relations without assuming that any one group dominates. It does this by introducing a wider neo-pluralist conceptualisation of governance and exploring the different political configurations beyond the 'traditional' boundaries of government. Therefore, the question should perhaps be rephrased – not 'Who governs?' but instead 'Who has the capacity to act and why?'. However, although urban regime theory recognises both a plurality of actors and the economic and political constraints within which they must operate, as noted by Cochrane (1999), its most glaring omission is in its lack of attention to marginalised and excluded citizens who remain shut out from these coalitions or 'regimes'.

The second account of power offered by Lukes therefore critiques the understanding of the boundaries of politics in pluralist accounts. The political system is widened to include consideration of the ways in which demands for change can be excluded, and dissipated, with the creation or reinforcing of barriers to 'public deliberation' of issues. This conceptualisation of power begins to address the ways in which agendas can be set to cover only 'safe issues' through 'non-decision making'. Pluralists suggest that power also shows up in conflict even if it involves apparent 'non-decisions' and the assumption that where there appears to be no conflict there is consensus, assuming that 'the interests are consciously articulated and observable' (Lukes, 1974: 20). This raises the question of whether observed decisions reflect overt and/or covert conflict. There may be compliance through overt negotiated settlements but these might also reflect coercion and manipulation. The second account of power therefore allows scope for recognising how political agendas can be shaped by the relationships that unfold between institutions and their practices, the state and the broader socio-economic landscape. But the actors involved might not even be consciously aware of these exclusionary biases.

The third conceptualisation of power begins to offer a 'deeper and more satisfactory analysis of power relations' (Lukes, 1974: 10). Power relations and the ways in which issues of control – and conflicts of interest – are kept out of the political process are not always identified and articulated. As Lukes argues (1974: 21), behaviouralists regard decision making in terms of 'choices consciously and intentionally made by individuals between alternatives', but in fact the bias of the system 'can be mobilised, recreated and reinforced in ways that are neither consciously chosen nor the intended result of particular individuals' choices'. Systemic bias is not sustained simply by a series of individually chosen acts, but also, most importantly, by the socially structured and culturally patterned behaviour of groups, and practices of institutions, which may indeed be manifested by individuals' (in)action. So, for Lukes, power is not just based on individual decisions but also on collective groups and organisational effects. Nor is it the case that power is only exercised in situations of conflict. Rather we need to look at how hegemony – the desires you have as projected onto and replicated by others – is reproduced: rather than power only being exercised in a conflict situation, it may be that 'the most effective and insidious use of power is to prevent such conflict from arising in the first place' (Lukes, 1974: 23). What Lukes is proposing here is that just because there is an absence of conflict we should not assume that consensus prevails. Lukes is implying the possibility of false or manipulated consciousness. 'Logics' other than conscious individual choice, such as the logic of capital accumulation, become more important.

Thus, one strand of critique of the 'downscaling' policy in governance, as suggested, centres on the new institutional structures surrounding the shift to 'partnerships' and 'quangos' and the contracting out or commodification of local services. The fundamental contention is that there is a real blurring between the public and private sectors, which conceals class conflict and inequality beneath an apparent convergence of interests, serving to undermine working-class constituencies and also resulting in a heightened control of the newly privatised polity by new (predominantly male) interests (Peck, 1995). Peck cites evidence of over 73,000 'gift' appointments under Conservative governments to a range of quangos. It should also be anticipated that the current Labour government will follow a similar line of political appointments. One witness to the Liverpool Democracy Commission referred to the 'emergence of a "new magistracy" comprising public servants and local worthies often involved in several partnerships, but with no direct accountability to the public' (Liverpool Democracy Commission, 1999b: 2). A fundamental problem surrounding the 'entrepreneurial city' therefore concerns the suspicion that exclusionary tactics are being used by coalitions, including partnerships, which are depicted as divorcing urban entrepreneurial policy from democratic, accountable structures.[4]

Nonetheless, some structuralist accounts, because of their economic determinism, still fail to identify the actual mechanisms 'that promote some interests and issues while dampening others' (Mollenkopf, 1996: 222). Neo-Marxist accounts therefore deal with these mechanisms in terms of how they generate 'systemic, cumulative, political inequality, which has a more profound impact on outcomes than the coalition patterns studied by pluralists' (Mollenkopf, 1996: 222) in two broad neo-Marxist schools of thought. One addressed the political logic of capitalist accumulation, and the other the role of the urban political system in terms of mitigating or controlling conflicts surrounding 'collective consumption' (public provision of services) and urban protest and social movements. While structuralist accounts ground urban politics in its broader socio-economic surroundings, Mollenkopf, among others, maintains that there is a tendency in such accounts towards functionalism (the state 'must' undertake activities that favour

---

[4] Again, Imrie and Raco (1999) claim that this new dispensation is not that different from previous local government elite decision-making processes, and that democratisation and accountability can be heightened in certain areas of governance.

capital), determinism rather than variation across space and time, structures subordinating agency and a reduction of urban politics to economic imperatives, which 'trivialises politics'. Some post-Fordist regulation analysis is more sympathetic to the construction of political imperatives, albeit in the context of shifting external economic environments. This goes some way towards Mollenkopf's (1996) proposal that analysis of urban politics needs to consider three distinct sets of interests: public sector producer interests, popular or constituency interests, and private market interests. But there is no ultimate reduction of urban politics to capitalism; rather, as Mollenkopf (1996: 228) suggests, any political 'entrepreneur' who wishes to exert influence on local government must deal with this plurality of voices and complex sets of players, which requires understanding of both 'the constraints and [the] opportunities that astute political entrepreneurs can seize'.

In poststructuralist accounts, however, the focus is not only on the question of whose interests prevail but also on that of how different actors perceive their interests. Alternative ways of being and doing are closed off by power relations apparently so secure and well established that both the subjugated and the dominant are unaware or incapable of imagining alternatives. Thus social rules, norms, values and practices play a critical role in concealing the reality of pervasive dominance and in defusing conflict (Kabeer, 1994: 227). This is not to propose individual and group false consciousness, but to suggest that conflict is avoided because of its high costs. Therefore a more multi-dimensional and fluid approach would allow attention to the socially embedded and complex nature of power. Foucault (1980) was concerned with developing a critique of the strategies through which modern society was able to discipline and control its population by using the knowledge claims and practices of the human sciences – criminology, sociology, psychiatry, psychology and medicine. He was particularly concerned with the intervention and administrative control through which the modern state defined itself. Foucault saw this as enabled by the discourses associated with intellectual thought, leading to the ordering and disciplining of the subject, and the decentring of the Cartesian self-knowing and self-conscious individual; individuals' ability to know themselves is restricted by the colonising force of different bodies of knowledge.

Throughout social theory the use of geographical metaphors has been widespread, and Foucault employs terms such as 'territory', 'domain', 'soil', 'region' and 'locality'. His specific use of spatial metaphors was designed to locate the relations that are possible between power and knowledge. Power is not a static, localised commodity; rather, these geographical metaphors reveal its circulation in a chain or net-like organisation (Foucault, 1980). The major implication for the theorising of participation at the local scale is that Foucault's analysis of power 'requires us to shift our concentration from the centre and national institutions such as the state *not because this enables the powerless to speak and be heard, but because those macro-spheres of authority are not necessarily the only focal conductors of power*' (Kothari, 2001: 141, emphasis added). According to Kothari, this more fluid and relational approach to power should disrupt dichotomies such as macro/micro, central/local, powerful/powerless. However, she also notes that

> the creation of dichotomies of power within participatory discourse (haves and the have-nots) allows the revealing of power not as social and political discourse or as embodied practice, but only as manifest in material realities. Thus participatory approaches can unearth who gets what, when and where, but not necessarily the processes by which this happens or the ways in which the knowledge produced through participatory techniques is a normalized one that reflects and articulates wider power relations in society. (Kothari, 2001: 141)

There is a need, according to this perspective, to understand the relationship between participant and observer as historically constructed through all sorts of rituals (Kothari, 2001: 143). Discourse, therefore, is never neutral; people 'construct problems, solutions and actions in particular ways that are congruent with existing relations of power, domination and the distribution of resources' (Atkinson, 1999: 70). This approach caters for a more nuanced discussion and analysis of 'power', because power is revealed as being constructed in situ. It is therefore highly relevant to thinking about participation in governance in the current context of regeneration.

Participation in Governance

Although the term 'participation' is common currency, and therefore appealing and attractive to diverse interests, is there any actual agreement as to what participation *is*? In other words, does its ability to mean all things to all people in fact obscure and confuse the term, and indeed obscure the multi-dimensionality of participation and what participation satisfies (Burkey, 1991)? In the conventional, some might say 'orthodox', internal critiques (Cooke and Kothari, 2001) introducing the concept, participation is usually regarded as either a goal to be achieved in and of itself, as a response to the problem of exclusion, or, more specifically, as participation in projects and programmes to overcome problems of exclusion (Gaventa, 1998: 51). So should participation be seen as a means or an end? Does it imply technical and managerial 'solutions' or social and political transformation? According to Oakley (1991), there are three broad interpretations of participation. One paramount consideration is the contribution that participation is able to make to predetermined programmes and projects (the means). A second concern is getting the organisations in place or the institutions right for development. A third is the 'end' of empowerment. Although this last interpretation usually recognises that a transfer of power is required (Atkinson and Cope, 1997), empowerment is often difficult to define or identify. It can be, for example, providing the skills and abilities to enable people to manage better and to have a say in, or negotiate with, existing development delivery systems. Or is it a more fundamental philosophy – the internal, visceral transformation of communities (Burkey, 1991; Oakley, 1991; Rhanema, 1992)? From the point of view of the policy makers at least, participation could be viewed therefore as both a means and an end:

- Involving people is an end in itself – giving voice, especially to (actually or potentially) 'socially excluded' individuals and groups, strengthening the capacity for independent action and intervention by these excluded neighbourhoods in regeneration initiatives; while
- Participation in the programme by such individuals and groups is also seen as a means of addressing some of the economic problems that they may be experiencing, through, for example, more sensitive training, improved educational attainment, and/or involvement in community-based economic development issues and projects, usually predetermined. In this scenario participation is usually for economic reasons, raising the issue of involvement in decision making, control of resources and benefits.

Over and above the management of social inclusion programmes, and monitoring their outputs, we should be looking critically at the political character of these programmes. Foucauldian perspectives on power and governance therefore propose that government – that is, the organisation of collective deliberation in liberal democracies – has two main components: first, various 'rationalities' that give rise to goals or objectives of governing authorities; and, second, techniques and mechanisms that aim to deliver these objectives (Murdoch, 2000: 505). The important point is that these rationalities are realised through practices that utilise governmental technologies, therefore politicising non-political or technical practices – such as participation. In reminding ourselves of Watson's three propositions regarding power, we should therefore be asking: what are the terms of regeneration programmes as constructs of power and political relations? In other words, what are the so-called 'excluded' considered to *lack*? Is it, crudely, money (state-mediated redistribution, including service provision), work (and/or education, as the principal means of state-mediated social integration and participation), or morals (the 'right' cultural and individual behaviours) (Levitas, 1998)? In a slightly different tradition, we could also suggest lack of power, voice and empowering political participation.

The focus on getting the excluded 'in' reflects a politics of inclusion based on 'insertion', 'inclusion' and 'integration', which, some argue, has an uncritical emphasis on integration. Jackson (1999) suggests that, despite this critique, 'the assumption that marginality is the problem remains pervasive' in Eurocentric social exclusion discourse. Rather than seeking outright integration, which is the commonest representation in the literature, there is a complex process of negotiation with the dominant culture and institutions, mediated through class, gender, ethnicity, religion and geography. These problems highlight the inadequacies of social inclusion agendas, which identify different groups but often lump them together as commonly discriminated-against 'excluded', with little evidence of harnessing their intrinsic worth and differences. This is most noticeable in the current promotion of 'inclusion' as paid work in the labour market (Levitas, 1998). These policies reflect prevailing attitudes foisted on the excluded and contain a range of contradictions. They imply that if you are 'out' or excluded, you do not have much to contribute. The valorisation of employment, important as it is, tends to eclipse different values and alternative contributions. Community members might be volunteering their time and energy, yet be registered as unemployed or economically inactive. Or, for example, reproductive labour outside the labour market might be valued by women, for its contribution to their sense of identity and relational networks, more highly than the supposed benefits of integration through employment-based social inclusion. What, then, does this tell us about being labelled 'excluded' when you are in fact extremely active? Inclusion should not just be understood in terms of adding efficiency to the economy. Indeed, the emphasis on inclusion through paid work undervalues those contributions which cannot simply be economised and above all subordinated to neoclassical economics.

Other criticisms of social exclusion discourse centre on the false binary opposition that juxtaposes the 'powerful' included against the 'powerless' and 'passive' excluded. Thus the dualist nature of social exclusion discourse can itself function as a controlling mechanism, focusing on whether you are 'in' or 'out' and therefore legitimising particular methods of getting you 'in'. Important implications follow from this for inclusion policies:

> The excluded are brought in, included, offered access to the resources and relations of power. The poor, by inclusion for example in employment, may become non-poor. Yet [for example] in gender terms what might this mean? Gender identities of women are positive, and valued by women, at the same time as they are valued in hegemonic ideologies. Might inclusion involve loss or transformation of these [and other] identities? (Jackson, 1999: 14)

The enthusiasm for a participatory culture and politics within regeneration is reflected in prevailing models of cooperation in governance. Bearing in mind the brief review of different interpretations of 'power', how does current enthusiasm for deliberative democracy therefore dovetail with the possibilities of a more democratic system of governance?

The pluralistic and harmonious view of power, a feature of the new institutionalisation of participation, as endorsed by New Labour, promotes collective decision making through rational agreement and communicative reasoning and a commitment to discussion and airing disagreements. It again flags up concerns about how the excluded should be brought 'in'. 'Novel cooperation processes', with non-hierarchical, round-table structures and a cooperative style of policy making, represent, on one level, the ascendancy of a politics of consensus in current urban regeneration. Yet how can we reconcile this harmonious view of human relationships with fundamental inequalities in bargaining positions? The aim of deliberation is to encourage a plurality of perspectives through, for example, cross-sectoral multi-agency partnerships. Then, apparently, discussion overcomes narrow self-interest and teaches individual participants to see their own position in relation to others. The argument appears attractive but places considerable faith in communicative reasoning, which, according to Amin (2000), has an air of 'procedural fetishism', 'a faith in the perfectibility of deliberative decision-making techniques'. We have to balance this belief in the ability of discussion to lead to consensus with entrenched self-interest and disparities in institutional capacity and the ability to manipulate and coerce agendas. Within these scenarios community participation reflects a politics of inclusion, drawing communities into governance structures in order to contain them through consensual politics of partnership deliberation and compromise. According to Amin, if an accord emerges out of a deliberative partnership arrangement, this will be the product of struggle and compromise – a contextualised achievement that is 'temporary and shaped by the interests and mobilised powers of the occasion – not the product of reasonable argument or moral enlightenment' (Amin, 2000: 6).

For other observers critical of social inclusion policies per se, and their stakeholder politics, predominant approaches fail to recognise fundamental inequalities: '[Social inclusion discourse] distracts attention from the essentially class-divided character of society, and allows a view of society as basically benign to exist with the visible reality of poverty. It does this by discursively placing the unwanted characteristics outside society' (Levitas, 1998: 188). The deliberative democracy approach is therefore considered to be at odds with a more critical perspective on participation which regards power and its acquisition as more of a zero-sum game in which there are inevitably winners and losers. Gaventa (1998) therefore cites another version of community organisation which functions at a grass roots level and is concerned with changing structural inequalities and power relations. Critiques more sensitive to political constructions and contestations of the urban entrepreneurial city landscape usually depict communities as engaged in a cultural politics of resistance through which protest shapes localised attachments to place and identity. To radical democrats, ensuring and achieving social justice ('genuine' participation) depends on more than consensus and should involve empowering counter-hegemonic forces through recognising the politics of participation as contestation and a shifting, unending process of identity formation. Promoting the autonomy of groups involved in collective action for empowerment sees power as relational and conflictual, with marginalisation inherently connected to the material and ideological hegemony of dominant classes and groups requiring fundamental structural transformation (Stokke, 1998: 223). Gaventa, for example, might concede that there is a rich history of voluntary organisation involvement in, and contribution to, Western society, but he questions the often uncritical promotion of voluntary organisations as always associated with a pluralist and open model of democracy because 'there is nothing inherent in the status of a voluntary non-profit organisation which leads it to work to remedy the inequalities or problems of society, or to strengthen the participation of the poor in dealing with development issues' (Gaventa, 1998: 25).

However, these perspectives also fail to move beyond a narrow conception of power as adversarial, to be 'taken' and 'possessed' through a politics of contest rather than consensus, which, again following Amin, still does not overcome blindness to embedded power, inequality, oppression or common ethico-political targets. In short, despite all the appeal to equality and social justice, there is little concrete to join the fragments of radical democrat resistance in order to contain the rich and powerful.

The Limits of Participation?

> [P]articipation, therefore, can not merely be proclaimed or wished upon [. . .] people [. . .]; it must begin by recognising the powerful, multi-dimensional, and in many instances, anti-participatory forces which dominate the lives of [. . .] people. (Oakley, 1991: 4)

Participation therefore has many guises, including the current context of neo-liberal restructuring and 'retreat of the state', which then creates the 'need' for a self-reliant poor to relieve pressure on subsidies and governmental responsibility. There are suspicions that social integration is bound up with Europe's dwindling welfare provision and that claims on resources and expenditure may be lessened through a social inclusion agenda that deflects attention away from state provision. We are only told that exclusion is bad because it threatens to disrupt the mainstream status quo, or because it is an undesirable condition of dependency, or, better, because it denies rights and participation, with numerous (insurmountable?) obstacles. Either way, the struggle for participation as an end represents an idealisation of that end.

The flourishing of 'participation' in the context of structural changes in the economy, and responses within state and civil society, is therefore context-specific, tied to accumulated meanings and ideological persuasions (Nelson and Wright, 1995). There are a number of fundamental dimensions and paradoxes within the participatory process. First, it involves the encounter between the 'hitherto excluded and those elements in the society that maintain or enforce exclusion' (Stiefel and Wolfe, 1994: 4) or those anti-participatory forces that exist within social structures. The contributors to Nelson and Wright's collection suggest that 'if participation is to be more than a palliative then it must involve shifts in power' (1995: 1). For Oakley (1991), meaningful participation implies the ability positively to influence the source of events. It cannot be meaningful unless it achieves power and challenges established interests, leading to direct access to resources and the decision making affecting those resources.

Another basic dilemma involves the contradictions of participation as a *mediated* situation (Rhanema, 1992), whereby individuals need to be 'free' and 'unbiased' in order for participation to be meaningful, unco-opted and uncoercive, yet all societies are structured along lines of class, race and gender. For Rhanema, genuine participation is not represented through its external and hence inevitably co-opted guise but instead by inner creative and spiritual qualities through an awakening of self-realisation, step-by-step transformation or praxis. It cannot therefore be determined from outside unless a community's own knowledge acts as the foundation for participation, otherwise it becomes a new form of domination. The same author suggests that there is a complex interaction between these communities and external agents which requires extreme caution and sensitivity, otherwise new dependencies are created and the poor cannot retain control.

Further contradictions surround the imperatives of urban regeneration programmes themselves, within which regeneration is brought about through the project cycle, reflecting budget constraints and time-frames designed to produce easily measurable physical and financial goals (Stiefel and Wolfe, 1994: 217). We should therefore scrutinise whether participation is required only in so far as it slots tidily into these predetermined and externally defined aims and objectives of a programme or project; 'participation is seen as yet another input to be programmed and managed along with other inputs' (Oakley, 1991: 30). The long-term creation and transformation of social relations within an area, and the wider structural constraints on this, are bypassed, particularly in the current context of development initiatives (Cleaver, 2001). Even here the argument for participation's benefits concerning efficiency, effectiveness, sustainability and empowerment is regarded as producing limited evidence (Cleaver, 2001; Oakley, 1991). We should therefore ask whether 'participation' is such a significant break from past urban development, or whether it seeks to incorporate and include those evading, or excluded from, a more thorough-going modernisation, while also generating a politically attractive slogan. Rhanema (1992: 124) questions whether participation represents any break from the 'colonisation' of 'top-down' approaches. Instead, he suggests, its current use is due to the perceived legitimacy that it brings to outdated and discredited ideas of transformation and change.

Participation is therefore regarded by many authors as inherently disorderly and conflictual, in contrast to the quantitative, and supposedly orderly, bureaucratic nature of 'planning', which attempts to contain the chaos of development (Stiefel and Wolfe, 1994; Nelson and Wright, 1995). Power, for these authors, cannot be given away. Instead participation involves the use of 'power to' in order to negotiate with and transform those 'hopefully willing partners who have structural and institutional "power over"' (Nelson and Wright, 1995: 18). These authors suggest that participation should therefore be transformative, again by asking whether people traditionally excluded are now recognised as legitimate knowers, or whether states and non-governmental organisations do not just regard them as having 'strong backs [volunteering labour and time] and deep pockets'. Are such people-centred perspectives transforming the apparatus of development or are the unforeseen consequences more effective?

Arnstein describes a range of 'ladders' of participation, based on her incisive observation which pinpoints what citizen participation *is*, namely, a redistribution of power. Otherwise it is an 'empty ritual' (Arnstein, 1969: 216). Its overall purpose should be to induce social reform. An updated version of the ladder (Burns et al., in Atkinson and Cope, 1997: 206) provides more nuanced 'rungs', including 'effective advisory board', 'limited decentralised decision-making' and three different types of 'control' ('delegated', 'entrusted' and, at the peak of citizen control and the top of the ladder, 'independent control'). Despite these nuances, Guijt and Shah (1998) maintain that the ladder metaphor conceals complex interactions between but also, crucially, within groups labelled as 'excluded' or the powerful 'included'. A more recent approach within the participation 'orthodoxy' problematises the notion of 'community' by incorporating notions of difference and diversity into a recasting of communities as complex, changing, heterogeneous entities reflecting competing rather than homogenised interests (Guijt and Shah, 1998). We should also therefore be more generally suspicious of accounts, particularly predominant in current regeneration policy, in which the concept of 'community' is invoked to denote consensus and common need (Nelson and Wright, 1995). The concept of 'community' is constructed following the involvement of the community in question in an activity involving another main party (or parties) – national or local state or non-state agency. There is usually a tacit assumption that the other party is the initiator of the activity (Desai, 1995), with the implication, once again, that the 'community', and particularly the way it participates, are creations of external definition and intervention rather than having any intrinsic meaning or straightforward definition. These interventions, depending on what they are targeting, will deploy either a positive or negative image of community. So, policies addressing community care will emphasise caring community characteristics, whereas those combating crime, 'antisocial' behaviour or exclusion will tend to represent the breakdown of community networks (Levitas, 1998). 'Community' appears to have positive, albeit besieged, qualities when we come to regeneration. 'Community participation' therefore straddles both the positive and negative uses of 'community', although there is a tendency in regeneration policy to represent the community, somewhat romantically, as homogenised, embodying collective interests pertaining to a geographically defined area. These problems therefore raise important questions concerning the role of power in participation within communities in equipping communities, or, more accurately, members of them, to 'take control of their lives'.

A recent major policy statement on the Labour government's commitment to neighbourhood renewal and regeneration, for example, now places 'community' involvement at the core of national strategy for social inclusion: 'The [National] Strategy recognises that sustainable renewal can only be achieved if it has community ownership. Full community involvement, starting where the community is, and with its priorities, is as important as improving public services' (Social Exclusion Unit, 2001: 71). Community involvement is therefore linked to relevance, leading to effective engagement and, hence, sustainability. Cost-effective measures also apparently emerge from downscaling (Social Exclusion Unit, 2001;

Department of Social Security, 1999). Yet, again, there is the undertone of this process legitimating policy restructuring through 'local' values:

> Our aim is to get away from the 'single-policy', 'top down' approach and to deliver policies in a way which is relevant to people's lives. Through local partnerships and through our consultation arrangements, we are actively engaging local people in the development and delivery of policies. We are breaking down organisational and institutional barriers to create imaginative joined-up approaches. (Department of Social Security, 1999, point 33, chapter 6)

Strategies to encourage local participation are evident in the large number of jobs created in local authority and regeneration agencies. 'Putting Communities First' is the bold declaration of Heywood New Deal for Communities, with the job description for the 'community development manager' insisting that 'the community must be at the centre of all our projects, plans and aspirations'. Elsewhere, advertisements for a 'project leader/officer' and a 'community development officer', and those concerning 'community involvement' and 'community-based care', state key objectives as, typically, liaising with public agencies and community service providers; encouraging the formation of local community groups; working with local groups in achieving community ownership; and introducing a practical and sustainable community development strategy that encompasses 'self-help' and 'best value'. Government offices will even take punitive actions 'if an LSP [Local Strategic Partnership – a single local body to be set up in each of the 88 local authority areas to receive the Neighbourhood Renewal Fund] did not take sufficient account of community views' (Social Exclusion Unit, 2001: 54). Dispersal of funding within the Neighbourhood Renewal Fund is contingent on LSPs being formed and with the preference that community strategies are designed. Yet a fundamental problem, as evidenced in this paper by the reluctance to prefix 'participation' with 'community', concerns the definition of 'community' and the criteria established for membership of the 'community'. Strategies such as the National Strategy for Neighbourhood Renewal also provide little, if any, detail on how residents might be involved in the design of service provision, despite aiming 'to involve people living in poverty in a participatory way, at all levels of governance and in all stages of planning' (Oxfam, 2000: 35).

Ladder analogies also contain normative assumptions, depicting participation as a gradient, with upwards movement desirable and necessary until the endpoint of 'independent control' is reached. Rather, we should be asking and observing how different players participate and why such forms are chosen, rather than prescribing strategies or identifying which rung of the ladder is being achieved (Guijt and Shah, 1998). Arnstein's ladder, nonetheless, does provide a checklist of what is, or is not, being achieved, a schema that can be applied to a wide range of 'target' institutions. It also raises questions of what Arnstein calls roadblocks or obstacles in the path of participation. For Oakley (1991) these are state structures and administrative obstacles, and also social obstacles, such as lack of skills, leadership and experience, which militate against communities' ability to take on the 'excluders'.

In a UK context, Atkinson and Cope (1997: 216) suggest that it is vital that 'the local community be involved at all stages of the urban policy process – problem definition, agenda-setting, goal-setting, policy appraisal, policy implementation, policy review, policy succession and policy termination'. It has been more common to set up the question of participation in terms of what it fails to do, and therefore to reflect on the shortcomings of the participatory process. Critical accounts do also exist within the more orthodox accounts of participation which draw our attention to the potential and actual political co-option, rhetorical statements about similar 'needs', goals and interests, and the coercion of free labour and volunteering time which the mantle of participation can conceal. However, for some authors, these critical perspectives still look towards improving techniques and tools to further the participatory project, rather than reflecting critically on participation per se: 'The question that stands out however, is how many such concerns need to be raised before participatory development itself comes to be seen as the real problem?' (Cooke and Kothari, 2001: 7).

Cooke and Kothari (2001) suggest that the discourse of participation itself unleashes tyrannical power in three principal ways: first, decision making and control instigated by participation facilitators override existing legitimate processes of decision making; second, there is a tyranny of the group, with group dynamics often reinforcing the interests of the already powerful; third, there is the tyranny of methods, with apparently neutral community mapping exercises tapping into boundless local knowledge actually concealing more than they reveal. The universal benefits and claims for participation can be exposed as specific and partial (Henkel and Stirrat, 2001: 174). Participants are brought into pre-existing exercises of power which structure the terms of engagement and can serve to reinforce existing relations of domination and control, demarcate what is 'reasonable', and even provide the language in which demands can be made (Atkinson, in Taylor, 2000). These social norms govern the terms of partnership engagement, through, for example, the strong imprint of political imperatives, and the conformity of public sector management approaches, including mandatory indicators defined from outside local areas (Taylor, 2000). There is also indirect control through auditing structures in UK regeneration policy and with it the formalisation of procedures. There is a distinct politics of participatory discourse, which is often insidious and concealing even if it is deployed unconsciously (Kothari, 2001; Atkinson, in Taylor, 2000). Subject positions and moral judgements – in other words, what can and cannot be done – are, therefore, already prescribed to participants before they participate. Many residents feel alienated, even belittled by these procedures and jargon.

The Way Forward: The Taste of Governance and (Re)Learning

With all these problems revealed, and the difficult question of 'who participates' (Jones, 2003) not even addressed, we turn now to the final issue of the crucial role of re-learning in regeneration. White (1996) has made the important point that although participation may involve sharing and a degree of negotiation, it does not necessarily involve sharing in *power*. How many current regeneration projects could, in fact, claim to involve genuine power sharing? For White, echoing Gaventa (1998), the price of 'mainstreaming' participation is its misuse and abuse, which potentially involves the incorporation of the excluded as a means of enabling control for governments and agencies. To avoid depicting participation as 'non-political', and therefore to lessen the effects of technical co-option, participation should be scrutinised within any particular context, by asking about its

- *form*: is it nominal, instrumental, representative or formal?
- *function*: is it merely cosmetic, a means or an end?
- *interests*: does it serve a 'top-down' or a 'bottom-up' agenda, or both? Does it serve different groups (from the 'top' and the 'bottom') in different ways? From the perspective of the 'top' it might produce legitimisation, efficiency, sustainability, or empowerment; from the perspective of the 'bottom' it might allow inclusion and leverage, incur costs, or be felt as empowering (White, 1996).

To get a sense of the dynamics and fluidity of this process, White shows how the interactions between different interests can change rapidly as an effect of participation, and suggests caution as to how 'interests' are constructed. Her overall point is that 'change hurts', and that for participation to be effective it should generate conflict. Otherwise, the failure to recognise the role of politics in participation renders it ineffective and indeed co-optive. Whereas for Cooke and Kothari (2001) this probably represents merely an internal orthodox critique of participation, and therefore an attempt to salvage the participatory project, it is my opinion, following Taylor (2000), that communities should be allowed access to the opportunities, including jobs, open to public sector officials, especially because residents do not have the easy option of 'exit' and because their areas depend to a far greater extent on public services (Taylor, 2000). Furthermore, 'residential neighbourhoods, understood as overlapping social networks rather than as spatial entities, are of particular significance for those who spend considerable amounts of time in and around the home: children, elderly people, female carers, the unemployed and other vulnerable groups' (Kearns and Forrest, 1998: 1). Residents have also been able to develop effective service management and regeneration organisations, providing themselves with an asset and income stream to bring as financial capital to the partnership table (Taylor, 2000).

So much is written about community capacity-building but we forget the capacity-building required of other institutional structures. We need therefore to consider, as (arguably) the strength of social inclusion discourse, democratising existing institutions and minimising what Amin (2000) calls domination in games of powers. Arguably, a strong representative national and local state is also essential for participatory democracy, and participation should not aim to replace the state. For example, Liverpool's Pathways area partnerships also gain support from local authority structures which are adapting to partnership working through producing flexible inter-institutional working and engaging communities. Each of the nine directorates within Liverpool City Council attached itself to at least one area partnership and set up a system of link officers in each directorate connecting across all 11 partnerships. Although this was approached with differing degrees of enthusiasm, and proved to be problematic in some of the areas, there were real benefits not only for most area partnerships but for governance more generally, as the council gained an appreciation of the 'feel for how communities work':

> part of using the Directorate support network was . . . to use the City Council as the accountable body which meant in effect that the City Council resources supported the partnerships through things like personnel, through things like IT, through things like finance, through things like training and development and all of those corporate resources . . . a lot of people have pulled on regeneration hats where probably previously they'd not really come across it as part and parcel of their ordinary work. But because they've got good management skills, those skills are transferable in a wide variety of situations and regeneration is a classic illustration. You don't need to be, you know, an Oxbridge Economist to do regeneration in a city like Liverpool. What you do need is to have a feel for how communities work and how you can make relationships work and how you make linkages . . . (Head of Leisure Services Directorate, Liverpool City Council, in Meegan, 2000: 24)

According to Meegan (2000), the developing relationship between Liverpool City Council and its previous 11 Pathways area partnerships (established in the context of Objective One funding) is also reflected in European Regional Development Fund bids, with the city council acting as the accountable body for a wide range of community-based schemes. An indicator of the success of this supportive framework is that the community stamp on projects has become increasingly clear over the course of the Objective One programme. Furthermore, whereas the chairs of the 11 partnerships were initially councillors or officers of the council, only two are now chaired by city councillors. Indeed, across Merseyside local residents and representatives of community organisations fill the great majority of these chairs and community involvement in these partnership boards is around 360 – a third of the total numbers involved (Meegan, 2000). Furthermore, Liverpool City Council is also providing the institutional framework for a code of conduct for community representatives in order to work through, and in future avoid, some of the existing problems concerning community representation and participation in partnerships.

Important issues of governance as a construction of social and political discourses obviously remain entrenched. But we should not be suggesting that communities must inevitably be co-opted and cannot themselves, like local authorities and agencies, learn different ways of acting and knowing. Alongside discussions of discursive power are key participatory strategies involving institutional mechanisms that enable the 'community' to be taken seriously by policy makers and donors. Giving community representatives on partnership boards, for example, power to score bids for potential projects appears to be one particularly effective tool. Indeed, for all the problems, a community participant in one of the few area partnerships that actually has extensive private sector involvement told me that outside agencies' obligations were tied to funding mechanisms and that 'the partnership has got to sell involvement to make it [Pathways] work'. In effect, the board must therefore reach consensus regarding appraised projects before they can be passed. 'If the council and the community haven't got it right', as one community board member put it, 'then they've got to get together and sort it out and that's good'. The crucial point is that these spaces of inclusion can themselves, during the process of negotiation, transform the bargaining positions of participants. Interaction in regeneration programmes and projects can take place at a range of levels – not only at board level but also through a number of working groups spinning off from sub-groups from each partnership board. In the example of Merseyside's Objective One 'Pathways to Integration' programme, sub-groups are responsible for more specific issues, such as 'environment', 'youth', 'physical development', 'community development' and 'childcare'. These groups involve residents and professionals. In one sub-group meeting, which addressed community educational issues, residents were very vocal in questioning the appropriateness of a large European-funded bid for computer courses and facilities. They considered the courses to be highly inappropriate for residents' needs. Without their approval, the bid could not proceed. Agencies and professionals had to respond to these criticisms. In another case, a community college had to alter its bid drastically in order to win approval for the bid. Once a bid has been scrutinised by the sub-groups, it is then passed on to the board level whereupon it is examined again. This process was described as a 'double whammy' by one resident, acting as chairperson of the local partnership:

> you've got local people, local people who are looking at the project from its inception, do you know what I mean, through to the board level . . . you've also got people who will send that sub-group individual projects for them to assess. I'm quite happy that people are confident enough, because they've been doing it for a while now. I'm happy that people are confident to sit down and do that in a professional manner and not be bamboozled and not be, you know, spoken down to like. Five years ago I'd say that would have been a problem but not now you know. (Jones, 2003)

Another community representative claimed that 'it's the first time ever that we've got a little bit of power'. There is no doubt that residents are aware that agencies now require their input and involvement, even 'need' it, at least in terms of the community role in scoring projects. Just as local authorities are adjusting to the new landscape of governance, so too are communities, as another community representative put it:

> It's, well, you know that you've got to work in partnership to get things done, and to be perfectly honest *we're learning to manipulate that situation*. It's plain common sense, you learn to manipulate the situation. The council are also learning that we can manipulate

the situation, they can't get grants unless we are involved . . . the power base has changed. Whereas we had to beg for every little bit we have now realised that without the community involvement they [council and agencies] can't go forward. (Jones, 2003, emphasis added)

Despite all the barriers to involvement, frustrations that mirror the problems of City Challenge and the Single Regeneration Budget (Atkinson and Cope, 1997), such as preset agendas, insufficient time for proper consultation, high levels of 'red tape' or bureaucracy, lack of administrative support in some areas, payment in arrears, tight timescales and, particularly for Pathways, the problem of finding match-funding, which initially clearly prevented more community-oriented bids, there was little sense in which these and many other active residents felt co-opted. It is perhaps remarkable that community representatives have not only immersed themselves in these alien procedures but have done so to such an extent that they now feel empowered to oppose councillors and professionals, thus potentially rejuvenating a moribund and failing system of representative democracy. Strategies of involvement, such as public meetings, clearly need to be reassessed, perhaps to base regeneration strategies on the spontaneity of wider forms of social participation rather than on the formalised and institutionalised variety, but many residents are obviously capable, with the right support, of expanding these spaces of participation in governance. However, complex social relations, time constraints and accumulated experiences – and perhaps dashed expectations of previous initiatives – also suggest the need to be realistic about the barriers to increasing participation and the myth of even 10 per cent, never mind 100 per cent, participation (Guijt and Shah, 1998), Furthermore, in cities such as Liverpool there is a historical pattern whereby community representatives are considered as delegated to act on behalf of communities. Given apparently low levels of involvement, we should focus on the quality and effectiveness of that involvement rather than merely quantifying the process (Jones, 1999). To go back to the initial polarised account of citizen participation/inclusion, we should also be asking those participating whether they 'choose' to be on the margins and to seek 'independent control'. Many, perhaps most, residents do not always seek to remain at the margins, as depicted in 'radical' accounts. Instead, we should be focusing on the particular circumstances and characteristics that surround participation in a given project, programme or locality. Often the level of intra-community conflict creates the need to establish a broader collective mechanism beyond the 'local', linked to a broader societal level in order to remind the 'included' of their obligations to equity. In the case of Pathways to Integration, community representatives also became adept, over time, at creating an influential pan-area partnership community body across the whole of Merseyside (see Meegan, 2000). Ultimately, according to the former head of Liverpool Council for Voluntary Services, Ed Murphy, who gave evidence to the Liverpool Democracy Commission's hearings (1999a), Pathways had given communities 'a taste of involvement in neighbourhood governance'. There is no reason to suppose that this taste cannot be improved on and extended.

Conclusion

Arguably, participation as inclusion in governance, with all its many 'roadblocks', disclaimers and health warnings, has superseded representative democracy in parts of Liverpool and other cities. While concerns remain over whether partnerships – in particular, public–private partnerships and finance initiatives – allow for genuinely collaborative working between agencies and residents (Liverpool Democracy Commission, 1999b), community participants are nonetheless playing an increasingly important role in these 'spaces of participation' that are regenerating cities and neighbourhoods and recharging governance. This is not simply about either co-option or resistance but about listening to the competing needs of residents within a diversity of situations. Nonetheless, in order to take advantage of these spaces of inclusion, renewed focus on social justice and citizenship is also required. Moreover, this needs to be actively encouraged through promoting capabilities and rights, as well as socialisation into collective responsibilities, citizenship and experimental democratic programmes (see Amin, 2000). We need to give a platform to the plurality of citizen voices and enable the movement away from approaches to urban governance that 'fix', standardise and distil social relations (of which the current fashion surrounding 'social capital' is a notable example). To reiterate an earlier observation, social exclusion and inclusion must be regarded as the interaction of the 'hitherto excluded and those elements in the society that maintain or enforce exclusion' (Stiefel and Wolfe, 1994: 4). We may therefore be relying too much on the 'local' as the appropriate scale to deliver the democratic city. For all the gains of certain micro-level urban regeneration programmes, we should also be thinking at a macro-level about capitalism, institutionally based exclusion and questions of equity, *in tandem with* the importance of grass-roots struggles. Area-based strategies are rightfully to be regarded as additional area-targeted redistributive measures, but they are not substitutes for macro-level policy which could also enhance social justice in the city. New fractions and interests are also the products of entrepreneurial politics, exacerbating existing social divisions and territorial inequalities (Hall and Hubbard, 1996).

A critical barometer of the success or failure of policies encompassed by the urban regeneration litany is, therefore, the extent to which communities can assert themselves within spaces of inclusion. Such assertion, however, as argued in this chapter, is contingent on the composition of the political and institutional space surrounding inclusion, as well as the particularities of the specific areas and communities. The literature and practice suggest that a shift in power is necessary for participation to make any real difference. This shift entails substantial re-learning on the part of agencies and communities alike. Fragile, uneven and contested as this process may be, there is evidence in Liverpool of an emerging new politics of urban regeneration centred on participation in governance. This new politics is transforming governance in our cities, arguably, to alter the ways in which policy-makers view communities and vice versa – but not necessarily in any predictable or co-opted way.

References

Amin, A. (2000), 'The Democratic City', paper presented at the annual conference of the Institute of British Geographers, January

Arnstein, S. (1969), 'A Ladder of Citizen Participation', *AIP*, July

Atkinson, R., and Cope, S. (1997), 'Community Participation and Urban Regeneration in Britain', in P. Hoggett (ed.), *Contested Communities*, Bristol: Policy Press, 201–21

Bell, M., and Franceys, R. (1995), 'Improving Social Welfare through Appropriate Technology: Government Responsibility, Citizen Duty or Consumer Choice', *Social Science and Medicine*, 40: 1169–79

Blair, T. (1998), Speech to National Association of Councils for Voluntary Service, London, www.nacvs.org.uk

Burkey, S. (1991), *Participatory Practice*, London: Zed Books

Cleaver, F. (2001), 'Institutions, Agency and the Limitations of Participatory Approaches to Development', in Cooke and Kothari (eds)

Cochrane, A. (1999), 'Administered Cities', in Pile et al., eds. (1999)

Cooke, B., and Kothari, U. (eds) (2001), *Participation: The New Tyranny?*, London: Zed Books

De Haas, A. (1998), 'Social Exclusion: An Alternative Concept for the Study of Deprivation', *Institute of Development Studies Bulletin*, 29(1): 10–19

Department of Social Security (1999), *Opportunity for All: Tackling Poverty and Social Exclusion*, London: HMSO

Desai, V. (1995), *Community Participation and Slum Housing: A Study of Bombay*, London: Sage

Foucault, M. (1980), *Power/Knowledge: Selected Interviews and Other Writings*, Brighton: Harvester Wheatsheaf

Gaventa, J. (1998), 'Poverty, Participation and Social Exclusion in North and South', *Institute of Development Studies Bulletin*, 29(1): 50–57

Gonzales, J. M. (2000), 'State-led Experiments in Participatory Development in Columbia' (paper presented to workshop on 'Local Politics and Democratisation in Developing Countries'), University of Oslo, November 16–18

Guijt, I., and Shah, M. (eds) (1998), *The Myth of Community: Gender Issues in Participatory Development*, London: Intermediate Technology Publications

Hall, T., and Hubbard, P. (1996), 'The Entrepreneurial City: New Politics, New Urban Geographies', *Progress in Human Geography*, 20: 153–74

Harding, A. (2001), *Cities and Power in the Global Age: Urban Theory Reconsidered*, London: Pinter

Henkel, H., and Stirrat, R. (2001), 'Participation as Spiritual Duty: Empowerment as Secular Subjection', in Cooke and Kothari (eds)

Imrie, R., and Raco, M. (1999), 'How New is the New Local Governance? Lessons from the United Kingdom', *Transactions of the Institute of British Geographers*, 24: 45–64

Jackson, C. (1999), 'Social Exclusion and Gender: Does One Size Fit All?', *The European Journal of Development Research*, 11(1): 125–46

Jones, P. S. (2003), 'Urban Regeneration's Poisoned Chalice: Is there an Impasse in (Community) Participation-Based Policy?', *Urban Studies*, 40(3): 581–601

Kabeer, N. (1994), *Reversed Realities*, London: Verso

Kearns, A., and Forrest, R. (1998), 'Social Cohesion, Neighbourhoods and Cities', paper prepared for Housing Studies Spring Conference, York: University of York, 15–16 April

Kothari, U. (2001), 'Power, Knowledge and Social Control in Participatory Development', in Cooke and Kothari (eds)

LeGates, R., and Stout, F. (1996), *The City Reader*, London: Routledge

Levitas, R. (1998), *The Inclusive Society*, London: Macmillan

Liverpool Democracy Commission (1999a), *21st Century City*, Liverpool: University of Liverpool

—(1999b), 'Partnerships', Chapter 2, unpublished

Lukes, S. (1974), *Power: A Radical View*, London: Macmillan

Madanipour, A., Cars, G. and Allen, J. (eds) (1998), *Social Exclusion in European Cities: Processes, Experiences and Responses*, London: Jessica Kingsley

Mayer, M. (1996), 'Post-Fordist City Politics', in LeGates and Stout (eds)

Meegan, R. (2000), 'The Governance of Inclusion: Pathways to Integration in the Objective One Programme for Merseyside', Workshop on Urban Governance, ESRC Cities: Competitiveness and Cohesion Programme, Bristol, 25–26 September

Mohan, G., and Stokke, K. (2000), 'Participatory Development and Empowerment: The Dangers of Localism', *Third World Quarterly*, 21(2): 247–68

Mollenkopf, J. (1996), 'How to Study Urban Political Power', in LeGates and Stout (eds)

Murdoch, J. (2000), 'Space against Time: Competing Rationalities in Planning for Housing', *Transactions of the Institute of British Geographers*, 25: 503–19

Musterd, S., and Ostendorf, W. (1998), *The Welfare State in Western Europe*, London: Routledge

Nelson, N., and Wright, S. (eds) (1995), *Power and Participatory Development*, London: Intermediate Technology Group

Oakley, P. (1991), *Projects People*, Geneva: ILO

Oxfam (2000), 'National Strategy for Neighbourhood Renewal: A Framework for Consultation. A Response from Oxfam GB' (www.oxfam.org.uk/policy/papers/neighbour.htm)

Peck, J. (1995), 'Moving and Shaking: Business Elites, State Localism and Urban Privatism', *Progress in Human Geography*, 19: 16–46

—(2000), 'Jumping In, Joining Up and Getting On', *Transactions of the Institute of British Geographers*, 25(2): 255–58

Pile, S., Brook, C. and Mooney, G. (eds) (1999), *Unruly Cities*, London: Routledge

Putnam, D. (1992), *Making Democracy Work: Civic Traditions in Modern Italy*, Princeton: Princeton University Press

Putzel, J. (1997), 'Accounting for the "Dark Side of Social Capital"', *Journal of International Development*, 9(7): 939–49

Rhanema, M. (1992), 'Participation', in W. Sachs (ed.), *The Development Dictionary*, London: Zed Books

Schrijvers, J. (1995), 'Participation and Power: A Transformative Feminist Research Perspective', in Nelson and Wright (eds)

Social Exclusion Unit (2001), *A National Strategy for Neighbourhood Renewal*, London: Cabinet Office

Stiefel, M., and Wolfe, M. (1994), *A Voice for the Excluded: Popular Participation in Development: Utopia or Necessity*, London: Zed Books

Stoker, G. (1995), 'Regime Theory and Urban Politics', in D. Judge, G. Stoker and H. Wolman (eds), *Theories of Urban Politics*, London: Sage

Stoker, G., and King, D. (eds) (1996), *Rethinking Local Democracy*, London: Macmillan

Stokke, K. (1998), 'Globalisation and the Politics of Poverty Alleviation in the South', *Norwegian Journal of Geography*, 52: 221–28

Taylor, M. (2000), 'Communities in the Lead: Power, Organisational Capacity and Social Capital', *Urban Studies*, 37(5–6): 1019–35

Tickell, A., and Peck, J. (1996), 'The Return of Manchester Men: Men's Words and Deeds in the Remaking of the Local State', *Transactions of the Institute of British Geographers*, 21: 595–615

Ward, K. (2000), 'A Critique in Search of a Corpus: Re-visiting Governance and Re-interpreting Urban Politics', *Transactions of the Institute of British Geographers*, 25(4): 169–85

Watson, S. (1999), 'City Politics', in Pile et al. (eds)

Webster, N. (2000), 'Local Organisations, Political Space and Poverty Alleviation', paper presented to workshop on 'Local Politics and Democratisation in Developing Countries', University of Oslo, 16–18 November

White, S. (1996), 'Depoliticising Development: The Uses and Abuses of Participation', *Development in Practice*, 6(1): 28–32

World Bank (1997), *World Development Report: The State in a Changing World*, Oxford: Oxford University Press

Part II: Perspectives

5. Gendered Perspectives

Colette Fagan

Women and men have different types of responsibilities and opportunities within the family and society. Women do most of the essential, but unpaid housework and the 'care' work involved in raising children, looking after adults who are ill or have disabilities, and helping older relatives and neighbours to manage their lives. Men's main responsibility is as the 'breadwinner', earning a wage to support their families. Elements of this 'breadwinner' arrangement of family life have been changing in recent decades. Most women now combine their domestic responsibilities with paid employment, often in part-time jobs, and it is now more socially accepted for women to have jobs when raising their children than in earlier decades. Many women are also lone parents, where the tasks of raising income and providing care are rolled into one. Yet the widely held social expectation is still that men should be the main earners and women the main carers in families (Brannen et al., 1994: 32–34; Warin et al., 1999). At the same time unemployment, job insecurity and widening wage inequalities in Britain mean that it is more difficult for men to fulfil the 'breadwinning' role. Men with few qualifications, men from ethnic minorities and those living in economically depressed areas are the most likely to be unemployed or constrained to low-paid and precarious employment opportunities. Men in these situations are under considerable pressure as they feel unable to meet the widely held expectation that they should provide for their families (Warin et al., 1999).

A number of studies have shown how gender inequalities within family life, labour markets and civic activities shape women's and men's experiences of living in cities (e.g., Bondi and Christie, 1997; Booth et al., 1996; Hanson and Pratt, 1995; Little et al., 1988; Taylor et al., 1996). Women are generally more geographically restricted to their neighbourhood than men and spend more of their lives in this locality due to the demands on their time associated with looking after children, other adults and housework. They travel shorter distances to work than men and are more dependent on very local job opportunities due to the combination of domestic responsibilities and lower incomes which constrain their access to transport (Tivers, 1988). As a result, the quality of their lives is shaped by local services and public transport more directly than men's. For example, transport costs and the logistical difficulties of travelling with young children make them heavily dependent on local shops and services. At night, women are less likely to leave the home than men, not just because of their responsibility for supervising any children, but also because of their greater fears of street crime, which produce a self-imposed curfew, particularly when public transport is poor or unaffordable (Taylor et al., 1996). Being more restricted to the local neighbourhood than men may mean that women cultivate more localised social networks and are more involved in daily life in the neighbourhood. But it may also make it difficult to sustain more dispersed friendship networks and limited mobility can contribute to loneliness and isolation.

The second set of issues is that women are largely responsible for managing family budgets and 'making ends meet', which in low income households often means skipping meals or going without other things in order to cushion the living standards of their children and partners (Pahl, 1989; Brannen and Wilson, 1987). More generally, the majority of adults who have to manage living in poverty or on low incomes are women. This is frequently due to childcare constraints on their availability for employment, in conjunction with women's wages and pensions being lower than those acquired by men (Glendinning and Millar, 1987; Walker, 1996). This feminisation of poverty is particularly visible among lone parents and the elderly: the majority of people in these circumstances have very low incomes and are women.

The relationship of working-age men to their neighbourhood is influenced to a large degree by whether or not they are employed. Employment, unless it is very local, takes men away from the neighbourhood for large parts of the day and week. In contrast, unemployed men have more time to spend in their neighbourhood and are more constrained to the locality due to their low income. It is well known that unemployed men do not fill their days by taking on tasks around the home or in the neighbourhood that are considered to be 'women's work', for if anything this would 'add insult to injury' given that unemployment means that they are already unable to fulfil the socially expected male role of 'breadwinner' (Wheelock, 1990; Morris, 1990). Thus, while unemployed women may have more domestic structure to their daily lives, and may develop social networks of support with other women around these domestic tasks, unemployed men's ways of coping with low income and being confined to the neighbourhood are likely to differ.

Finally, in all types of neighbourhoods women and men have different types of contact with the state. Women's domestic roles bring them into more contact than men with statutory agencies such as schools, health services and social services on behalf of the people they are looking after. Experience of crime and contact with the police also differ by gender (Mooney, 1997). Men commit the majority of crimes, account for the majority of victims of violence in public places, and are generally the focus of policing strategies, which target surveillance on groups of men, particularly young men. Women, on the other hand, come into contact with the police as victims of domestic violence and other crimes, or as a result of supporting children or partners who have experienced crime or been arrested.

These gender differences coexist with shared experiences in women's and men's lives. The material and psychological well-being of both sexes is heavily influenced by their income and the quality of their environment, housing and local services. Both sexes suffer material deprivation from unemployment and living in economically deprived neighbourhoods. And there is little gender difference in the extent of psychological stress that comes from unemployment, or in the high proportion of the unemployed who believe that having a job is important for reasons other than money, such as self-respect and social status (indeed, the unemployed have a higher normative employment commitment than people with jobs) (Rose, 1994; Gallie et al., 1994).

This opening discussion has drawn out gender differences in people's lives and their experiences of their neighbourhoods in circumstances of low income and unemployment. These issues informed a recent study of two economically disadvantaged neighbourhoods in Liverpool regeneration (Andersen et al., 1999) which was part of a broader research programme of the Joseph Rowntree Foundation on area. The study areas were Dingle and Speke, both of which are covered by Partnership urban regeneration programmes. This chapter focuses on one part of the project: people's perceptions and concerns about their neighbourhoods and what they wanted in order to improve their neighbourhoods and to inform regeneration policy initiatives and evaluation. Focus groups were used for this part of the research, as this method has the advantage of providing a space for the participants to develop the focus of the discussion around their own concerns and priorities, and in more detail than is possible in structured research tools such as survey questionnaires.[1] The small-scale nature of this research means that the results cannot be interpreted as numerically representative of the whole population in the localities being studied. However, the issues that emerged are salient for informing debates about social exclusion and urban regeneration initiatives, and for the design of any subsequent larger-scale studies of this topic.

Women, Men and Economically Disadvantaged Neighbourhoods: The Liverpool Case Study

The focus group discussions were organised around broad themes: what 'neighbourhood' meant to the participants, what they thought would improve their neighbourhoods, and their perceptions of the regeneration programmes in their area. In much of the discussion of these issues there was little difference by gender; instead the overriding finding was that women and men shared a common assessment of their neighbourhoods and what would improve their quality of life.

[1] Twelve focus groups were held (six in each area). Participants were recruited through contacts established during the exploratory early stage of the research. Some groups were already constituted and participants known to one another, while others were formed from a number of different sources. In both areas the groups consisted of two youth groups (one male, one female), two groups of elders (one male and one female in one area, one female and one mixed in the other areas), a mixed-gender group of local people who were all actively involved in a tenants' and residents' association, and a women-only group.

However, the gendered division of responsibilities and resources was the taken-for-granted backdrop and reference point in the discussions, echoing Taylor et al.'s (1996) finding in their study of Manchester and Sheffield, where women discussed their routines and strategies for 'dealing with' the established social order. In our study the existing gender division of labour particularly shaped the contributions made by women with children and those who envisaged becoming mothers when discussing their lives and what would improve their neighbourhoods.

Perceptions of the neighbourhood

There was little gender difference in how residents defined the boundary of their neighbourhood. As well as the geographical boundary people drew in terms of which streets fell into which area, a large element of the definition of the locality was through definition of what it was not in order to identify 'their patch'. Another similarity between women and men was the value that they attached to their local networks of family, friends and neighbours. These social networks were a key part of the meaning attached to 'neighbourhood' and 'community' and were seen as central to enhancing the quality of the fabric of everyday life in terms of companionship and support on a day-to-day basis and in managing critical events. Many residents from both areas volunteered examples of how they had helped, or had been helped, by neighbours and friends in times of bereavement, domestic crises such as the electricity being cut off, or more mundane events such as running errands or looking after one another's children. Others mentioned the importance of daily contact such as chatting and greeting people on the street for making them feel that they belong in their neighbourhood. This sense of 'neighbourliness' and 'community' was attributed to the roots people had from living in the area for long periods. Conversely, there was a concern that these networks break down when young people have to leave the area to find somewhere better to live, as was happening in Speke.

Women and men from both localities also identified similar problems with their neighbourhood. They were concerned that the housing quality was deteriorating, particularly when empty properties were not re-let, and that there was a shortage of local shops and services (particularly in Speke). A second set of problems which the residents were quick to raise was the level of crime, drug dealing and lack of safety in public spaces. Finally the behaviour of children and teenagers was an issue raised in the discussions. One aspect of this was a perception that young people lacked discipline and respect for others and that their rowdy street behaviour, vandalism, drunkenness and so forth had a negative effect on life in the neighbourhood, which the police were ineffective in controlling. The lack of facilities for young people was also discussed as contributing to this problem.

One gender difference is that women had more specific concerns about the need for childcare services, particularly after school and in school holidays. Women were frustrated that the services that existed were largely targeted at mothers on training courses. They thought that it was disruptive that access to formal childcare services was only available for the duration of periods of training and that it was difficult or impossible to arrange childcare so as to find or hold down jobs. In this context, many women felt that it was preferable to rely on informal arrangements with nearby family and friends; this was less disruptive for the children, and the other advantage was that the children already knew the women who were looking after them. At the same time, they also discussed the difficulties of arranging and maintaining these informal arrangements among themselves when employment circumstances, illness and other events meant that things often needed to be reorganised and renegotiated. Given the shortage of good quality and affordable childcare, a major concern that women had was the growing emphasis that the government's 'welfare to work' policy is placing on getting lone mothers into employment:

> [They] want women to go back to work but how can a woman go back to work without a crèche or after-school facilities?

> [It] worries me very much, that thing about making a mother go back to work. It could be a situation that if your benefit is going to get slashed unless you get this job and you're in a panic . . . you'll give your child to anyone.

Thus the main difference that emerged between women and men was rooted in the direct responsibility that women have for looking after children, and the support networks that they mobilise around this activity.

Support networks and self-help among women

Women maintain and develop particular types of neighbourhood networks rooted in their care providing role and because more of their time and activities are centred around their local area. This is often the springboard for their involvement in local campaigns related to improving the area (Bondi and Peake, 1988). We were told about a number of examples of informal networks being mobilised around particular self-help initiatives. Women volunteered comments in both single-sex and mixed-sex focus groups which indicated a greater awareness of the link between their gender and their community roles, although it should be noted that men might have been more forthcoming if we had included men-only focus groups for all age groups.

Women in Speke had organised themselves and successfully campaigned for a health centre, which had developed from their shared experience of the lack of local services for their children and taken root from their school-gate discussions about the problems this caused them. Another group of women had got together with the idea of running a summer play-scheme at the local community centre which the council was planning to close for the summer due to staff shortages. The women felt let down when the council blocked this initiative: not only did they think they had a lot of experience to offer from looking after their own children, but part of the reason for their connection with the centre was that they were doing, or had recently completed, training courses as childcare workers. In Dingle, women had also tried on a number of occasions to get funding to convert old buildings into childcare centres, crèches or community cafés, all with limited success. Where women in Dingle had been successful was in setting up a tenants' group and establishing one of the first housing cooperatives despite council opposition:

> They didn't think we were capable of controlling all this money, they didn't think we could do it. I mean, at the end of the day it was mostly women that did it.

More generally, women observed that it is mainly women who are active in the day-to-day running of voluntary and community organisations and self-help initiatives in their neighbourhood:

> [The] men put the suits on and try to be helpful but basically the women run the houses and the homes . . . They also run all these types of groups . . . At the PTA meetings it's always women there.

Few women questioned this division of labour, but some linked men's lack of involvement to male unemployment. One woman explained why she felt men were much less involved in support networks and self-help within the neighbourhoods:

> They've got no role, no place, there's nothing that they can do, there are no jobs and if they've got money then they're the odd one out and they can get into drinking or drugs . . . You can't seem to get them involved with the kids, even to get little football teams going or anything like that, you can't. When we were young there were boxing clubs and the football and all that, they have nothing now.

So, while a minority of men are active volunteers involved in community organisations and campaigns, it seems that it is mainly women who take the initiative as an extension of their existing networks and responsibilities for looking after their families and neighbours.

For both women and men it is not easy to sustain the energy and membership of self-help groups, and access to information and financial resources is usually critical. While money and professional advice can often be mobilised from within middle-class communities, such resources are much harder to generate in poor neighbourhoods. As one Dingle resident explained, it is common for groups to raise small sums of money, but trying to get something bigger or a grant is very difficult.

What did women and men think would improve life in their neighbourhoods?

Not surprisingly, residents identified the root cause of the problems in their neighbourhoods as a lack of money. One aspect of this was a frustration with the council's lack of resources and a perception that the council rarely took into account what the spending priorities of the residents were. Spending under regeneration initiatives was also met with a large degree of cynicism and disillusionment, again because residents felt they had no power to influence the decisions. But it was not just that residents wanted more say in how available public resources were spent; they wanted to be able to earn a living. Women and men wanted jobs to improve their own standard of living and because they believed that if more people in the neighbourhood had jobs this would solve many of the poverty-related problems.

The lack of jobs in Liverpool in general, and more so in these two localities, made it difficult for both sexes to find work. Aside from the depressed labour market, other factors created further obstacles for women and men in their quest for employment. Women in Dingle mentioned that some informal work could be had but the money was only enough to supplement rather than replace their benefits. If they did work informally to make the family budget go further they were in constant fear of having their social security benefits reduced, even if many of these employment opportunities were small and short lived. A larger complaint was that when regeneration initiatives created jobs in the neighbourhood, these jobs never went to local residents despite their applications. Women and men felt strongly that if these jobs went to local people it would have a major, positive impact, however temporary some of the jobs might be. The benefits would not just be that more people had jobs, but local recruitment would increase the community's involvement in, and knowledge of, the regeneration project in question.

Aside from more opportunities to help themselves through employment, both women and men wanted the problems of crime and drugs to be tackled. They wanted more effective policing strategies, such as locally based community officers and more police on local patrols. A number of preventive measures were also mentioned: more facilities for children, quicker lets of empty houses to prevent them becoming drug dens, expulsion of known drug dealers, and better street lighting and public transport. They also wanted more local shops and amenities, and a frequent comment was the sense that the neighbourhood was dominated by community-based organisations trying to generate services in the area rather than the services themselves: 'too many organisations and not enough shops'. The lack of shops was particularly mentioned by women, in connection with the cost and hassle of taking their children on public transport to shop further afield.

Time and again, women said that better childcare – including after-school care for older children – would make a big improvement in their lives. Many also said that they could not take jobs because of the problems of arranging childcare. One woman from Dingle also wanted more 'little jobs' for schoolchildren to keep them occupied, and to give them some financial independence. As she pointed out, this would give them some means to purchase their own designer clothes, relieve the pressure on their parents' purse, and so reduce family tensions:

> They come in and say 'Mum, can we have this', and I say 'No, I can't afford it, get yourself a little job', but there are no little jobs for them and then they're bored and they get at you, and you get at them, and it's not fair on them.

All residents wanted more things for children to do, including young people themselves (see Chapter 7 below). Adults, particularly older ones, wanted parents to exert more control and discipline with the children. Women with children said it was important for different activities to be provided for different age groups: they wanted summer schemes for 11–15-year-olds, and something separate for the older children. Art classes, sports centres and drop-in centres were all mentioned. They also pointed out that youth clubs were generally dominated by boys and so excluded girls, an experience that young girls also mentioned. Some suggested that this was an issue that youth leaders needed to tackle with the boys, while others wanted to see 'girls only' provision on certain sites and for certain activities. Better facilities for children would not benefit only the children, but also women. Indeed, one group of women said that they had plenty of things to do to entertain themselves in their neighbourhoods (visiting friends, going out, relaxing at home), but what they needed was space away from their children: 'I would just be happy sitting in the house without the kids!'

Maintaining and improving the quality of housing was another major concern. Particularly in Speke, women were frustrated about the number of empty council houses. They talked about how houses and gardens that were well looked after by the occupants were allowed to fall into disrepair if the occupants moved out because the council left the house empty for too long. Often the children took over the empty property and vandalised it. On a number of occasions one or more women had noticed a newly vacated property and had approached the council requesting a transfer. In all instances they had been told that it was already allocated, only to then see it lie vacant for months, being vandalised in the process. The women also had many examples of how long it took the council to get round to doing essential repairs, and their anger and despair when caught in such situations. While there may be valid reasons for properties being left vacant or for delays in repairs, such as a lack of funds for repairs or the procedures of allocation systems, what residents experience is the deterioration of their environment. Not only did people want the housing and surrounding environment improved for the direct positive impact that this would have on their lives, but for the important, if less tangible, fact of changing the area's image: 'If they did all the houses. Yeah, make it look pretty . . . people aren't afraid of pretty things.'

Women – but not men – volunteered that they wanted a drop-in support centre for the times when they needed help and advice on matters from someone other than their family and friends. They were unanimous in their opinion that this support service should be 'disguised' to protect them from the stigma of using it, for example as part of a health centre rather than under the direct gaze of social services. Both women and men also thought that there should be more day centres and services for the older members of the community.

Finally, while some expressed the opinion that there were enough training courses in the area already, and that it was a lack of jobs, not skills, that was the problem, others suggested that a wider range of skills and training courses would be helpful. In this context the theme of mutual help emerged on several occasions, with suggestions that the skills and resources of residents could be used to provide some forms of training, as well as organising childcare and other activities for young people.

Conclusions

The economic and political restructuring involved in the shift from 'Fordist' to 'post-Fordist' production regimes is exacerbating spatial and social relations of inequality in cities (Pacione, 1997; Jewson and MacGregor, 1997). Service sector expansion has failed to compensate for job loss in manufacturing fuelling a concentration of unemployment in northern metropolitan areas. This unemployment is borne disproportionately by those with few formal educational qualifications, young people with limited work experience, older men who lost their jobs as manufacturing declined and ethnic minorities (Green, 1997). It is this job shortage, not poor skill levels, that is the main cause of the high levels of unemployment in Liverpool and other major cities (Turok and Edge, 1999). Many of the jobs that are created in the urban service industries are part time, low paid and precarious. Unemployment and insecure employment, combined with the withdrawal of public services with the political restructuring of the welfare state, are producing starker lines of inequalities between regions, cities and neighbourhoods within cities.

In this context, women and men in our study had clear opinions about what would improve the quality of their lives in their neighbourhoods. These were basic and unsurprising requirements: they wanted jobs, and improvements to the buildings, amenities and transport connections in their areas. They recognised the severely disadvantaged nature of their neighbourhoods, but also valued the networks of support that they had in these localities. A common complaint was that their opinions, local knowledge and skills were neglected or marginalised in regeneration programmes. This lack of involvement needs to be addressed, as sustained community consultation and participation are important for urban regeneration initiatives to succeed (see Pacione, 1997; Booth, 1996; Geedes, 1997).

The focus in this chapter was gender. Women's and men's circumstances, identities, desires and social networks are also shaped by age, ethnicity and other characteristics (Foster, 1997). And within any community there are conflicting concerns and priorities as well as common interests (Moore, 1997). Nonetheless the gender division of labour and resources continues to be a pervasive feature which shapes men's and women's lives. In this study, common concerns among women and men prevailed over differences when talking about their neighbourhoods and the improvements that they wanted to see. The differences that emerged were based on women's shared experiences of their care-providing role. Looking after children typically involved them in informal networks of reciprocal arrangements and favours, and a major concern for women was that the lack of public childcare services presented a major obstacle to their employment. It was also women's care-providing role and networks that typically formed the basis for their getting involved in local campaigns and community organisations.

Women's care-providing work is vital to the social fabric in all neighbourhoods, yet it is still often invisible or ignored in urban planning. While there was some progress through the 1990s in incorporating women's interests into planning consultation and decision making, women are still under-represented in these areas. More effort needs to be put into redressing this gender imbalance through connecting with the 'informal' political sphere of local activity where women's efforts and experiences are often concentrated (Booth, 1996).

References

Andersen, H., Munck, R., et al. (1999), *Neighbourhood Images in Liverpool: 'It's All Down to the People'*, York: Joseph Rowntree Foundation

Bondi, L., and Christie, H. (1997), 'Gender', in Pacione (ed.)

Bondi, L., and Peake, L. (1988), 'Gender and the City: Urban Politics Revisited', in Little, Peake and Richardson (eds)

Booth, C. (1996), 'Women and Consultation' in Booth et al. (eds)

Booth, C., Darke, J., and Yeandle, S. (eds) (1996), *Changing Places: Women's Lives in the City*, London: Paul Chapman Publishing

Brannen, J., Mészáros, G., Moss, P., and Poland, G. (1994), *Employment and Family Life: A Review of Research in the UK (1980–94)*, Employment Department Research Series No. 41, Sheffield: Research Strategy Branch, Employment Department

Brannen, J., and Wilson, G. (eds) (1987), *Give and Take in Families: Studies in Resource Distribution*, London: Unwin Hyman

Foster, J. (1997), 'Challenging Perceptions: "Community and Neighbourliness on a Difficult-to-Let Estate', in Jewson and MacGregor (eds)

Gaillie, D., Marsh, C., and Vogler, C. (eds) (1994), *Social Change and the Experiences of Unemployment*, Oxford: Oxford University Press

Geedes, M. (1997), 'Poverty, Excluded Communities and Local Democracy', in Jewson and Macgregor (eds)

Glendinning, C., and Millar, J. (eds) (1987), *Women and Poverty in Britain*, Brighton: Harvester Wheatsheaf

Green, A. (1997), 'Income and Wealth', in Pacione (ed.)

Hanson, S., and Pratt, G. (1995), *Gender, Work and Space*, London: Routledge

Jewson, N., and MacGregor, S. (eds) (1997), *Transforming Cities: Contested Governance and New Spatial Divisions*, London: Routledge

Little, J., Peake, L., and Richardson, P. (eds) (1988), *Women in Cities: Gender and the Urban Environment*, London: Macmillan

Mooney, J. (1997), 'Violence, Space and Gender: The Social and Spatial Parameters of Violence against Women and Men', in Jewson and MacGregor (eds)

Moore, R. (1997), 'Poverty and Partnership in the Third European Poverty Programme: The Liverpool Case', in Jewson and MacGregor (eds)

Morris, L. (1990), *The Workings of the Household*, Cambridge: Polity Press

Pacione, M. (ed) (1997), *Britain's Cities: Geographies of Division in Urban Britain*, London: Routledge

Pahl, J. (1989), *Money and Marriage*, London: Macmillan

Rose, M. (1994), 'Skill and Samuel Smiles: Changing the British Work Ethic', in R.

Penn, M. Rose and J. Rubery (eds), *Skill and Occupational Change*, Oxford: Oxford University Press

Taylor, I., Evans, K., and Fraser, P. (1996), *A Tale of Two Cities: Global Change, Local Feeling and Everyday Life in the North of England. A Study of Manchester and Sheffield*, London: Routledge

Tivers, J. (1988), 'Women with Young Children: Constraints on Activities in the Urban Environment', in Little, Peake and Richardson (eds)

Turok, I., and Edge, N. (1999), *The Jobs Gap in Britain's Cities: Employment Loss and Labour Market Consequences*, London: Policy Press

Walker, C. (1996), 'The Feminisation of Poverty', in Booth, Darke and Yeandle (eds)

Warin, J., et al. (1999), *Fathers, Work and Family Life*, London: Family Policy Studies Centre

Wheelock, J. (1990), *Husbands at Home: The Domestic Economy in a Post-Industrial Society*, London: Routledge

6. Ethnic Minority Perspectives[1]

Ola Uduku

This chapter reviews and describes the experiences of the heterogeneous Black or ethnic minority community (taken to mean residents of non-Caucasian extraction) in Liverpool. It gives a short historical background and overview of the settlement and development of the Black community in Liverpool. It then goes on to evaluate the situation of the city's contemporary Black community, considering its structure and the community's success in its acquisition of employment, housing, education and improved health in relation to the general population.

By way of case study analyses, the chapter will discuss histories of two different ethnic minority communities, the Somali and the Chinese, who have been predominantly resident in and associated with distinct parts of Liverpool (Granby Toxteth and Chinatown respectively) over a considerable part of the twentieth century. Their contrasting experiences and contemporary position in society indicate many of the issues that all ethnic minority groups in Liverpool have to deal with.

The chapter then provides a critical analysis of the community's shortcomings and achievements in effectuating integration and parity with the generality of Liverpool. It also considers the community's success in maintaining connections with its 'transnational' origins and its role in contributing to the viewing of Liverpool as a uniquely multicultural metropolis from the past to contemporary times. Finally it considers what potential issues and scenarios might affect the community in the future.

[1] The writing of this chapter would not have been possible without the contributions and help of many. In particular I am grateful to Polly Green of the Pagoda Chinese Community Association, Nigel Reed of Pine Court Housing Association, Wally Brown, Principal of Liverpool Community College, Brian Wong of Liverpool Chinatown Business Association, and Bill Maynard of Urban Splash, for making time for extended interviews with me. I would also like to thank Graham Chang of *Brushstrokes* magazine for the information sent and his email correspondence. A number of discussions were anonymous and of a much shorter duration, but were of equal importance in creating this document. The figures and statistics given in the text are attributable to Merseyside Information Service, within Liverpool City Council, or to the Office for Population and National Census figures from 1991, unless stated otherwise. Finally I wish to thank Gideon Ben-Tovim for being willing to read through several drafts of this paper, and for many important comments and constructive suggestions.

Commentators on Liverpool's Multi-ethnic Character

Much has been written about Liverpool's past; paradoxically, however, there has been little published about the incidence of Black and Asian migration and settlement from a historical perspective. A considerable amount of information about this can, however, be garnered from the historical records of shipping activities in Liverpool, for example from the records of the Blue Funnel Line (serving China and much of South East Asia) and the Elder Dempster Line (mainly serving West Africa).[2] There were also a number of commissioned social welfare reports, such as the Fletcher Report (1930) and the Caradog Jones Survey (1940), whose controversial findings and recommendations gave a particularly negative view of the Black community in Liverpool. There have also been the semi-historical accounts of writers and residents, such as Dickens (1898) and Hocking (1879) who both provide snapshot (albeit fictional) views of Liverpool's minority resident groups and their lifestyles.

More recently the history of ethnic minority communities in Liverpool has been most associated with the social deprivation and lack of social services provision that was especially acute in Liverpool in the 1970s and 1980s. Authors such as Ben-Tovim have well-documented evidence of this (Ben-Tovim, 1980; Ben-Tovim et al., 1986; 1988). The three significant 'riots' which took place in the 1970s and 1980s in the Granby Toxteth ward, where much of Liverpool's Black African-Caribbean community resided, also resulted in an increase of publications and writing on the community and socio-political influences in the area.

Even less has been documented about the Liverpool Chinese community, the exceptions being the two histories produced by Loh and Craggs (1986) and Wong (1989). The two ethnic minority housing associations, the Pine Court Housing Association (Chinese-run) and the Steve Biko Housing Association (African-Caribbean run, now defunct), were also set up during this period. These initiatives produced a limited amount of literature relating to the reasons for their being set up to cater specifically, but not exclusively, for minority groups from the Chinese and African-Caribbean communities.[3] Similarly the Pagoda Chinese Community Centre was set up in the early 1980s with the specific remit of providing access to social welfare services for the Chinese community.[4]

The most recent writing on Liverpool's ethnic minority neighbourhoods has been by Uduku and Ben-Tovim (1998). Loh and Craggs (1986) and Wong (1989) similarly give documented accounts of the history of the Chinese community and its residential characteristics, and a document has been produced focusing on 'Care in the Chinese Community [in Liverpool]' (Wing Kwong, 1994). At a city-wide

[2] For a discussion on Liverpool seafarers see Frost, 1992, Chapter 7, and the preface to Frost, 1994.

[3] CDS Housing Association Annual Report and Accounts, 1998; Pine Court Housing Association Annual Report and Accounts, 1995, 1998, 1999; Steve Biko Housing Association Annual Report and Accounts, 1995. Communication with Wally Brown (Principal of Liverpool Community College), 9 October 2000, confirmed that there had been earlier initiatives such as the 'Ujaama House' in the 1970s, but these had also had a short life.

[4] Interview with Polly Green (administrator, the Pagoda Chinese Community Centre), 14 January 2000; Pagoda Leaflet (c.1998).

level there has been a considerable amount of analysis of Liverpool's regeneration efforts in the recent past, but this has generally focused on the city centre and specific communities of interest, such as the Eldonian community, and has not included Granby Toxteth or (until recently) Chinatown.[5]

Granby Toxteth, however, retains its post-riots notoriety in the local press, with articles still written regularly about crime in the area.[6] Chinatown, conversely, receives generally limited but in more recent times relatively positive publicity. Initially this centred on the new housing association's redevelopment efforts in the area and in the work of the Chinese community centre. More recently, the focus has moved to the area's regeneration and linkage with the Rope Walks Partnership's Urban Initiative £40 million regeneration scheme (Rope Walks Partnership, 1999).

It is possible that, with the current regeneration initiatives in Granby Toxteth, the neighbourhood will also begin to receive more positive media attention. Thus far, the local press has publicised the new housing and the 'multi-faith' school, Kingsley Road Community School, that has been built in Granby Toxteth. There are also a number of local history writing and recording initiatives that are being carried out by the local community and by others. This can only help to further the rehabilitation of the area and its redefinition as a location of 'regeneration'. The local neighbourhood Granby Toxteth Residents' Association is also still closely involved in the neighbourhood's transformation with its plans for a local African-Caribbean market to be established on vacant land in the area and also its attempts at regenerating the neighbourhood (Granby Toxteth Residents' Association Annual Report, 2000).

Liverpool's Chinese (a term used to describe both China-born Chinese and also South East Asians of Chinese extraction from Vietnam, Singapore, Malaysia and farther afield) have little published or recorded information about themselves.[7] During the launch of the new Chinese Arch at the entrance to Chinatown, the local library and the Liverpool Chinatown Business Association (LCBA) produced a pamphlet documenting the development of the Chinese community in Liverpool (LCBA, 2000). With its new ties with the Rope Walks area, and other funding organisations, there is increased interest in the local history of the Chinese in the area.[8]

---

[5] For the Eldonians, see Cowan et al., 1988. A search for articles in the *Guardian* and the *Independent* from January to June 2000 came up with 17 articles on Toxteth and three on Liverpool's Chinatown. Only one out of the 17 identified (*Independent*, 4 March 2000) talked about the regeneration of the fringes of Toxteth. All three articles identified about Chinatown talked about its recent regeneration (*Independent*, 5 February 2000, *Independent* and *Guardian*, 31 March 2000).

[6] Using the same survey method, of the 17 articles on Toxteth identified in the *Guardian* and *Independent*, 15 had some reference to crime, riots, or the deprived nature of the area. In the local papers, the *Liverpool Echo* and *Daily Post*, over the 6-month period, three main (front-page) references were made to Toxteth; two had to do with death and violence, and the third concerned the misrepresentation of the area (*Liverpool Echo*, 28 January 2000, 13 March 2000; *Daily Post*, 20 June 2000). The articles on the Chinese community were positive articles about the Chinese New Year and the new arch (*Liverpool Echo*, 7 February 2000, 31 March 2000).

[7] An exception is *Brushstrokes*, a joint Manchester/Liverpool Arts Council-funded Chinese magazine.

[8] Confirmed during an interview with Brian Wong of the LCBA, 19 September 2000.

From the above it is clear that there is a dearth of information about Liverpool's major ethnic minority communities residing in the southern part of the city, the African-Caribbean and South East Asian communities. Much of the information that does exist was written during a short period in the mid-1980s, that is to say, in the aftermath of the 1981 disturbances. This was a time when there was intense analysis of the conditions and events surrounding the disturbances, and hence interest in and funding for research in this area. Since that time there has been a sparse amount of research published. Recently, however, the regeneration programmes that are taking place in both Granby Toxteth and the Chinatown area have again resulted in the release of funds which have encouraged new research interest in the area.

'The Black Community'

'The Black community' is a catch-all phrase used to describe the varied residential population of Liverpool who are not categorised as 'white'. As might be expected, this community is neither homogeneous in its ethno-cultural make-up nor in its class structure. Clearly, then, members of this so-called 'community' may have very little in common, although by being classified as 'Black' they do have an ascribed identity and invariably have a shared experience of being different from the majority, and of the tensions and difficulties this situation can often cause. The 1991 census returns further confirm that the Black community in Liverpool is considerably dispersed, although still concentrated mainly in the south of the city (OPCS, 1991). While the three inner-city wards of Granby, Arundel and Abercromby have significant ethnic minority populations, more than 20 per cent of Liverpool's Black population lives outside of these wards (OPCS, 1991, specifically Arundel, Granby and Abercromby data-sets). This is significant when one considers the experience of the Black community that still resides in and around central Liverpool.

In this chapter we are concerned with the quality of life and everyday experience of Liverpool residents of colour in the city. The history of Black residence in Liverpool has been described by others, such as Law and Henfrey (1981), Fryer (1984), Murphy (1995) and that of the Chinese community by Loh and Craggs (1986) and Wong (1989). These accounts tend, however, to be specific to the authors' area of interest; thus a comprehensive general history has yet to be produced. There are, however, key issues that are central to the history of Black residence and settlement in Liverpool that all groups acknowledge.

Most important is Liverpool's relationship with countries of the former British Empire, the USA and countries further afield on account of its importance as a seaport. While much is known about Liverpool's involvement in the slave trade, today most of Liverpool's Black residents are descendants of residents who arrived in Liverpool after this grim period. The 'legitimate' trading companies, including Lever Brothers, John Holt and McIver, all had substantial trade relationships with African, West Indian and South East Asian countries, which involved the purchase of raw materials at source and their shipment to the UK, with Liverpool being a major shipping port. Elder Dempster and Blue Circle Lines were the key shippers of goods from Africa and China/South East Asia respectively. Frost (1992; 1994) has documented the experiences of the West African seamen who were involved in this trade, while Lawless (1994) discusses the recruitment of seamen from former British Somaliland. In recent decades, further global displacement as a result of wars, famine and more recently economic migration has also significantly contributed to the composition of the Black community.

From the mid-nineteenth century onwards, the Black community settled in the areas around the south docks, in the vicinity of the current location of the Chinese community around Cornwallis Street (see Figure 1). The African-Caribbean community's movement to its current neighbourhoods of Granby, Arundel and Abercromby took place in stages from the end of the Second World War, as a result initially of the bombing of the docks area towards areas north of the south docks. The movement continued towards Parliament Street and the university neighbourhood which had a preponderance of cheap rentable accommodation and access to neighbourhood shops and businesses. This move came about partly through forced relocation as a result of urban clearance, and also because of land acquisition and consolidation by Liverpool University, as Simey (1996) describes and university records suggest (Holford, 1949–50).

Granby Toxteth went on to become the heart of the Black community from the late 1950s up until the present, as many of those who had lived in rented accommodation in and around the Abercromby Square/university precinct area moved on to the area due east of Parliament Street. Originally a smart upmarket suburb of Liverpool inhabited by shipping magnates and ambassadors, and the site of a number of religious buildings, since the 1920s the area had become associated with the growing Liverpool Jewish community. This community began to move out at the end of the Second World War to more suburban areas of Liverpool and farther afield. The African-Caribbean community and other ethnic minority groups moved into Granby Toxteth as these earlier communities moved out.

Since its heyday in the 1950s as a major multicultural neighbourhood, the Granby Toxteth area has experienced the decline in population evidenced elsewhere in Liverpool. Limited population change occurred as a result of the effects of slum clearance and decanting schemes that took place on a low level in the area in the 1960s and 1970s. The growing levels of local unemployment and a movement of the more affluent members of the community to more suburban areas further increased this population decline.

Most noteworthy to the outside world were the series of riots in 1973, 1981 and 1985 that served to brand the community as a 'racial' hotspot. Reports and analyses of the riots have been discussed earlier, and in more detail by others (see Gifford, 1989). The results of these events were significant in creating the negative imagery of the area and the subsequent economic 'postcode redlining' which still bedevils the neighbourhood today. They also further hastened the depopulation of the locale, as many residents who could afford to move did so.

This sets the contextual background to the case study analysis and discussion

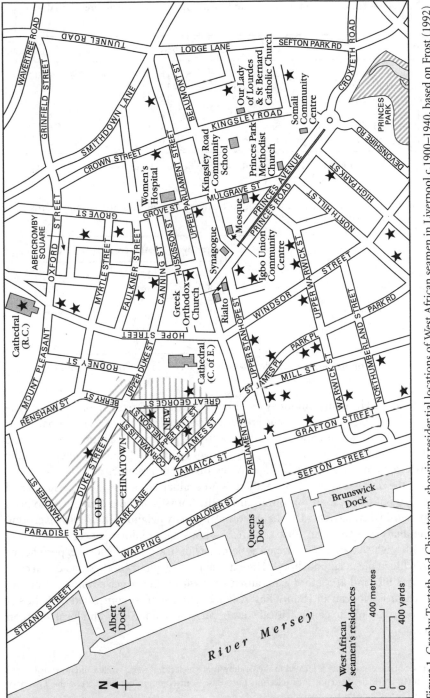

Figure 1. Granby Toxteth and Chinatown, showing residential locations of West African seamen in Liverpool c.1900–1940, based on Frost (1992)

Table 1: Population of Granby Toxteth and Abercromby wards (including Chinatown) as of 1997

Ward	Granby	Abercromby	City average
Pop. aged 0–1	212	111	180
Pop. aged 1–4	801	427	712
Pop. aged 20–24	1,024	2,145	1,152
Pop. aged 34–40	750	574	892
Pop. aged 44–60	565	388	663
Pop. aged 80–84	175	111	274

Source: Gina Tomlinson, Merseyside Information Service, Liverpool.

Table 2: Unemployment percentage rates for Granby Toxteth and Abercromby wards (including Chinatown) as of 1997

Ward	Granby	Abercromby	City average
Male rate	22.8	17.7	13.6
Female rate	8.8	6.4	4.3
Total rate	16.4	12.4	9.1
Under 25s (as % of total)	27.8	24.1	28.3
Long-term unemployed (as % of total)	33.9	31.7	29.4
All long-term unemployed (as total %)	61.7	55.8	57.7

Source: Gina Tomlinson, Merseyside Information Service, Liverpool City Council.

that follow. The ethnic minority communities discussed remain located primarily in the South Liverpool inner-city area generically called Toxteth.[9] The Somali community in particular continues to have a strong presence in Granby Toxteth. The Chinese community has its locale, 'Chinatown', within walking distance of Granby Toxteth, in the newly named 'Rope Walks' district of the inner city.

In the discussion that follows there is an evaluation of the life experience and qualities of two case study communities, the Somalis and the Chinese, who both live within distinctively identifiable ethnic minority neighbourhoods in Liverpool. The analysis focuses on four key areas – housing, employment, education and health – which have been selected as being key indicators of the local experience of daily life in the neighbourhood. The experience and quality of these factors in each group's life, and at a more generalised level within the larger ethnic community (African-Caribbean and South East Asian, respectively) are contrasted with the situation city-wide, to gain a critical view of provision of facilities and local views on this.

[9] The Somali community is located in the Granby Toxteth electoral ward, while Chinatown is located within the Dingle ward for local election purposes. Both communities are within the Liverpool Riverside parliamentary ward.

The Somali Community in Liverpool

What is now Somalia was up until the 1960s a divided country comprising British-governed Somaliland with its administrative capital in Aden, and Italian-governed Somalia, which had Mogadishu as its capital city.[10] Being in part a British protectorate, Somalia had substantial trade relations with Britain during this period, and many Somali men enlisted as merchant seamen and worked as crew on ships sailing to Europe (see Lawless, 1994). Many such sailors settled in British ports, such as Liverpool, Cardiff and Bristol. Liverpool and Cardiff now have significant Somali communities that can trace their existence to this colonial period.

The widespread famine experienced by Somalia in the 1980s brought about the second phase of Somali settlement in Liverpool and elsewhere in the UK. Because Liverpool and other cities already had established Somali communities in their midst, the city councils were able to ensure that families in the UK with relatives caught in the famine were reunited. Many other Somali refugees were also resettled in these cities where it was felt that there was already an adequate support network in place.

By the 1990s, therefore, Liverpool had a significant Somali community, who lived predominantly in the Granby Toxteth area of the city. While the community is well connected to the neighbourhood, with a number of Somali clubs, groups and associations, and while most Somalis have adequate housing, there remain deep-seated problems. A recent report (Foundation for Civil Society, 2000) on Somali life in Liverpool highlighted the serious problems of unemployment, poor education and isolation experienced by most of the Somali community, the majority of whom have now lived in Liverpool for more than a decade.

Discussions with members of the community and researchers suggest that there has been little real improvement in the community's position since the 1980s. It is acknowledged that the community has received funding from various sources for 'development projects', but the implementation of such projects and their subsequent success have been poor. The Liverpool Foundation Report's evaluation of the situation presents a poor picture of contemporary life in the Somali community. Issues related to education, qualifications and unemployment levels within the community remain the most intractable, despite the targeted programmes that have been implemented to address these problems.[11]

At the launch of the report, members of the community had a chance to air their views. It was illustrative to note that all the formal speakers were male, most were over forty years old, and none felt that the report had adequately covered all aspects of the poor state of Somali life in Liverpool. Local Somali perceptions of life in Liverpool were not positive. The Somali community's experience of Liverpool is

[10] French Somaliland, the Ogaden, and the southern part of Somalia were also colonised. At independence, however, they became the independent State of Djibouti, the Ogadaan disputed territory (with Ethiopia), and part of Kenya's Northern Frontier Division respectively.

[11] The European Social Fund (1998) report describes one such programme, which was stated to have been of limited success.

often considered unique, due to its particularities. Their experience is, however, similar to that of many other minority communities in Granby Toxteth. Most are from former British colonies with previous trade links with Britain, which had long-established 'seafarer' communities in Liverpool dating from early in the twentieth century. Prominent among these would be the Yemeni, the Kru, the Nigerian, and the West Indian communities. The language issue does separate the Somali community from other Black Liverpool communities, since most, having lived in British colonies, would have been conversant in spoken English. The Yemenis, however, had similar linguistic differences to the Somalis.

The characteristics of the Black ethnic minority communities throughout Liverpool are similar; all suffer from poor levels of service provision and institutional back-up. Their demographic structures are also similar, comprising a significant stratum of older males, a younger generation comprising family units, a significant group of dual heritage residents with multicultural affiliations, and significant numbers of single parents (OPCS, 1991). The overall experience of the community in Liverpool would therefore seem not to have changed much in the past 50 years. It remains located primarily in a few central inner-city electoral wards and ill provided with institutional services, commercial infrastructure or local employment opportunities. Recently, however, there has been a blurring of the boundaries of the traditionally 'Black' areas, as urban upgrading schemes and university expansion have resulted in the gentrification and institutionalisation of buildings on the fringes of the neighbourhood.

Education, health and socio-economic conditions in Granby Toxteth vary in quality and provision. The neighbourhood in the past could boast of three primary schools and a secondary school, Paddington Comprehensive, nearby. All three Board schools have now closed, but recently a multi-faith school has opened, a first for Liverpool. Paddington Comprehensive School, only opened in the late 1960s, closed down in the early 1980s, partly because of the reluctance of parents in nearby 'white' neighbourhoods to send their children to a perceived 'Black school'. Shorefields, the state comprehensive school that has since Paddington's closure had Granby Toxteth within its catchment area, has in the past had a poor educational attainment record. It has, however, in recent years recorded a significant upturn in its attainment and assessment levels. It is yet to be seen how this will impact on the much diminished Black community, whose members often cite, as the reason influencing their decision to leave Granby Toxteth, the need 'to give our children a better education'.[12]

Despite the proximity of both Liverpool John Moores University and Liverpool University, access to tertiary education remains low and poorly funded. Thus the Charles Wootton College, which had a working relationship with the city's universities and provided access qualifications for local youths in and around Toxteth, has closed down due to administrative problems and an inability to secure funding. The Elimu Study Centre, which provides remedial study support for the dispro-

---

[12] Interview with Ms K. Dixon, August 2000.

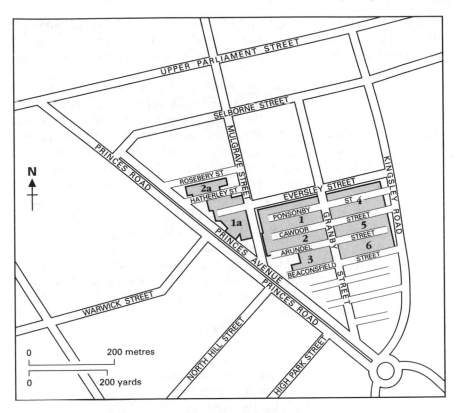

Figure 2. Granby Toxteth, showing areas of upgraded housing
Source: Riverside/CDS and LHT Housing Associations in collaboration with Wilkinson
Hindle, Halsall, Lloyd Architects.

portionate number of excluded school pupils in the community, continually struggles for funding. Despite the fact that the demographics of the area show that there
are a disproportionate number of single-parent families in the neighbourhood,
affordable nursery and kindergarten places remain limited and oversubscribed.
This is ameliorated somewhat, however, by the extended family network that still
exists, such that grandparents are willing to take over the care of their grandchil-
dren while parents go out to work.

Housing in Granby Toxteth also remains in a parlous state. A substantial part of
the neighbourhood is being redeveloped as part of a joint EU Single Regeneration
Budget/city council funded urban regeneration initiative. However, there remain
a substantial number of properties within the area that require upgrading or
demolition. The redevelopment is being carried out by the three housing associations operating in the area, who are also the major property owners. Their redevelopment efforts have not, however, gone unchallenged. There was a public
inquiry into the original development plans which resulted in the retention of part
of Granby Street, the main commercial thoroughfare in the new plan, and the stay

of demolition of some housing.[13] It is likely, however, that with the redevelopment there will be substantially more accommodation. This will in turn lead to the incorporation of new residents in the area who will further alter the area's demography and cultural mix.

Granby Toxteth is well served with health facilities; there are clinics, a day-care centre for pensioners, and a spinal injuries rehabilitation unit. Despite this, the area scores poorly on health indicator surveys in Liverpool. A youth 'foyer' project has also been built on the borders of the neighbourhood. Within Granby Toxteth there also exist a number of ethnic minority community associations and clubs such as the Igbo Union, the Somali Community Centre and the Caribbean Community Centre. The distinction here is that most of the ethnic minority associations are run on a voluntary basis with minimal or no funding from Liverpool City Council. The Catholic, Anglican and Methodist churches have a presence in the area, with the latter, Princes Park Methodist Church, having a successful youth centre, which has been running for more than two decades.

The synagogue and Greek Orthodox church are still in operation but cater for minority groups of worshippers who no longer live within the area, although they hold services there regularly. The mosque on Mulgrave Street was built within the last decade and serves as the central mosque for Merseyside. It is well attended and serves as a focal point for the local and regional Islamic community as a place of worship and meeting.

The commercial and economic activities within the area are particularly sparse. From being a thriving multicultural commercial street in the 1960s, Granby Street has lost its post office, bank, and all of its specialist shops. All that remain now are a few general stores, which sell local groceries and African, halal and other international produce. The current official redevelopment plans do not include the upgrading of the street or any plans for commercial activity within the area.[14] The residents' group's international market proposal would, therefore, if successful, be the only commercial development for the inner area.

The Chinese Community in Liverpool

Reputed to be the oldest in Europe, Liverpool's Chinese community remains located in one of the most historic neighbourhoods in the city. Today's Chinatown centres around Cornwallis Street and Great George Square. This is close to the historic epicentre of the original Chinatown that had been part of the seamen's lodging areas, centred around Cleveland Square and Pitt Street in the south docks area (see Figure 3). The old Chinatown had mainly been frequented and inhabited by sailors from China, South-East Asia and Africa, as it was close to the south docks, where most

---

[13] Public inquiry into the redevelopment of the Granby Triangle, 24–26 June 1997.

[14] The perimeter of Granby Toxteth has undergone considerable redevelopment with the rebuilding of the Parliament Street buildings within the 'Rialto Triangle', and the Parliament Street/Lodge Lane buildings at the 'Boundary' layout.

cargo from Africa and Asia would have been offloaded in the late nineteenth and early twentieth century. After the sustained bombing during the blitz in the Second World War, large parts of the area were cleared, and residents decanted to outlying housing estates in the late 1940s and early 1950s. A new housing estate was then built on the periphery of the area in the 1960s, while what was left of Chinatown remained in a near-derelict state, much of the property being in private hands.[15]

The resurgence of the 'new' Chinatown, which has produced a boost in commercial activity, increased residential numbers and increased provision of social facilities, has taken place over a relatively short period. Much of the improvement of the neighbourhood has resulted from the efforts of the LCBA in bringing commercial investment into the neighbourhood. A number of restaurants and small businesses have been set up recently, with more scheduled to open in the future (Brian Wong, pers. comm.). Associated with this has been the construction of affordable, rentable housing by the Pine Court Housing Association. This has resulted in the reinhabitation of the area by a varied mix of Chinese and non-Chinese residents who had either lived in sub-standard housing or had moved back into Chinatown from outlying housing estates in the city. There is also a self-catering student hostel for Liverpool John Moores University in the newly regenerated neighbourhood.

A number of social support services are also available within the community. Most prominent among these is the Pagoda Chinese Community Centre. This is an umbrella venue for a number of Chinese community functions and activities. Among these are a bilingual Chinese–English nursery school, a benefits advice group, an after-school study group, the Liverpool Chinese Youth Orchestra and a regular Chinese lunch club for the older residents. There are also separate Chinese community centres; a Chinese-language Sunday school, which has run for more than two decades from its current premises in Duke Street; and the Chinese Gospel Church, which is the main centre for the Chinese Christian community on Merseyside.

There is also a health centre and a Catholic primary school in the neighbourhood. The school has a good reputation and is well attended by members of the community and children from elsewhere in Liverpool. There are plans to open a herbal medicine shop in the area. A number of local shops also provide for the needs of the community; there is a large wholesale Chinese supermarket, a Chinese travel agent, and a number of accountants and smaller food stores.

Most recently there has been the successful completion of a Chinese arch, reputed to be the tallest outside China, which stands at the entrance to the new Chinatown. There are also plans afoot for the further development of the community, which is now officially twinned with (and thus has a special socio-economic relationship with) the city of Shanghai in China. Many of the current developments taking place

---

[15] Information about the Chinese community has largely been gathered from the following sources: interview with Brian Wong (Liverpool Chinatown Business Association), 19 September 2000; interview with Nigel Reed (CDS Housing Association, on secondment to Pine Court Housing Association), 19 January 2000; and interview with Polly Green (administrator, the Pagoda Chinese Community Centre), 14 January 2000.

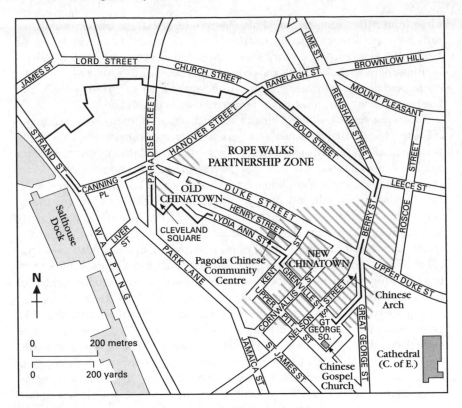

Figure 3. Rope Walks Partnership Zone including present Chinatown
Source: LCBA (2000).

in and around Chinatown are being done in association with the Liverpool Rope Walks Partnership. The Partnership has access to £40 million from the EU (through European Social Fund 'Objective One' funding) to help finance and 'kick-start' socio-economic development projects in the designated deprived area of downtown Liverpool, which covers part of Chinatown (see Figure 3).

Not all the development in the area, however, has been as successful or as socially inclusive as might be expected. The emphasis remains on the commercial as opposed to the social in the redevelopment of the area. Aside from the new housing, there has been only a limited amount of recently built social infrastructure (clinics, schools, social centres, etc.); furthermore what does exist is often in need of substantial upgrading. The area's success as an investment opportunity has brought in a number of Liverpool's building developers, who are moving their development sphere from the city centre core to areas such as Chinatown on its outskirts. However, the developers' activities are often profit-driven and commercial in nature, with a limited or non-existent social remit.

As a result of these activities the Chinatown community in Liverpool is enjoying a demographic increase as more Chinese and other residents are moving back into the neighbourhood. There is also an increased amount of socio-economic activity in the area. This is not restricted to increased numbers of customers at Chinese restaurants; it includes the daily influx of children from as far as the Wirral and Chester to the bilingual nursery school, a number of food shoppers, and other users of various local services.

The reinvigorated space that the new Chinatown now occupies has served to transform the lifestyle and public perception of the Chinese community in Liverpool. The newly constructed Chinese arch serves as a symbolic marker of the resurgence of the neighbourhood. Its size and bold, colourful design signal the resurgence and changes taking place in the area. Chinese identity in Liverpool today has become positive; the annual Chinese New Year Festival has become a major crowd-puller for residents of Liverpool and further afield. The commercial activities around the new arch suggest the existence of an economically successful and socially viable community.

However, social data on the Chinese community resident in Liverpool still show that there remains a high level of unemployment, and a lack of uptake of social care and welfare benefits by many residents (Polly Green, pers. comm.). Furthermore, not all housing in Chinatown today is of a very high standard; there still exist a number of dwellings above or behind the shops of particularly poor quality. There is also still a significant 'underground' community of poor Chinese who, because of immigration irregularities and language barriers, fall through the social welfare net, remaining unrecorded, and unable or afraid to access these services. The success of the community in improving its wider public image is thus yet to be effectively channelled into improving the lot of the poor within its midst.

Finally it is noteworthy that the successful regeneration of the community has been driven from within the local community, with the efforts of the city authorities often being secondary in the process. The relative success of the Chinese community in bringing about positive change, despite major obstacles related to its location, prevailing trends of out-migration, and its marked linguistic and cultural difference from the mainstream community, makes this case study particularly interesting.

Analysis

In Liverpool, as a port city, one might conclude that all residents are in effect minorities given the varied backgrounds and histories of many Liverpudlians, and therefore identity should have no sociological baggage in the city. Unfortunately this is not the case. This is especially true for ethnic minority residents. In Liverpool, as in many other cities, the 'melting pot' theory does not hold true.

In general most 'white' migrants have become assimilated within the mainstream residential and cultural life of Liverpool.[16] Substantial numbers of

---

[16] Possibly the Irish Catholic community could be seen to constitute a separate identity in parts of the north of Liverpool, with its strong ties to the Catholic Church. However, Irish Catholics are well integrated into the life of the city and can be found residing in various other neighbourhoods in Liverpool.

recognisable ethnic minority groups, such as the African-Caribbean and Chinese case-study communities, have continued to reside in discrete urban neighbourhoods, separate from the mainstream residential community in Liverpool. Many individual members of these communities have become residents of outlying suburban areas but the main locus of each community has remained centred within a specific geographically circumscribed area. Such areas have had and continue to retain a historic association with the minority group.

The two case studies clearly highlight the successes and shortcomings of the existence of minority communities in Liverpool. What is common to both the Chinese and the African-Caribbean communities is their separate existence and 'otherness' to the majority population in Liverpool. The 'rich-mix' scenario documented in London has little direct application here, and a significant resident middle class of either community is yet to emerge.[17]

The experience of the Somali community in Liverpool is particularly depressing. Somalis have lived in Liverpool for nearly a century, yet they remain on the margins. Somalis, discussing their plight in early 2000, presented a bleak picture of missed opportunities and a lack of constructive engagement on the part of the city with their community (Foundation for Civil Society, 2000). The new generation of Somali children are likely to have a lower educational attainment than their parents, and unemployment in the community is running at more than 50 per cent.

The Somali community, though often cited as being 'fragmented' in nature, retains its unique identity. There are a number of Somali organisations and groups that cater to the needs of the community. Most social services leaflets are also now translated into Somali. There are also successful advocacy groups for Somalis available at hospitals and other institutions, which ensure that there are simultaneous translation services available to all users of facilities.

Access to information, however, does not in itself improve the socio-economic condition of Somali residents. There has also been a significant improvement in the housing of Somalis and other ethnic groups in the Granby Toxteth area, largely as a result of the triumvirate of housing associations which own more than a third of all housing stock in the neighbourhood. For large Somali families this has been particularly beneficial, as several larger than usual housing units were built to accommodate a number of such families.

Economically, however, the community has fared badly. Unemployment remains high and the various government schemes to encourage the young to gain access to higher education and subsequent employment have had limited success. The youth of the Somali community can be seen with other Granby Toxteth youths on most days 'hanging out' on the street corners with no visible work to do.

The situation between Somali and other Black youths and the police is better

---

[17] 'Rich Mix' is the title of a report produced by the University of East London to describe the vibrant community life in the East End of London (Joseph Rowntree Foundation, 1998). 'Multicultural' USA has for long been characterised by a large Black middle class in cities such as New York and Washington.

than it was in the 1980s. There have been no similar disturbances in Liverpool on the scale of the 1981 'Toxteth' riots. The national statistic, however, remains true in Liverpool: young Black men of whatever ethnic origin are more likely to be stopped by the police than any other group. Somali residents and other Black Liverpudlians are also disproportionately represented in indicators of poverty and deprivation. There are a large number of single-headed households in the Granby Toxteth area, and the neighbourhood scores highly on Liverpool's social deprivation index (Liverpool City Council, 1995).

The Somali community remains to a large extent a separate group, which has yet to assimilate or integrate with mainstream Liverpool society. The issues of culture and religion are the most visible factors that separate the community. Most Somalis are strict Muslims and Somali women wear traditional Islamic head-dress. There are now successful Somali women's groups although the community remains strongly patriarchal.

The Somali community is also involved in the international food shops and newsagent dealerships which are beginning to attract ethnic minority entrepreneurs in and around the Granby Toxteth neighbourhood. Other traditional areas of employment and integration for ethnic minority workers in the UK, such as the minicab and taxicab industries, remain conspicuously devoid of Somalis and other African-Caribbean minorities in Liverpool. There is a nascent Somali middle class, who, like other successful Blacks, have moved out of the Granby Toxteth area. However, for conferences, special events, and every Friday, most Somalis and other Muslims return to the Granby neighbourhood, to the mosque on Mulgrave Street for prayers. Sites of social intermingling (outside of work relationships) with the wider Liverpool community remain restricted to schools, sports grounds, and clubs.[18]

The Somalis, in common with most of the African-Caribbean community in Liverpool, have still to be accepted within mainstream business circles and remain excluded from much of Liverpool's economic life outside of the Granby Toxteth locale. Thus the new Granby market proposal is located within the boundaries of the neighbourhood, and the Black presence in the city outside of Granby remains almost non-existent. The Somali and wider African-Caribbean community are yet to harness the organisational strength needed to influence successfully the redevelopment of the locale, which is taking place with limited involvement on their part. Similarly local development programmes have been unable to achieve total success, due in part to the lack of united community leadership and engagement with the programme providers in identifying the community's specific needs.

The Chinese community case study provided a different picture of ethnic minority life in Liverpool. The group designated as being 'Chinese' in fact comprises a more cosmopolitan collection of residents of Asiatic descent from the

---

[18] 'Casablanca', a former nightclub, used to be a major site for multicultural association. The club scene in Liverpool now is relatively mixed although the Afro-Caribbean youth have a few specific clubs that they frequent.

Chinese mainland, Hong Kong and elsewhere in South East Asia, although the majority are now likely to have come from mainland China.[19] While they appear now to have been phenomenally successful in regenerating their neighbourhood, they also have had to suffer the effects of segregation and 'ghettoization' in their residential and socio-economic activities.

Employment has remained relatively stable for many Chinese residents who are self-employed in the area. Younger Chinese, however, suffer the same problems as other ethnic minorities, with access to jobs outside the 'traditional' Chinese sector proving difficult. Also there remains a language barrier for many older Chinese and recent migrants who speak little or no English. The Pagoda Chinese Community Centre and the recently instituted employment trust deal with these and other problems facing the population.

The sense of physical separation from elsewhere in Liverpool remains very much in evidence. Aside from the new housing that has been built, the majority of the residents of the recently built Liverpool John Moores University hostel are of South East Asian extraction. The Pine Court Housing Association does rent to tenants who are not necessarily of East Asian or Chinese extraction, so there is a fairly varied 'tenant' community around Chinatown. The rundown housing estate nearby has predominantly local 'white' residents. Richer Chinese businessmen and professionals do not live in Chinatown, and there are Chinese businesses elsewhere in Liverpool. The Chinatown area, however, remains predominantly Chinese in nature, and the central focus for the Chinese community on Merseyside.

The effect of the Rope Walks Partnerships development remit on the area has been significant. Chinatown has benefited from being within the boundaries of the partnership area, while the partnership is seen in a positive light as being involved in the upgrading and redevelopment of an ethnic community neighbourhood. However, as a by-product of this and Chinatown's successful regeneration, new private loft apartments and private housing are being developed by commercial property investors in association with the city council. This is likely to have an uncertain effect on the local community, since the new loft-dwellers are likely to be more affluent than the existing residents, and predominantly white rather than Chinese.

Ethnic minority experiences and lifestyles in Liverpool can be different, as this analysis has highlighted. However, there are key issues that define the lifestyle of ethnic minority communities. Most remain segregated in residence, and have higher unemployment and poorer social infrastructure than other city residents. Despite these drawbacks, most of Liverpool's ethnic minority communities remain in existence and have their own support networks, often run as private clubs or associations, which look after the needs of their members.

The Chinese community's Pagoda Centre has been particularly successful in attracting local authority funding to run its activities, which provide a broad

---

[19] Chinese migration to Liverpool, like that of the Somalis, took place in stages, with the Hong Kong Chinese being in the majority at an earlier period (Brian Wong, pers. comm.).

spread of services for the local community, from nursery facilities to elderly people's dinner clubs. In the case of the Somali community, as with other African-Caribbean groups in Granby Toxteth, this support network is less developed. There are, however, a number of clubs and organisations that attend to the needs of the ageing, predominantly male population. The Somali Association on Granby Street has been successful in getting the local authority to provide the local 'meals on wheels' service for Somali elders on a regular basis. There are, however, few other agencies that have been able to provide a range of facilities and activities for the community comparable to those available in Chinatown.

These differences in the two communities' development outcomes and their future in the light of Liverpool's re-emergence as a (multi)cultural metropolis, evidenced by its successful bid to become European City of Culture in 2008, will be considered in the final section of this chapter.

Conclusions

In this chapter, I have sought to develop an understanding of the process of ethnic settlement and integration within Liverpool. This has been achieved by giving a contextual overview of Liverpool's major ethnic minority groups, the African-Caribbean and the South East Asian, and the case study analyses of the Somali and Chinese communities. The chapter has gone on to present a current perspective on the residential situation of each community. Despite their different settlement patterns, the two still show a number of common features, as well as the stark difference of each group's present development strategies. In this final section I shall consider the possible future settlement trajectories of these communities.

Contextually the two groups studied bear similarities with other ethnic groups who have assimilated more successfully (such as the Irish and Greek communities) or moved out of metropolitan Liverpool (the Jewish community). The historical records of the settlement of the Granby Toxteth area from its establishment in the mid-nineteenth century attest to this. The area now designated 'Chinatown' was also in the past home to a more mixed, multicultural population, due to its proximity to the south docks and the location of a number of international seamen's hostels in its vicinity.

The provision of social services, including educational, health and local services such as post offices, has historically been limited in both areas. Furthermore, the housing stock in each neighbourhood had been historically poorly maintained and, until the current regeneration efforts, had suffered the effects of demolition and 'redlining', leading to a state of dilapidation with rows of housing being left uninhabited. Economically, while there had been periods in the past during Liverpool's maritime eminence when both areas had boasted shops and small businesses, there had been a marked decline in economic activity in both neighbourhoods until the late 1990s.

Assimilation in terms of settlement patterns (meaning the ability to move to and live in traditionally 'white' Liverpool neighbourhoods) has, it seems, always been possible for minority groups who are Caucasian. For the Chinese and the African-Caribbean populations, this was, in the past, less easy. A limited number of relocations and removals were undertaken by the city council in the 1960s and 1970s. These were generally unsuccessful since the outlying housing estates were predominantly white and racism was (and remains) a problem. Effectively, then, Granby Toxteth and (to a lesser extent) Chinatown became designated racialised spaces. Today, however, the Chinese community has more members resident outside Chinatown than within. Although the African-Caribbean community and Liverpool-born Blacks of mixed race are well represented in the Granby Toxteth census statistics, significant numbers of Black people also live in the southern suburbs outside the Granby Toxteth area.

In Chinatown the economic imperative grew stronger, as the more affluent Chinese and South East Asian communities moved into Liverpool's suburbs, setting up Chinese restaurants and take-aways in these areas also. The result has been the regeneration of a more economically active Chinatown, initiated and developed by the local Chinese business population, with the recent development of housing association residential accommodation in the area and a central Chinese community centre with city council backing.

In Granby Toxteth this development has been much weaker; there is only a vestigial presence of commercial activity within the area, although the bordering areas of the neighbourhood have experienced a marked revival and gentrification. The fringe bordering the University of Liverpool has been upgraded and is now interspersed with student self-catering accommodation, while the Parliament Street boundary has seen significant new infrastructure in the past decade. This includes the new Women's Hospital, a youth 'foyer' hostel scheme, the new Rialto, a shopping/office/residential complex, and developer housing.

The net effect of this has been to improve the real estate value of the area, through the upgrading of its perimeter infrastructure. This has effectively placed the focus for the council and real estate developers on the core of Granby Toxteth. This is being done in piecemeal fashion, via a new joint housing association-funded residential estate, and a new local authority-funded school. These and other separate developments are yet to become linked as part of an overall scheme, and the neighbourhood is yet to have a clear regeneration strategy, as has happened through the Rope Walks area's strategy, which includes a development plan for Chinatown and other neighbourhoods.

It would seem that within Liverpool these two communities are likely to retain their individual ethnic identities, as is clear with the ongoing regeneration of both neighbourhoods that acknowledges their particularities. Granby Toxteth, though much slower in its regeneration efforts than Chinatown, retains a significant African-Caribbean and mixed race population, with a support infrastructure such as its mosque, ethnic minority community centres, and churches.

In the case of Chinatown, the historical links of the community with the area are evident in the buildings that housed historical locations for the community, such as 'The Nook' reputed to be 'the first Chinese-run pub in Liverpool'. Granby

Toxteth, though not originally an African-Caribbean neighbourhood, has an undeniable association with Liverpool Black history, as a location of the riots, and of many of the seamen's clubs, educational and cultural clubs which still function as sites of community association. Furthermore, the still significant Black population suggests that any migration elsewhere will only take place slowly, due to the existing support infrastructure in and around the area.

The ethnic minority residential settlement pattern and development in Liverpool differs considerably from other cosmopolitan urban centres such as London, in that it remains still very localised to areas of historical settlement or transitional neighbourhoods such as Granby. The areas both still have strong historical ties with families who lived within these neighbourhoods. Gentrification and the erasure of street names have been slow to take place in the core areas of both neighbourhoods. Both have retained their identities although existing side by side with predominantly white neighbourhoods, and institutions such as Liverpool University. The peculiarities of residence and settlement in the city have served to maintain the spatial segregation originating from the traditional foreign seafarers' old docks neighbourhoods.

This may be set to change with the rise of Liverpool inner-city real estate prices and the regeneration efforts going on in each neighbourhood. Current demographic trends and the city's young profile suggest that the younger population and students are less residentially discriminating, evidenced by the success of inner-city apartment developments and city-centre residential accommodation for students. The effects on Granby Toxteth and Chinatown are already apparent as ethnic minority students often choose to live in these neighbourhoods because of their support infrastructure. There has also been a return of the middle classes to the fringes of Granby Toxteth, where the Georgian terraced housing has undergone considerable upgrading and regeneration, and hence increased in value. The development of the Hope Street Festival, key tertiary academic institutions and a thriving café and bar culture in the area have all been instrumental to this process.

Chinatown's regeneration provides a unique example in Liverpool of locally led regeneration being successful in forming alliances with other funding and regeneration sources. The decision of the growing Chinese-speaking middle class to retain links with Chinatown via the commerce, schools, cultural centres and housing is also unusual. In Liverpool earlier successful minority groups migrated out from the inner city retaining minimal links. This Chinatown model, however, has been successful internationally in cities as different as Johannesburg and San Francisco. The African-Caribbean community has yet to achieve the equivalent (as, for example, in Brixton), and in Liverpool great efforts are being made to retain the Black identity in the face of rapid regeneration and demographic change within Granby Toxteth.

Possibly the historical roots of ethnic minority settlement in Liverpool are so entrenched in a segregationist past that the models of residence are more 'colonial', bordering on those of the American South or the colonial port cities such as Cape Town, Lagos and Singapore, where residential separation was enforced. This is in contrast to the more laissez faire modes of settlement found in mainland Europe. Possibly, then, Liverpool would much prefer a neatly ordered, albeit regenerated, series of ethnic neighbourhoods and would eschew the less spatially ordered 'Finsbury Park' model of layering and integration of multi-ethnic communities that embodies the current thinking on harmonious living.

It is likely, however, that these and other issues relating to place and identity will remain as crucial as they have been in the past to each community's engagement and relationship with metropolitan Liverpool today. The buildings may be upgraded, pulled down, or rebuilt; new residents may move in and regeneration schemes begin; but the communal memory and association with each neighbourhood are set to remain alive.

References

Ben-Tovim, G. (1988), 'Race, Local Politics and Urban Regeneration – Lessons from Liverpool', in M. Parkinson, B. Foley and D. Judd (eds), *Regenerating the Cities – The UK Crisis and the American Experience*, Manchester: Manchester University Press

Ben-Tovim, G., Brown, V., Clay, D., Law, I., Loy, L., and Torkington, P. (eds) (1980), *Racial Disadvantage in Liverpool: An Area Profile*, Liverpool: Merseyside Area Profile Group

Ben-Tovim, G., Gabriel, J., Law, I., and Stredder, K. (eds) (1986), *The Local Politics of Race*, Basingstoke: Macmillan

Brooks, G. E., Jr (1972), *The Kru Mariner in the Nineteenth Century: An Historical Compendium*, Liberian Studies Monograph Series Number 1, Liberian Studies Association/Department of Anthropology, University of Delaware

Caradog Jones, D. (1940), *The Economic Status of Coloured Families in Liverpool*, Liverpool: Liverpool University

Cowan, R., Hannay, P., and Owens, R. (1988), 'Community-led Regeneration by the Eldonians: The Light on Top of the Tunnel', *Architects Journal*, 23 March, 37–63

Dickens, C. (1898), *The Uncommercial Traveller*, London: Chapman and Hall

Fletcher, M. (1930), 'Report of an Investigation into the Colour Problem in Liverpool and Other Ports', Liverpool: Association for the Welfare of Half Caste Children

Foundation for Civil Society (2000), *The Somali Community in Liverpool: A Report for a Commission of Enquiry Chaired by the Bishop of Liverpool*

Frost, D. (1992), 'The Kru in Freetown and Liverpool: A Story of Maritime Work and Community During the 19th and 20th Centuries', unpublished PhD thesis, University of Liverpool

— (1994), 'Racism, Work and Unemployment, West African Seamen in Liverpool 1880–1960', *Immigrants and Minorities*, 13(2–3), July/November

Fryer, P. (1984), *Staying Power*, London: Pluto Press

Gifford, Lord (1989), *Loosen the Shackles – Report of the L8 Enquiry into Racial Disturbances in Liverpool*, London: Karia

Hocking, S. K. (1879), *Her Benny*, London: Warne

Holford, W. (1949–50), 'Proposals for the Development of a Site for the University of Liverpool', Liverpool: Liverpool University

Joseph Rowntree Foundation (1998), *Rich Mix – Inclusive Strategies for Urban Regeneration*, Bristol: The Policy Press/York: Joseph Rowntree Foundation

Laitin, D. D., and Samatar, S. S. (1987), *Somalia, Nation in Search of a State*, Boulder, CO: Westview Press

Law, I., and Henfry, J. (eds) (1981), *A History of Race and Racism in Liverpool 1660–1950*, Liverpool: Merseyside Community Relations Council

Lawless, D. (1994), 'The Role of Seamen's Agents in the Migration and Employment of Arab Seafarers in the Early 20th Century', *Immigrants and Minorities*, 13(2–3), July/November

LCBA (Liverpool Chinatown Business Association) (2000a), Chinese New Year Festival promotional leaflet, Liverpool: LCBA

— (2000b), promotional flyer 'Liverpool Chinatown – a Gateway to Europe', Liverpool: LCBA

Lewis, I. M. (1965), *Modern History of Somaliland, From Nation to State*, London: Weidenfeld and Nicolson

Liverpool City Council (1995), 'Neighbourhood Renewal Assessment (Granby Area) Executive Summary', Liverpool: Liverpool City Council

Loh Lynn, I., and Craggs, S. (1986), 'A History of the Chinese Community in Liverpool', Merseyside Area Profile Group, University of Liverpool

Murphy, A. (1995), *From Empire to the Rialto – Racism and Reaction in Liverpool, 1918–1948*, Birkenhead: Liver Press

OPCS (Office for Population Census Statistics) (1991), *Census Local Base Statistics for Granby*, OPCS

Rope Walks Partnership (1999), publicity brochure

Sherwood, M. (1994), 'Strike! African Seamen, Elder Dempster and the Government 1940–42', *Immigrants and Minorities*, 13(2–3), July/November

Simey, M. (1996), *The Disinherited Society: A Personal View of Social Responsibility in Liverpool during the Twentieth Century*, Liverpool: Liverpool University Press

Uduku, O., and Ben-Tovim, G. (1998), 'Social Infrastructure Provision in Granby Toxteth', Race and Social Policy Unit, Liverpool University

Wai Kam Yu (2000), *Chinese Older People: A Need for Social Inclusion in Two Communities*, report for the Joseph Rowntree Foundation, London: The Policy Press

Wing Kwong Lau (1994), *Care in the Chinese Community: The Way Ahead*, Liverpool: Chinese Community Development Association

Wong, M. (1989), *Chinese Liverpudlians: A History of the Chinese Community in Liverpool*, Birkenhead: Liver Press

7. Youth Perspectives

Barry Goldson

[It] is worth remembering that half of the world's population, yes, half, is under 22 years of age and 34 per cent of the world's population is under 15 years of age.

(Bird and Ibidun, cited in Willow, 1997: 1)

[P]olicies and services at national and local level have often *failed to consult young people* or involve them in the design and delivery of public services. This [. . .] makes young people feel alienated.

(Social Exclusion Unit, 2000a: 9, original emphasis)

It is hypocritical to lament a perceived lack of social and political responsibility among young people and, at the same time, to deny them opportunities for effective engagement in democratic processes.

(Lansdown, 1999: 10)

The institutions, structural arrangements and policies that influence, if not determine, transitions from 'childhood', through 'youth' and into 'adulthood' have been fundamentally reshaped and redefined through the 1980s and 1990s. The cumulative impact of radical change in relation to employment, education and training opportunities; welfare services; housing and domiciliary arrangements; health profiles; social security benefits; family forms; and criminal justice interventions has meant that the processes of 'growing up' and passing into 'adulthood' have become more hazardous and insecure for identifiable constituencies of young people. For working-class and disadvantaged children and young people, such change has invariably been accompanied by the experience of systemic and institutionalised forms of exclusion (Goldson, 1997; MacDonald, 1997). In this respect black working-class young people have been especially disadvantaged (Goldson and Chigwada-Bailey, 1999: 56–62). Coles (1995) describes this process as the 're-structuration of youth' within which the linked economic phenomena of de-industrialisation and structural unemployment have impacted on young people with a particular vehemence. Too many young people are now condemned to what Westergaard (1992) has called 'outcast poverty', and for the first time in many generations in the UK defined sections of the young cannot assume that their standard of living will be higher than that of their parents. Indeed, the very terms '(working-class) youth' and 'social exclusion' have almost become interchangeable in contemporary sociological and social policy discourse: the one implies the other.

144

Children and young people who live in and around the city are particularly, although not exclusively, exposed to such exclusionary processes, and those growing up in identifiable urban regions face especially marked levels of disadvantage. The Child Poverty Action Group notes that 'some areas, most notably Merseyside, suffer from a combination of high degree, extent and intensity of poverty to produce particularly severe socio-economic problems in "concentrated poverty" areas' (CPAG, 1997: 17). Indeed, Liverpool – the 'most deprived local authority district' in England according to the Social Exclusion Unit (1998: 16) – is the site of many such 'concentrated poverty areas'. Liverpool has been witness to economic decline on a 'devastating scale and pace' (Meegan, 1993: 60) which has 'left the city with huge economic and political problems' (Lane, 1997: 26). The city is the only British mainland area that has the European Union's Objective One status and it has functioned as a 'laboratory' for urban policy experimentation and regeneration initiatives for decades (Andersen et al., 1999: 6). Furthermore, within Liverpool, as with other major urban centres, poverty is not evenly distributed and particular ward districts and localities endure 'concentrated' forms of multiple disadvantage.

The primary purpose of this chapter is to review the extent, nature and consequences of poverty in relation to young people in urban settings, and to consider the impact of state policy on the same. Moreover, by focusing on two 'concentrated poverty areas' in Liverpool – Dingle and Speke – the chapter will engage with the conceptualisations of disadvantaged and excluded young people in relation to their neighbourhoods, and their reflections on area-based regeneration initiatives. By drawing together the wider analysis of youth poverty and state policy with the specific Liverpool-based research, the chapter will conclude by considering the potential for youth participation within area-based regeneration.

The State of Disadvantaged Youth

> A significant minority of young people today experience a wide range of problems and acute crises [. . .] The scale of these problems is in many cases worse than this country's past experience and worse than other apparently comparable countries. The problems are concentrated in, but not confined to, the most deprived neighbourhoods.
>
> (Social Exclusion Unit, 2000a: 12)

More than 20 years of neo-liberal social and economic policy have created crisis conditions for too many young people as the 'United Kingdom' has become increasingly disunited, divided and polarised. At the end of the 1970s 7 per cent of children and young people lived in households with no adult in work and one in ten lived in 'poor households': those with a total income of less than half of the national average after housing costs. The corresponding figures today represent a threefold increase on both counts (Social Exclusion Unit, 2000a: 15). Indeed, poverty afflicting children and young people has increased more in Britain since

1980 than in any other Luxembourg Income Survey country for which there are data, and the prevalence of such poverty is now higher in the UK than it is in any other country in the European Union (Bradshaw, 1999; see also CPAG, 1998; Joseph Rowntree Foundation, 1998; 1999; Shropshire and Middleton, 1999; Gregg et al., 1999; Jones and Novak, 1999). Fitzpatrick and her colleagues refer to the 'double disadvantage of youth' whereby young people have suffered disproportionately relative to adults, and young people living in areas of multiple deprivation have suffered more acutely still (Fitzpatrick et al., 1998: 1). Inevitably, within such generalised patterns of intensifying poverty and inequality lie the specificities of disadvantage that define and detail the contours of young people's everyday lived realities.

Substantial numbers of young people have become disengaged from state education. Poor achievement at one end, and spiralling permanent school exclusions at the other, mark the points of a desperate educational continuum. In 1998, 31,000 young people left school in England and Wales with no qualifications (Howarth et al., 1999), during a decade that was also witness to an extraordinary increase in the numbers of young people permanently excluded from education (Parsons, 1996). Swelling numbers of young people are 'zero status', that is not in education, training or employment (Roberts, 1997). The rate of youth unemployment consistently rose throughout the 1990s, and, according to the 1999 Labour Force Survey, 18–24-year-olds endure unemployment at twice the rate that applies to older workers (cited in Howarth et al., 1999: 42). Furthermore, not only have employment opportunities for young people substantially diminished, but their rights to claim state benefits have simultaneously been systematically eroded (Novak, 1997).

Such adverse economic conditions, and the concentration of such conditions within bounded urban spaces, necessarily produce problematic social symptoms. Adolescent mental health problems are apparently becoming more widespread and more acute (Coppock, 1997), and the rates of self-harm and suicide among young people have increased, especially for working-class males without work (West and Sweeting, 1996; Howarth et al., 1999). The number of illicit drug users aged 15–24 continues to rise, and heroin is the main drug used by over half of the young people commencing treatment programmes in England (Department of Health, 1999). Lansdown (1999) detects a burgeoning 'culture of disaffection' among young people and recent surveys provide some evidence for this. Fitzpatrick et al. (1998: 2) observe that 'disadvantaged young people are least likely to exercise their political rights', a conclusion also reached by a recent Demos report which noted that 'in effect [. . .] an entire generation has opted out of politics' (cited in Lansdown, 1999: 9; see also British Youth Council, 1998). Indeed, even the most cursory review of research evidence confirms that increasing numbers of young people are literally excluded: from education, from the labour market, from state benefits, from 'community' participation, and from the democratic process at both the local and the national level.

The State and Disadvantaged Youth

> Some of these problems are the result of broader social and economic changes. But Government policies have not responded as effectively as they could have.
>
> (Social Exclusion Unit, 2000a: 9)

The point has already been made that the hostile socio-economic circumstances that challenge and confront young people can largely be understood with reference to over twenty years of neo-liberal state policy. Indeed, while global economics and the transfer of capital across international markets – what the Social Exclusion Unit refers to above as 'broader social and economic changes' – comprise the macro-context, it is difficult to avoid the conclusion that national state policy has directly contributed to the creation and consolidation of crisis conditions for the disadvantaged young. Moreover, the state has an ambivalent relation with disadvantaged young people, located as it is within a complex politic. On the one hand the government has little hesitation in declaring its intention to eradicate child poverty in order to ensure that 'no matter who they are [. . .] each young person has the best possible start in life and the opportunity to develop and achieve their full potential' (Social Exclusion Unit, 2000a: 5). Yet, on the other hand, the state has become increasingly impatient with young people who live at the sharp end of exclusionary socio-economic formations. Such impatience is manifested through pious and decontextualised moralising (in relation to teenage pregnancies, for example) at one end of its continuum, and a populist authoritarian appeal to 'toughness' through its 'no more excuses' agenda at the other (Home Office, 1997). This latter point is most vividly expressed by the government's responses to 'antisocial behaviour' in general (Social Exclusion Unit, 2000b), and youth crime in particular (Goldson, 1999; 2000), through which it has implemented a range of correctional, punitive and interventionist policies which ultimately rely on institutional and custodial 'remedies' (Goldson and Peters, 2000; Moore, 2000). The unequivocal endorsement of prison as a primary response to youth crime, for example, is evident in recent statistics. Between 1993 and 1996 there was a 30 per cent increase in the number of young prisoners (under 21 years old) and between 1995 and 1996 the number of children and young people (aged under 18 years) incarcerated rose by 34 per cent (White and Woodridge, 1998). Indeed, an uneasy ambivalence lies at the core of state policy in respect of disadvantaged youth, and the 'velvet glove' that seeks to comfort and appease anxieties in relation to child poverty covers a particularly cold 'iron fist' which clamps down hard when the young poor transgress. The contradictory detail of such ambivalence is too complex to unravel here but acknowledging its very existence is critically important.

What is less complex is the current administration's stated commitment to 'joined-up' practices and the provision of 'best value' services. The fact that 'emerging evidence suggests that, on average, the state spends 14 per cent less money on young people in the most deprived areas than on the average young person' is thus problematic (Social Exclusion Unit, 2000a: 49). Equally, the government has condemned poor strategic policy coordination and the fragmented nature of service delivery, at both central and local levels:

It is no-one's job to ensure coherent design and delivery of Government policies on young people at risk [. . .] there is no permanent youth policy, cross-Whitehall Ministerial Committee or official network [. . .] there is no single point of contact [. . .] inside departments responsibility is fragmented too [. . .] it is almost impossible to find out about other services or initiatives at local level [. . .] agreeing joint priorities appears to be just as difficult [. . .] young people get shunted from agency to agency [. . .] *too often the specific needs of young people are not given sufficient attention in the way regeneration programmes are designed and bids for such funding put together.* (Social Exclusion Unit, 2000a: 53–56, emphasis added)

Through a coordinated series of policy developments and 'plans' including Children's Services Plans and 'Quality Protects' initiatives, Education Development Plans, Behaviour Support Plans, Special Educational Needs Plans, Early Years and Child Development Plans, Youth Justice Plans, Crime and Disorder Strategies, Drug Action Plans and Health Improvement Programmes, together with a range of 'New Deals', the government is addressing the perceived needs of disadvantaged young people. Central to its youth strategy is the stated objective that

young people should leave secondary school equipped for the challenges of the 21st Century. Young people must be prepared for life in the fullest sense – *learn how to contribute to* their family, *their community* and the wider society [. . .] learn to respect themselves and those around them and so become caring and *active citizens* – adults to be proud of. (Department for Education and Employment, 2000: 8, emphasis added)

Indeed, the responsibilities of 'citizenship' and 'education for citizenship' form a primary focus of government objectives. The government has invested £40 million in the Millennium Volunteers project in order to promote volunteering among young people. More significantly, it established a Citizenship Advisory Group with Sir Bernard Crick as the Chair, with a remit to 'provide advice on effective education for citizenship in schools, to include the nature and practices of participation in democracy; the duties, responsibilities and rights of individuals as citizens; and the value to individuals and society of community activity' (Crick, 1998). Within a democracy, of course, responsibilities are meant to be accompanied by rights that apply equally to all citizens, and rights are normally expressed through relations of meaningful consultation, participation and engagement. It is precisely such relations that tend to elude the poorest and most disadvantaged young people and area-based regeneration initiatives are no exception.

Disadvantaged Youth in Liverpool: Excluded from 'Cityzenship'

Liverpool, as has already been noted, comprises an urban geography permeated with multiple and interlocking forms of disadvantage. This section of the chapter is informed by research undertaken in two of Liverpool's poorest areas: Dingle and Speke (Andersen et al., 1999). The northern edge of Dingle is situated within half a mile of Liverpool's city centre and the area conforms to popular images of a traditional working-class inner-city area. Speke lies approximately eight miles southeast of the city centre and the area comprises an archetypal outer estate; in fact it is one of the largest self-contained housing estates in England. The research was an integral part of a wider inquiry which explored people's experiences of living in disadvantaged neighbourhoods and examined the impact of, and level of participation in, area-based regeneration initiatives (Forrest and Kearns, 1999). For the purposes here I intend to summarise some of the key issues that emerged from a series of single-gender focus group discussions with young people in Dingle and Speke, with particular emphasis on their perceptions of local identity, their experience of disadvantage, and their sense of civic engagement, community participation and contribution to area-based regeneration.

Local identity

Almost all of the young people in the focus groups had lived all of their lives in either Dingle or Speke. They expressed mixed feelings about their neighbourhoods. In both areas young people articulated dissatisfaction with the physical infrastructure and this concurs with wider surveys of poor neighbourhoods (Howarth et al., 1999: 82):

> The area itself is getting worse. You walk around and look at how many derelict buildings that there are around here. It gets worse with every generation. (Male Focus Group: Dingle)

> nothing happens it just gets worse, nothing gets better . . . No one will want to live here . . . All the houses are getting boarded up because people are leaving and no one wants to move in. (Female Focus Group: Speke)

However, the young people were also extraordinarily attached to the social dimensions of their neighbourhoods and place-based identity was very strong, if at times paradoxical. In this sense the people and the security and support that they convey compensate, at least in part, for the poor physical fabric. As Kearns and Forrest (1998: 13) have observed 'residents of poor neighbourhoods spend more time in their local areas than do residents of wealthier neighbourhoods' and the sense of community cohesion and neighbourliness is an important source of belonging for the young people:

> Everyone has lived here all of their lives haven't they? I've lived in my house since I was born . . . We have a history together . . . Yes, most people that live here have been here most of their lives. They all grew up together. Our parents grew up here and they know each other from their childhood . . . The families have other generations here and our old fellas hang around together. (Male Focus Group: Dingle)

One young person contrasted the experience of living in Dingle with his observations of a middle-class Liverpool suburb:

> I've been working all day in Maghull. Now that's one bad place. It's clean but I wouldn't
> want to live there because of the atmosphere. Everyone keeps themselves to themselves
> in all the houses. No one knows anyone, like your neighbours. Down here . . . everyone
> knows one another and they talk, but there they don't, you never see next door neigh-
> bours talking . . . It's just dead. No one even looks at you. They don't socialise. (Male
> Focus Group: Dingle)

Indeed, despite the contemporary sociological preoccupation with individuation, anonymity and social fragmentation (Beck, 1992; 1998; Furlong and Cartmel, 1997), the young people from Dingle and Speke consistently emphasised class-grounded forms of solidarity, mutuality and community cohesion as forming the basis of their coping and support strategies:

> We all hang around together and if someone is in trouble we all help . . . we all help one
> another . . . (Male Focus Group: Dingle)

Triple disadvantage

I referred earlier to the 'double disadvantage' conceptualisation of youth (Fitzpatrick et al., 1998). The young people in the Liverpool focus groups endured all of the exclusionary processes that have been discussed above but additionally they articulated a form of triple disadvantage rooted, first, in living in Liverpool; second, in living in a poor neighbourhood in Liverpool; and third, in being young and living in a poor neighbourhood in Liverpool.

First, the overwhelming consensus among young people within and across all of the focus groups was that the popular external image of Liverpool was nega-tive. The young people felt that media representations of Liverpool – in both news and drama – serve to perpetuate stereotypical images underpinned by construc-tions of criminality and fecklessness. 'Scouser' has become a term of ridicule and insult:

> To them you're just a scouser . . . on TV though the scousers are always really bad people.
> (Female Focus Group: Speke)

Many of the young people described experiences of being outside Liverpool and attracting negative attention on the basis of their accent:

> People say 'get back where you're from' and everything. They always go, say when you go
> on holiday somewhere, they always go 'Oh watch them, watch where their hands go,
> watch what they put in their pockets'. (Female Focus Group: Dingle)

Second, the young people described how the disadvantage that results from the negative external image of Liverpool per se is further compounded by unfavourable impressions that people have of their neighbourhoods *within* the city. The sense of living in a 'marked' community shapes the everyday experi-ences of young people from Dingle and Speke and it has both a practical and an emotional effect:

They think that we are all dead common and rough. They say don't go there because they'll rob your car . . . If you go to places where you hire stuff, they won't do it. They tell you that they won't go into Speke. Because we live down here people think that we are all druggies and that . . . I know people who have gone for jobs and as soon as they say they're from Speke they know that they won't get it . . . They've got a bad feeling about us, I don't know what it is. They think we are all scallies and that and we don't get on with anyone. Speke is just the same as everywhere else . . . It makes you really angry though when they are saying things about you and where you live . . . It makes you feel that you're nothing. (Female Focus Group: Speke)

There are girls in our school . . . and their Mums won't let them come down to this area . . . we wanted our mate to come down and she said 'No, my Mum won't let me go because of the area and things that go on'. Say there's one drug dealer they blame everyone else for being a drug dealer and everything. It's the same with robbers. Yeah, you're either a robber a drug dealer or someone who has shot someone or a scallie. That's what we are to them. That's what they think we are. (Female Focus Group: Dingle)

Moreover, the young people felt that such negative conceptualisations within the city extended to politicians, local authority officials and regeneration professionals:

They don't do anything for anyone. As long as the council pays them that's all that matters . . . Nobody's interested. They are just leaving us to rot like they are leaving Speke to rot really . . . I don't think that anyone is really bothered about Speke . . . We're out of the way here aren't we? We are on the edge really, on the edge of society . . . We are just on the edge, it's like the last stop in Liverpool. (Male Focus Group: Speke)

It's just wasteland where a park had been but it had been destroyed. Not destroyed, just left, they didn't look after it. They knock things down but don't even think about rebuilding them and then the ground is left and it's all rough and that. The land is just left with no use at all. It looks bare. (Male Focus Group: Dingle)

Third, the young people from both Dingle and Speke believed that the external and internal forms of negativity in respect of their city and neighbourhoods are further intensified by virtue of their very youth. They reported spending a lot of their time 'on the street' and, as a youth worker explained, they have little alternative:

It might be a point of finding somewhere where they can meet. I can guarantee that in Speke if I got three young people to stand on a certain corner at any given time, that would increase five-fold, there would be fifteen young people standing there within an hour or so . . . there are no specific areas that people have got to call their own in Speke. They have got a youth club but there are people who are 'unclubbable', they don't feel happy being associated with a club. That doesn't make them bad, it just makes them different. (Youth Worker: Speke)

However, groups of young people gathering together on street corners in this way traditionally attract the attention of adults, and are invariably problematised.

Although they did not welcome this, some of the young people expressed insight and understanding:

> I can understand because if there was a gang hanging around outside my house, I wouldn't like it either. I'd want them to be moved. The old people don't like it because they do get scared. You know that you are not going to do nothing but they don't and they get frightened. (Female Focus Group: Speke)

However, the young people strongly objected to what they perceived as indiscriminate police harassment:

> We used to hang around in a bus stop . . . we found a little bus stop and we just used to hang around there at the arches. There are no houses around there so we didn't get moved on. But then the police came and they took our names and everything because we were sitting in a bus stop! But we weren't vandalising it or anything. We were just sitting there . . . Sometimes they'll just come up to us and search us for no reason when we're not doing anything. If you are sitting at the arches they'll hassle you but they won't be looking for the real trouble . . . they are not from Speke themselves and they have the attitude towards Speke to start with. (Female Focus Group: Speke)

> The police are a bit harsh like . . . They ask you loads of questions . . . Most people have probably been pulled for nothing haven't they in here like? . . . They know who the scallies are but they just pick on everyone. They take it out on people because they can't get the right ones. (Male Focus Group: Speke)

> You could be standing on the corner and they just come up and nearly pin you up against the wall. And for nothing. It's all for nothing. (Male Focus Group: Dingle)

Area-based regeneration as exclusion

The remarkable thing about the young people in Dingle and Speke is that their conceptualisations of area-based regeneration, together with their expectations and aspirations, are unremarkable. They are very grounded and 'ordinary'. Throughout the series of focus group discussions it became increasingly apparent that the young people want to be listened to and taken seriously; they want opportunities to participate and engage in regeneration initiatives; they want to see real, maintained and sustainable environmental change in their communities; they want to see the development of appropriate community resources; and, above all else, they want to be able to look forward to futures in which employment is a realistic prospect. Such findings have emerged from other similar studies of disadvantaged young people and they 'demonstrate how mistaken crude assumptions regarding the "differentness" of the young poor are' (Jeffs and Smith, 1995: 69).

Young people have more than enough experience of being 'done to'. As a youth worker commented in relation to regeneration consultation meetings:

I believe that young people should be at these meetings, they are part of the community, not simply in the community, they are part of that community . . . There are always people trying to do things for the young people, and again I don't knock that, but what I would be more in favour of is young people actually doing things for themselves. They are not helpless, they do have ideas, and some have very good ideas and there are some who want to get involved. They have always been restricted in the past by saying that we will do that for you. (Youth Worker: Speke)

Providing opportunities for young people to participate actively is complex but necessary if notions of active citizenship and civic engagement are applied. Moreover, as Fitzpatrick et al. (1998) found, while there are important convergences between young people's and adults' priorities for youth within regeneration processes, there are also some striking differences. Adults do not, and simply cannot, accurately represent the interests of the disadvantaged young and this is particularly the case in relation to regeneration 'professionals':

It's falling on deaf ears really though, isn't it . . . who do these people, those who decide what to put the money into, who do they ask where it should go before they do it? . . . I don't know what they spend it on. Just arts and stuff and nobody's interested in arts . . . they just do what they want to with all that money and power. Most of them aren't interested in the things that everyday people want like most of us around here. We're not interested in art . . . it's not going to create jobs is it? . . . It's the people who live here who need to be asked . . . They just come up with a big pot of money and want to spend it on the first thing that comes into their heads without asking anybody . . . If people knew that their say definitely meant change . . . they'd all be there wouldn't they? (Male Focus Group: Speke)

Yeah, but they don't listen to us, we wouldn't get any say in the matter . . . we should be able to talk to them, tell them what we want. They should listen to us. Yeah, and they should come and talk to us instead of people who are older than us, they need to see the kids. They always talk to someone else. (Male Focus Group: Dingle)

The young people expressed their frustration with the perceived deterioration of their communities and the need for regeneration strategies to provide sustainable and real environmental improvements:

They must have created about 200 jobs planting trees, they should ask the community first and find out what they want and then maybe they could invest it into a business which would create more business. As long as those trees are growing the problem is out of sight . . . it may make things look a bit more pleasant but behind those trees everybody is in the same situation, it's just the outside, the problems are on the inside, the side that no-one sees. (Male Focus Group: Speke)

However, the young people aspire to employment and/or the realistic prospect of employment above all else:

I just want to get a good job really and just be happy. I don't want to be on the dole . . . it's like asking us what we want to be when we are grown up. We already are grown up. (Male Focus Group: Speke)

Give people more jobs. Yeah, get more jobs for people in the area . . . Build new businesses and all that. That would make more jobs and the people would be able to enjoy
themselves . . . The kids would get a better education because there would be jobs for
them when they leave school. Speke would get more money and then it would have a
better reputation because people say that if you come from Speke you're on the dole and
that, so it would be different. (Female Focus Group: Speke)

At one level the focus groups present a bleak picture of non-participation and
poverty of environment for the young people in Dingle and Speke. Area-based
regeneration initiatives appear to confirm rather than alleviate their excluded and
marginal status. At another rather more optimistic level, and despite the sense of
'triple disadvantage', the young people articulate a strong place-based identity
and they value the socially grounded support within their neighbourhoods.
Furthermore, they have considered views about their environments which, given
the opportunity, they are well able to express and explain. This should not surprise
us and it is consistent with the findings from related studies elsewhere (Fitzpatrick
et al., 1998; Freeman et al., 1999; Willow, 1997). What is perhaps more surprising,
and at loggerheads with repeatedly stated elements of government policy, is that
area-based regeneration processes continue to exclude the perspectives of disadvantaged young people.

Including the Excluded: Youth Participation and Area-based Regeneration

The opportunity to genuinely participate is a right, a civil right, a human right, a right
of citizenship.

(Cockburn, 1998)

[C]ommunities belong [to] and are shaped by young people too.

(Willow, 1997)

The government is ostensibly committed to facilitating the participation of *all*
young people, 'consulting and involving them in policy development and service
delivery' (Social Exclusion Unit, 2000a: 81). Equally the concept of 'neighbourhood management' is one of New Labour's 'big ideas' in 'tackling social exclusion'
and 'will form a key part in its National Strategy for Neighbourhood Renewal'
(Joseph Rowntree Foundation, 2000: 1). This initiative will involve delegating significant decision-making powers to neighbourhood level, with a strong emphasis
on involving the community in planning and implementing services. Equally, it
will require a willingness to give local people the power and *responsibility* to take
action in their neighbourhoods. Such developments are not unproblematic for
poor communities: there are obvious dangers in shifting the burden of responsibility from the state and its agencies to the level of the neighbourhood, dangers
that should neither be ignored nor minimised. However, the policy developments
also offer some potential for the democratisation of neighbourhoods and the
inclusion of previously excluded groups. Indeed, at the national level there may

be a need to 'Bring Britain Together' (Social Exclusion Unit, 1998) but, as Forrest and Kearns (1999: 49) have noted, 'the main task in many disadvantaged neighbourhoods is to bring the community together by building links between constituent groups'.

Herein lies some opportunity for the meaningful participation of the young poor, but this will require overcoming the challenges and issues that have been signalled throughout this chapter. Past experience offers little comfort in this regard. Much has previously been made of formal rights in respect of young people. In 1991, for example, the UK government ratified the United Nations Convention on the Rights of the Child, which conferred a range of participation rights on children and young people and a responsibility on government to publicise the Convention actively and widely among young people (Hodgkin and Newell, 1996; Willow, 1997). However, a recent survey of over 2,000 young people found that 75 per cent had never heard of the United Nations Convention, and almost all of the rest said that they had heard only a little (Alderson, 1999). Moreover, in commenting on youth councils and participative youth forums, Matthews and Limb (1997) have observed that 'non-participation is endemic in the UK [. . .] young people are seemingly invisible on the landscape'.

Where attempts have been made to engage the participation of disadvantaged young people in regeneration initiatives, youth forums have constituted the favoured mechanism and this makes this latter point particularly significant. Following their study of 12 urban regeneration initiatives Fitzpatrick et al. (1999: 11) concluded that 'youth forums differed widely; they ranged from high-profile and well-organised forums backed by generous funding and linked directly to decision-making processes to loose groupings with no independent resources'. It is of little surprise that the best resourced youth forums yield the most effective results in terms of youth participation, and Fitzpatrick et al. (1999: 12) note that 'where youth forums are promoted as part of the governance of a regeneration strategy it needs to be recognised that successful involvement will not come without substantial resources and staff dedicated to the job'. Even well-resourced youth forums, however, confront formidable challenges intrinsic to regeneration processes and community politics. How are the representativeness and accountability of such forums to be established and maintained? Disadvantaged young people tend not to comprise a readily cohesive and consistent constituency. Self-selective processes and/or hand-picking methods are unlikely to produce truly representative bodies. How might youth delegates be represented throughout the decision-making machinery without being marginalised and intimidated within the inevitable complexity of overlapping partnerships, interlocking structures of boards and committees, and the relative formality and jargon-based nature of discussions? Indeed, 'many adults who accept the validity of youth involvement have yet to translate this into change in their own behaviour to let young people into decision making. They expect young people not to participate on their own terms but to adapt to existing structures, processes and language' (Fitzpatrick et al., 1999: 12). Such difficulties should not prohibit attempts to engage young people but they signal the complexity in so doing. The research suggests that there is a great deal of value in other forms of less intensive and shorter-term participation including surveys, conferences and focus groups, which also serve to allow larger numbers of young people to contribute and express their views. Such initiatives are valuable; however, they should not be seen as a legitimate substitute for forum and committee representation but rather as a complementary set of processes. Moreover, as Arnstein incisively observed over thirty years ago, 'participation without redistribution of power is an empty and frustrating process for the powerless. It allows policy holders to claim that all sides were considered, but makes it possible for only some of those sides to benefit. It maintains the status quo' (cited in Henderson, 1995: 62).

Clearly there are no quick-fix solutions to the complex and multifaceted forms of exclusion endured by young people living in disadvantaged neighbourhoods. At the level of area-based regeneration there is much more to learn in respect of meaningful youth participation: how to make organisational structures more receptive and responsive to youth involvement; how to engage in sustained serious dialogue; and how to make participative practices appropriate and effective. There is some evidence that lessons are being learnt at both the central government level (Hodgkin and Newell, 1996; Social Exclusion Unit, 2000a) and the local government level (Willow, 1997; Fitzpatrick et al., 1998; 1999) in this regard. Such lessons include recognising that consultation is a complex process and not a simple one-off event; understanding the need for dialogue and feedback loops and being prepared to act on the perspectives offered by young people; ensuring that participative opportunities apply to *all* young people including those (perhaps especially those) who are apparently most 'disengaged'; and thinking imaginatively and laterally in creating a range of methods for youth participation that do not simply replicate adult processes, structures, procedures and timescales.

Conclusion

> Over the last two decades the gap between the 'worst estates' and the rest of the country has grown. It has left us with a situation that no civilised society should tolerate [. . .] for too long governments have simply ignored the needs of many communities [. . .] a new approach is long overdue.
>
> (Social Exclusion Unit, 1998: Foreword by the Prime Minister, Tony Blair)

It is widely acknowledged that deepening and widening forms of poverty and inequality have disfigured human relations and communities across the UK in its most recent history. We also know that such corrosive socio-economic formations are unevenly distributed. Particular regions, cities within regions, neighbourhoods within cities, and demographic constituencies within neighbourhoods are disproportionately afflicted. Furthermore, we know that young people have especially borne the brunt. Growing up poor, with the pervasive presence of exclusionary processes, blights the lives of too many young people in cities such as Liverpool.

Despite the fact that young people comprise a very substantial proportion of the population, we know that they are at best marginal to area-based regeneration initiatives, and at worst effectively excluded from them. Where does this leave notions of 'citizenship' and 'education for citizenship'? If 'big ideas' are to make any meaningful impact on everyday lived realities then area-based developments have to engage with disadvantaged young people. This will require overcoming the resistance, or indifference, to the extension of youth participation in regeneration policy and practice. It will also require re-balancing policy priorities at central and local government levels. Indeed, despite rhetorical constructions of youth participation within contemporary policy discourse, practical reality has witnessed a far greater emphasis on the surveillance, control and regulation of young people. Young people, almost by definition, are increasingly associated with the 'antisocial' and conceptually confined to the 'disorderly'. The evidence from the Liverpool research, together with many other studies that have focused on disadvantaged young people, confirms that their unequivocal 'pro-social' energies, aspirations and convictions are stultified and suffocated by exclusionary processes. There are deep-rooted complexities, tensions and contradictions here but they must be tackled if 'Building a Better Britain' is to represent more than a politically seductive catchphrase.

References

Alderson, P. (1999), *Civil Rights in Schools, ESRC Children 5–16 Research Programme Briefing*, http://www.esrc.ac.uk/curprog.html

Andersen, H., Munck, R., et al. (1999), *Neighbourhood Images in Liverpool: 'It's All Down to the People'*, York: Joseph Rowntree Foundation

Beck, U. (1992), *Risk Society: Towards a New Modernity*, London: Sage

— (1998), *Democracy Without Enemies*, Cambridge, Polity Press

Bradshaw, J. (1999), 'Children 5–16: Growing into the 21st Century Research Programme', paper presented to the Economic and Social Research Council Conference 23 February 1999, Royal Horticultural Conference Centre, London

British Youth Council (1998), *State of the Young Nation – Seen and Heard*, London: British Youth Council

Cockburn, T. (1998), *Children and Citizenship in Britain — A Case for a Socially Independent Model of Citizenship*, London: Sage

Coles, B. (1995), *Youth and Social Policy*, London: UCL Press

Coppock, V. (1997), '"Mad", "Bad" or "Misunderstood"?', in P. Scraton (ed.), *'Childhood' in 'Crisis'?*, London: UCL Press

CPAG (Child Poverty Action Group) (1997), *Not to be Ignored: Young People, Poverty and Health*, London: CPAG

— (1998), *Poverty: Journal of the Child Poverty Action Group*, No. 101, London: CPAG

Crick, B. (1998), *Education for Citizenship and the Teaching of Democracy in Schools: Final Report of the National Advisory Group on Education*, London,

Department for Education and Employment, Quality and Curriculum Authority

Department for Education and Employment (2000), *Connexions: The Best Start in Life for Every Young Person*, London: Department for Education and Employment

Department of Health (1999), *Statistical Bulletin July 1999 – Statistics from the Regional Drug Misuse Database*, London: Department of Health

Fitzpatrick, S., Hastings, A., and Kintrea, K. (1998), *Including Young People in Urban Regeneration. A Lot to Learn?*, Bristol: Policy Press

— (1999), 'Young People's Participation in Urban Regeneration', *Childright*, 154: 11–12

Forrest, R., and Kearns, A. (1999), *Joined-Up Places? Social Cohesion and Neighbourhood Regeneration*, York: Joseph Rowntree Foundation

Freeman, C., Henderson, P., and Kettle, J. (1999), *Planning with Children for Better Communities*, Bristol: Policy Press

Furlong, A., and Cartmel, F. (1997), *Young People and Social Change: Individualisation and Risk in Late Modernity*, Buckingham: Open University Press

Goldson, B. (1997), 'Locked Out and Locked Up: State Policy and the Systemic Exclusion of Children "In Need" in England and Wales', *Representing Children*, 10(1): 44–55

— (ed.) (1999), *Youth Justice: Contemporary Policy and Practice*, Aldershot: Ashgate

— (ed.) (2000), *The New Youth Justice*, Lyme Regis: Russell House Publishing

Goldson, B., and Chigwada-Bailey, R. (1999), '(What) Justice for Black Children and Young People?', in B. Goldson (ed.), *Youth Justice: Contemporary Policy and Practice*, Aldershot: Ashgate

Goldson, B., and Peters, E. (2000), *Tough Justice: Responding to Children in Trouble*, London: The Children's Society

Gregg, P., Harkness, S., and Machin, S. (1999), *Child Development and Family Income*, York: Joseph Rowntree Foundation

Henderson, P. (ed.) (1995), *Children and Communities*, London: Pluto Press

Hodgkin, R., and Newell, P. (1996), *Effective Government Structures for Children*, London: Calouste Gulbenkian Foundation

Home Office (1997), *No More Excuses – A New Approach to Tackling Youth Crime in England and Wales*, London: Home Office

Howarth, C., Kenway, P., Palmer, G., and Miorelli, R. (1999), *Monitoring Poverty and Social Exclusion 1999*, York: Joseph Rowntree Foundation

Jeffs, T., and Smith, M. (1995), 'Youth', *Developments in Sociology* (11), Lancashire: Causeway Press

Jones, C., and Novak, T. (1999), *Poverty, Welfare and the Disciplinary State*, London: Routledge

Joseph Rowntree Foundation (1998), *'Findings' March 1998 – Income and Wealth: The Latest Evidence*, York: Joseph Rowntree Foundation

— (1999), *'Findings' March 1999 – Child Poverty and Its Consequences*, York: Joseph Rowntree Foundation

— (2000), 'Neighbourhood Management's Role in Tackling Social Exclusion', *Findings in Focus, January/February*, York: Joseph Rowntree Foundation

Kearns, A., and Forrest, R. (1998), 'Social Cohesion, Neighbourhoods and Cities', paper prepared for Housing Studies Spring Conference, University of York, 15–16 April

Lane, T. (1997), *Liverpool City of the Sea*, Liverpool: Liverpool University Press

Lansdown, G. (1999), 'Investing in Democracy: Young People and the Political Process', *Childright*, 154, 8–11

MacDonald, R. (ed.) (1997), *Youth, the 'Underclass' and Social Exclusion*, London: Routledge

Matthews, H., and Limb, M. (1997), 'The Right to a Say: The Development of Youth Councils/Forums within the UK', *Area*, 30(1): 66–78

Meegan, R. (1993), 'Urban Development Corporations, Urban Entrepreneurialism and Locality', in R. Imrie and H. Thomas (eds), *British Urban Policy and the Urban Development Corporations*, London: Paul Chapman

Moore, S. (2000), 'Child Incarceration and the New Youth Justice', in Goldson (ed.)

Novak, T. (1997), 'Young People, Class and Poverty', in H. Jones (ed.), *Towards a Classless Society?*, London: Routledge

Parsons, C. (1996), 'Permanent Exclusions from Schools in England in the 1990s: Trends, Causes and Responses', *Children and Society*, 10(3): 177–86

Roberts, K. (1997), 'Is There an Emerging British "Underclass"? The Evidence from Youth Research', in MacDonald (ed.)

Shropshire, J., and Middleton, S. (1999), *Small Expectations: Learning to be Poor*, York: Joseph Rowntree Foundation

Social Exclusion Unit (1998), *Bringing Britain Together: A National Strategy for Neighbourhood Renewal*, London: The Stationery Office

— (2000a), *Report of Policy Action Team 12: Young People*, London: The Stationery Office

— (2000b), *Report of Policy Action Team 8: Anti-Social Behaviour*, London: The Stationery Office

West, P., and Sweeting, H. (1996), 'Nae Job, Nae Future: Young People and Health in a Context of Unemployment', *Health and Social Care in the Community*, 4: 50–62

Westergaard, J. (1992), 'About and Beyond the Underclass: Some Notes on Influences of Social Climate on British Sociology', *Sociology*, 26: 575–87

White, P., and Woodridge, J. (1998), *The Prison Population in 1997. Home Office Statistical Bulletin 5/98*, London: Home Office

Willow, C. (1997), *Hear! Hear! Promoting Children and Young People's Democratic Participation in Local Government*, London: Local Government Information Unit

8. Elders' Perspectives

John Lansley

To write about older people in a book about the city is to raise the question of whether city living is any different for older people than it is for any other group of adults. Whom do we regard as older, why do we regard them as different and why, above all, do influential groups in society treat older people as problematic?

The first of these questions is indeed seldom asked. A review of studies in the geography of old age (Harper and Laws, 1995) cites a number of papers about older people in rural settings, but none specifically about people in urban situations. Many of the studies that have been done have concentrated on housing design, rather than looking at issues of urban or neighbourhood living. Urban living may then be regarded as normative for older people as it is for anyone else, though we might want to ask whether living in *cities* differs from living in other urban environments. The city is not just a large town: it also implies something beyond the urban about governance and a certain quality of life.

But the question of who is old comes close to the root of the matter. Being – or rather, being regarded as – old is not a simple matter of chronology, since this bears little relationship to people's abilities and patterns of behaviour. Nor is it a reflection of people's physical or mental capacities or decrepitude, which vary widely through the second half of the lifespan. Rather, being old is a cluster of attitudes, on the part of the individual and of the social contacts within which he or she is enmeshed, and which are formed both by individual stereotypes and by the broader factors that underlie social and economic relationships.

These two patterns of perceptions of ageing are well illustrated in the history of gerontological theory. Most gerontology in the early post-war period was based on the pathology of later life. It was observed that older people's social contacts diminished over time, and this role loss (Havighurst, 1963) was initially treated as a state to be remedied with increased social activity. Further studies, however, led to the development of an alternative theoretical model, that of disengagement (Cumming and Henry, 1961). In this analysis, role loss was treated as a natural and beneficial process which enabled the ageing body and psyche to reduce their activities in preparation for the final disengagement of death.

By contrast, a second generation of gerontologists, represented by Estes and Minkler in the USA (Estes, 1979; Minkler and Estes, 1991; 1998) and Phillipson and Walker in Britain (Phillipson, 1982; 1998; Walker, 1981; Phillipson and Walker,

1986), reversed the analysis. Using what they described as a political economy approach, they asked whether the cause of disengagement, which clearly does take place, was the decline in the powers of the individual, or whether it was a process of exclusion imposed by, and in the interest of, the economic concerns of society. Retirement was a necessary method of dealing with a surplus of potential workers in society, and once people had retired, although they might be treated as a reserve army of labour, their relationship to the means of production had fundamentally shifted. Since they were no longer producers, or, in many cases, consumers because of the loss of income that retirement created, they were rather treated as fodder for what Estes (1979) called the 'Ageing Enterprise': a therapeutic industry that structured the lives of older people into a pattern of dependency on formal or informal services.

This model, like its predecessors, is also limited. Recent postmodernist inquiry (Phillipson, 1998; Wilson, 2000) has questioned how satisfactory is an analysis that many older people would themselves reject, on the grounds that they 'don't feel old' (Thompson et al., 1990) and do not behave as though they were controlled by a system of structured dependency. If the older people in the present study appear to suffer from that social exclusion that is the mirror image of disengagement, we need to enquire whether that exclusion is primarily caused by age or by other social divisions that in fact unite them with, rather than dividing them from, their neighbours in Dingle and Speke. The lives of most of these older people appear to be actively supported by a range of informal networks (Wenger, 1989) deriving from kinship ties, coeval relationships, and general neighbourliness.

We thus approach the study with questions about:

- How far older people are a distinct and different group within the local communities;
- How far they are socially excluded, and, if so, whether this exclusion is specific to their age status;
- Whether their lifestyles and culture differ significantly from those of other residents of the two neighbourhoods;
- How far older people are in need of support, and, if so, where that support comes from.

Older People in the City

Our study did not allow anything like a total view of older people and cities. We only dealt with two extremely deprived neighbourhoods. The lives of older people in other neighbourhoods, in the city centre, or in the suburbs, might be very different. To speak of older people and the city, then, requires a great deal of refinement and modification: which people, and consequently, which parts of the city? This is relevant for four reasons:

First, the immediate living environment of older people is important for them, since it is where they will probably spend a higher proportion of their time, compared with, say, those who leave the immediate neighbourhood each day to go to work. While some older people – the WOOPIES (Well-Off Older Persons) and their ilk (Meade, 1989: 12; Falkingham and Victor, 1991) – may be highly mobile and welcome the opportunities for greater mobility that retirement brings, many older people do not possess their own car and are reliant on public transport (Warnes, 1992). This in its turn is likely to be reflected in shopping patterns (Smith, 1991), leisure activities and social contacts, as well as setting time limits to visits further afield. So the experience of the city is partly controlled by the degree of access and type of location that people enjoy.

The second issue, related to this, is the way in which particular areas of the city may be seen as 'belonging' to certain groups of people, or are contested territory between them. The city centre at night, for example, is often seen as the territory of young people. There is also the issue of how cities seek to present themselves: Vesperi (1985) quotes a consultant's report to the City of St Petersburg, Florida, to the effect that the city had an image of being *dominated* by older people, and that it should 'reestablish [its] image as a community of young, *progressive* citizens' rather than of the older people who 'appear to aimlessly walk around downtown St Petersburg during working hours' (Vesperi, 1985: 45, cited in Laws, 1993 [Laws' emphasis]). What areas may older people claim, where are they placed by others, where are they excluded from, and what are the processes that determine these things?

Third, there is the geography of sentiment: people want to go on living in an area because of the memories it holds for them, or the social life that it represents (Rosser and Harris, 1965; Sixsmith, 1990). Equally, if they choose to move away on retirement this may be justified in terms of their friends having already left or because of a sense that the area has lost its value to them (Karn, 1977). If they have lived in a house for a long time, they will have invested in it not only physically and financially, but also emotionally, and they may have very mixed feelings even when, for example, a housing association renovates the property, or when they are moved to a similar house in the next street (Clark et al., 1991: 32).

Fourth, the city, though not unique in this respect, generates a sense of neighbourhood for many people. This relates not only to geographical sentiments, a recognition of familiar bricks and mortar, but also to a sense of reciprocal relationships. The Seebohm Committee's definition of community still has relevance:

> The term 'community' is usually understood to cover both the physical location and the common identity of a group of people [. . .] The notion of a community implies the existence of a network of reciprocal social relationships, which among other things ensure mutual aid and give those who experience it a sense of well-being. (Seebohm, 1968: para. 476)

Later life could be seen as a time to call in some of one's reciprocal debts, but that in turn is to suppose that one's debtors are still present in the locality. The length of time of residence and stability of other residents may thus be of major importance as people get older. Studies have tended to concentrate on the near residence of kin, and indeed there comes a point in dependency when this may be of over-riding importance, but at an earlier stage of semi-dependency, neighbours may be crucial and we shall see in the later discussion how important they were to those whom we interviewed.

These issues lead to consideration of broader sociological questions. Any person's experience of a city will be influenced by their social status. How are we to ascribe elements of age, as opposed to such other elements of class, gender and 'race' to explanations of their lives?

Background

Why do people come to live in cities, and what are the implications of that move? Despite the criticisms levelled against it, Cowgill's theory of modernisation (Cowgill, 1974) still gives a coherent account of the process and of its limitations. His basic thesis is that the modernisation (i.e. technologising) of manufacturing and other industrial processes has led on the one hand to the growth of cities, and on the other hand to a decline in the status of older people, who are seen to lack the knowledge, education and skills to participate in these new methods. The theory is open to a number of criticisms: it oversimplifies historical processes (Fennell et al., 1988; Bond and Coleman, 1990) and it is substantially a gendered theory in its emphasis on employment status (though Palmore [Palmore and Whittington, 1971; Palmore and Manton, 1974] claims to have taken the case of women into his calculations separately). Further, although this may explain why people moved into cities in the first place, and the changing status and roles that this may have given to older people (Anderson, 1974) – a process that is still rele-vant in countries that are 'modernising' today (Tout, 1989) it tells us only a limited amount about people who live in British cities today, and whose families are likely to have been urban dwellers for several generations.

In all cities, housing has not just aged: the social composition of those living in it has changed over time in terms of class, age and family size. Areas move up and down the housing market as decay or gentrification takes place. In Liverpool this was exacerbated by Second World War bombing and the flight to the suburbs and to dormitory towns by the middle classes. As the city expanded, former villages were absorbed, with changes in lifestyle for existing residents. New industries were created (and sometimes subsequently collapsed again). Patterns of housing tenure altered: private landlords declined in number and were replaced by owner occu-pation for some and new landlords, whether city council or housing association, for others. And through all of this, wider economic and social changes were having a massive effect on people's lives.

Although these points are sufficiently obvious, it is important that we should be aware of these demographic, geographic and historical variations when we examine older people in the city. What we are confronted with is not a standard population distribution, but particular cohorts located in particular places as a consequence of urban policies, and who continue to age in their different settings, whether these are places where they have always lived, or places to which they have been moved in consequence of some urban policy decision. They may, in consequence of relocation, be more compelled to rely on their contemporaries for support rather than on the whole local community. Specific patterns of urban demography have developed as a consequence of these movements: we need to take them into account when considering the sociology of any given older population, while at the same time asking how far such cohort effects may fade out over time.

To summarise, life for older city dwellers may cover a wide range of housing experiences. An older person may have lived in the same house for a long time, but have experienced great social changes in the area in which they live, or may have moved at different stages of their lives to very different settings – or they may have *been* moved, often with little consultation about their wishes, and required to rebuild their social relationships in their new settings. This is different from the kin-linked working-class communities described by sociologists of the 1950s and 1960s, though it does relate to the new estates to which the subjects of those studies were being moved (Townsend, 1957; Rosser and Harris, 1965). The recent Keele University study, revisiting Bethnal Green, Woodford and Wolverhampton (Phillipson et al., 2000) gives a fascinating account of how the same areas may have changed over a period of sixty years. We need to develop a social policy of neighbouring and friendship that is much more sensitive than most approaches to date by social services and health authorities, who still seem to work on the basis of individual cases' support networks rather than with any recognition of how urban policy can itself determine that social environment (Wenger, 1984; 1990; 1992).

A significant feature here may be a shift from intergenerational to intragenerational social relationships. On the one hand, greater longevity means that there are more coevals to relate to, while on the other hand the formalisation of relationships by age bands may be a consequence of the physical separation of work and residence: young people go to work elsewhere in the city, leaving elders reliant on other elders for their social contacts. Obviously, this is not just the case for city life: small retirement townships may compel coeval relationships much more strongly (Karn, 1977). And the ageing of society will have its own implications in terms of expanding the numbers of elders who can choose to associate with one another. Jerrome (1992), for example, has argued that elders associate together in clubs, church groups and the like, because they feel excluded by other sectors of society and find among their own contemporaries people with whom they can share their values and understandings of life. At issue here is the question of which people, or what social forces, determine who we have as neighbours. None of us is totally free in this regard, but the people in our study were perhaps less free than most.

The Liverpool Study

As part of the Liverpool study we held discussions with four focus groups of older people, two from Dingle (one group consisting of users of a day centre) and two from Speke. The Speke groups were single-sex (one group of men and one of women), both involved in a church-based community centre; the other Dingle group was of women and again linked to a local church. Obviously, these groups do not give anything like a total picture of the range of elders in these two areas, nor are these districts representative of the city as a whole. In particular, none of the people we talked to was a member of a minority ethnic group.

Earlier chapters have described the two study areas and how the histories of those areas affect the lives of their residents. There are no simple continuities of generation succeeding generation in the same location. In the case of Speke, an estate built in the 1930s and 1950s, as with some similar Liverpool estates, one can see cohort movements: some of the people whom we interviewed had moved there as young families in the 1950s or 1960s and had spent their adult lives there. Their children, on the other hand, have moved away in search of employment, so that Speke now has half the population it had in the 1960s. It has been subject to demo-lition, restructuring of three-storey maisonettes as two-storey houses, and a small amount of sales to sitting tenants: for the most part, though, Speke has one local authority landlord, although recently, ownership of housing stock has passed into housing association control.

In Dingle, an inner-city working-class area, there has been a much more mixed housing history. Some areas were subject to large-scale slum clearance; others became general improvement areas; housing associations and cooperatives, private developers and the city council have all been involved in the renovation and new-build of the current housing stock. There is a mixed ownership pattern, though owner occupation is low; different landlords – city council, housing association and private – have different priorities and agendas, and tenants vary greatly in the length of time they have lived in the area.

These are certainly urban civic dwellers: how do they regard their urban life? We asked them questions about three areas of life: neighbours and the neighbourhood, the physical environment and its maintenance, and regeneration and consultation.

Neighbourhood

'Community' is a highly contested term, but it remains a concept with which people construct their understanding of their own lives. The Speke older women focus group started its account of community attachment with a flourish:

> With regard to the people I don't think you could have a better area.
> That's right.
> We've got plenty of burglars.
> The girl in the Wine Lodge got her throat cut on Saturday night.
> The people.
> It used to be so lovely.
> These [other members of the focus group] are all Speke people, and we're all good friends . . . and we know that if any of us were in trouble we could go to them.
> We all live where we can get to each other.
> We've got phones.

This exchange brings out nicely the dualism of many attitudes towards people's home areas: yes, there are burglars and throat-cutters, but against this there is a long-held belief in local community life – 'the people', the source of help in times of trouble, even though, in practice, evidence for this may rely on a small friendship group. They spoke warmly of one another in the group, and implied that they had other long-standing neighbours for whom this was also true. A comment from the organiser of a visiting scheme for older people in Speke is relevant:

> We don't get a lot of referrals from Speke. They will say 'my daughter only lives down the road', or 'my grand-daughter will do the shopping' . . .

But, like their fellows in Dingle, the Speke elders are also aware of the limits to community: there are those without family, those who live on their own, those who lock themselves in at night. Going to bed early may be a sign of loneliness, or of a need to lock yourself in securely. It can also be caused by fuel poverty:

> She goes to bed at eight o'clock . . . she hasn't got the money to keep the gas going . . . You may as well be in bed than using all the electricity and gas keeping the place warm . . . Look at all the old age pensioners that go and sit in the likes of Asda, on the benches, because it's warm.

'Community', then, is determined by such factors as primary relationships, particularly at family level (though family mobility may be placing more of these responsibilities on coevals), the physical environment and those charged with looking after it and, to a decreasing extent, the working community – decreasing not in terms of retirement but because of the decline in the number of available jobs. Speke, which was built with its own industrial estate, has seen virtually all those factories close.

Neighbourliness is based on mutuality and we were given plenty of examples of this:

> You can always find someone who will help . . . Say, the lights go off or you have a flood or something, or you get locked out, you will always find somebody who will do something. For instance, she [another member of the group] lost her key the other night: well, what did we do but wake her neighbour up, and he practically crawled up the wall and he managed to get in through the window. These are the so-called scallies [rogues] and they're always willing to help.

> There's a girl in our road who was left on her own just before Christmas; she had three children with another on the way . . . We went to town and even got money towards groceries and things, and we got beautiful cards from her thanking us and saying that the children had never had a Christmas like it.

But not all neighbours are like that and not all relationships are based on this kind of mutuality. A lot of complaints were made about new tenants being moved into the area, particularly one-parent families whose children were seen as being out of control. These uncontrolled incomers were seen as a major change to the area:

I've got a problem family put by me. I feel sorry for the two boys, because they don't seem to bother with them at all . . . It's not their fault, they're just not taught what's right.

You used to kill to get into our road . . . It's still smashing . . . but you start going up [it] and, I've got nothing against families with young children, but . . . they have no control over them, they just let them do what they want.

'It's still smashing': here lies the ambivalence of many of the attitudes as we heard them. Yes, the area is run down physically; jobs are a thing of the past; the council has given up on repairs; shops are closing; but still, so the message goes, the people are great – but some of the people are less great than others.

People are perhaps clinging to the people they know and the relationships they have. Out-migration of younger kin is clearly an issue in an area with high unemployment, irrespective of any more general issues of geographical mobility. Kin networks appeared to be declining: sons were moving off to the south coast in search of jobs; daughters, on the other hand, were staying more locally – perhaps living in Runcorn (a new town in Cheshire, 12 miles from Speke) but calling in frequently on the way to or from work. Even those who at first gave an impression of isolation sometimes turned out to have considerable family support. One day-centre user acknowledged that her son, who lived out in the suburbs, called in most days, and was going to redecorate her flat over the summer – 'But I don't like to ask him to do too much, because his wife doesn't like it . . .'

Finally, we need to recognise the role of institutions in the neighbourhood. Dingle was rich in a wide variety of voluntary and statutory agencies, at least some of which offered support to older people. Speke had considerably fewer. In both cases, while recognising that we drew three of our focus groups from groups who met on church premises and therefore may well give a biased response, the role of the churches appeared to be important in both expressive and instrumental ways. As Jerrome (1992) has pointed out, churches offer an important meeting place for elders, and the groups we met were regularly attending lunch clubs and other social events, whether or not they attended services. The Speke church, in particular, had a large programme of social care, carrying out basic support such as help with transport, picking up shopping and prescriptions, and generally keeping an eye on people. In Speke and Dingle there are very few resident 'professionals' other than the local clergy, who are in a position to offer advice about how to deal with officialdom and other professionals. One clergyman closely involved in the community commented that many of the local people were likely to go off the deep end in meetings with officials, and he had to do an interpretative job in order to maintain communication channels.

Environment

In both places there were three main themes: boarded-up houses, closure of shops, and inadequate and badly maintained public services. These issues have been described in other chapters and they will not be repeated at length here, beyond noting that the perceptions of the older people were very similar to those of other residents. Rather, we shall comment briefly on how these issues affected older people specifically.

As regards housing, most of those we talked to had lived in their houses for many years and they consequently had an attachment to their homes based on memory and sentiment, as well on the house's current physical condition (Sixsmith, 1990). All the same, the fact that older people spend more time per day in their homes than younger people who are out at work means that the physical condition, in relation to such aspects as heating, ease of mobility and security, is important (Clark et al., 1991).

Shops are another important item for older people, particularly those with limited mobility and the decline of shopping facilities in Speke, the closure of the Co-Op supermarket in Dingle, or the arson attack on a corner shop near the homes of two of our respondents had meant that shopping was much more difficult for them. In an age when shopping is increasingly geared towards the car owner who visits the supermarket once a week, or even the computer owner who orders deliveries from a website, the shopping patterns of older people appear to the big commercial powers as an irrelevance (Vincent, 1999).

There were other environmental issues in Speke. Attitudes polarised around two projects: the redesigning of the park and planting trees on the main road at the edge of the estate. The park had been a valued resource, perhaps particularly for older people:

> . . . it was a lovely park. There were bowling greens, tennis courts, the lads could play football. And suddenly they moved in and there were these hills being built, so I asked the man who was doing it, and he told me that it was a long-term thing: we'd see how it would be balanced out and be landscaped in a few years, but it's ridiculous! Nobody goes there now, only some people walking their dogs . . . and when it goes dark you daren't go in there.

It was later acknowledged that damage to the rose garden and the bowling green had been due to vandalism, but the main culprit was seen to be the council. The planting of trees along Speke Boulevard, the main road on the edge of the district, by the Partnership programme was treated with well-nigh universal scorn:

> You know they're planting all these trees down the Boulevard, well, someone said to me, the reason they're doing that is to hide Speke!

Services, again, seem to be moving away. Speke in particular had lost its police and fire stations, adding to their sense of isolation. Dingle was better provided with resources but people questioned who really used them. One respondent commented about the local sports centre:

> They come in their posh cars and park, it's so expensive that the local people can't afford to use it. To have a swim it's nearly £2. So unless you are working you can't afford to go,

which is so sad when it's in our area. It's supposed to be our sports centre: is it heck! It's really for the suburbs.

Two valued local amenities in Speke were the Credit Union and the Minor Injuries Unit. These had both been created by local people, either through their own mutual activities or by pressuring the health authority: 'Everything we've got, we've fought for'. This is not a perception unique to the older residents, but it is certainly one that they shared.

Regeneration

Again, there was little to distinguish the attitudes of older people from those of other groups over discussions about the regeneration of the two areas. Some members of the male Speke focus group had attended early consultative meetings but had concluded that the views expressed at those meetings were not being taken seriously by those responsible for the scheme, and had stopped attending.

> People feel let down . . . When this Speke Garston [Partnership] first started up . . . the turn out was quite good. People from the community were there asking questions, but after a while there was no-one going because they felt that their questions were not being answered. They thought . . . they had no say in how the money was spent, and nobody was listening to what they wanted, [so] they stopped going.

Older people were as concerned as others about the state of their areas – perhaps more so, because they had lived there longer, and they spent more time there. There may be more nostalgic belief in the good quality of both community spirit and the physical quality of the areas, particularly in Speke, in elders' responses, because of this temporal element. With this goes a belief in a style of local government which, it was suggested, had now disappeared, but which can be illustrated in the changed nature of Speke Park. In the old days, it was said, there used to be park keepers, who not only maintained the physical fabric of the parks, but also policed standards of behaviour. Now things have changed. In a seminar given to our research group, Ray Pahl commented in passing that park keepers were being replaced by community workers. The future of areas was now in the people's own hands. As we have seen, there was considerable local scepticism about this claim. But it also suggests a required shift in civic behaviour. If you want things to happen, you have to participate. It won't be done for you. Contrast this with the municipal socialism of the post-war years. It may have been paternalistic, and it almost certainly did not give such good levels of provision as people, looking back, now believe. But it was based on consensual attitudes about standards and kinds of provision. People may now 'participate' in plans for their local communities and complain when they are not listened to sufficiently. But is this in part a second best: would many people, and perhaps particularly older people, prefer not to have to participate, if they could have decent local services in the first place? The contrast between the park keeper and the community worker seems symbolic of a fundamental shift in civic life.

Conclusion

This chapter began with a series of questions about older people in cities. Many of these questions remain. We have, after all, only described the views of very small numbers of people living in what are in many ways quite atypical areas of Liverpool. Within that setting, however, certain points may remain.

One immediate issue is one of historical demography. In Speke, as we have seen, there were people who had lived there for anything from 20 to 40 years. They had arrived on what was then a new estate with young families and were now in their sixties and seventies, with their families grown up and often moved away. There were still some areas with a high proportion of older residents, though that was now breaking down, and in some areas there were uneasy relations between older residents and more recent incomers. In Dingle, by contrast, where there had been much more mixed developments and redevelopments over a longer period, the pattern of location and length of residence were much more mixed. Even here, though, there were complaints about new arrivals who were, it was claimed, unable to control their children.

It appears, though we need more study of our findings, that where there has been an age cohort living together for a long period, they have tended to develop coeval horizontal patterns of relationships – possibly reinforced if their children have moved away from the area. This pattern of social networks is somewhat different from those described by Wenger (1989) and other writers and we should emphasise that three of our focus groups were composed of fairly fit 'young elders' in their sixties and early seventies, with only slight support needs. If they had had serious needs, a different pattern of support relationships might have emerged, depending more, perhaps, on kinship support.

At the other extreme, we may also note that the nature of relationships in the two areas was much more tightly structured around neighbourliness than has often been proposed by sociologists such as Abrams (Bulmer, 1986). Against Cowgill's (1974) claims for modernisation, which seem in part to be descended from Tönnies' *Gemeinschaft/Gesellschaft* dichotomy, social relations in Dingle and Speke seemed to remain firmly in the *Gemeinschaft* tradition of close, multifaceted mutual relationships. We can attribute these partly to a high level of need for mutual support, and partly to sentiment about an area in which people may have lived for a long period.

From this we derive questions about the lifestyles of older people. Do they differ, on the one hand, from those of older people in other parts of the city, or, on the other hand, from those of other people living in these two areas? From the questions we asked, it appears that older people have much in common with their fellow residents in Speke and Dingle. If there are differences between age groups, they are differences of upholding traditions of 'good' neighbourly behaviour, of valuing a history of good supportive relations which have become part of their sense of living in these areas – and, interestingly, these attitudes appeared more marked in Speke than in Dingle. Their lifestyles were formed, for the most part, not because of their age, but because of their common experiences of developing strategies to combat social deprivation, which have grown up over many years.

Things were not, in reality, as simple as that. These were people who were supporting one another, and who were reliant – and probably would be more so in the future – on family help. But they still regarded themselves as independent and active: like so many other older people, they 'didn't feel old'.

And finally, there is the question of access to city resources. Put bluntly, these are areas of the city that are seriously deprived of basic resources that most of us take for granted: shops, transport, jobs, house repairs, and adequate statutory services of all kinds. The significant point here seems to be that deprivation is experienced not according to people's age, but according to their social class. These are the kinds of deprived urban working-class communities that the Bethnal Green school wrote about in the 1950s and 1960s. In such a setting, age becomes largely irrelevant: we had the same kinds of responses from all age groups. Disengagement becomes not a matter of the individual social psychology of ageing: rather we see areas of the city which have been structurally disengaged from the rest of the city, and whose residents are seeking to re-engage. This is social exclusion with a vengeance, for all social groups in the area. The primary awareness and identification of our older respondents was as residents of Dingle or Speke. For such people, social policy responses need to be based on general social improvements, rather than specific policies for older people. Their chances of 'escape', as suggested by proponents of 'loose' communities rather than the old 'tight' groupings, may be fewer than those of other people, but then they don't want to escape. 'It's a smashing area . . .' – if only.

References

Anderson, M. (1974), *Family Structure in Nineteenth Century Lancashire*, Cambridge: Cambridge University Press

Bond, J., and Coleman, P. (1990), *Ageing in Society: An Introduction to Social Gerontology*, London: Sage

Bulmer, M. (1986), *Neighbours: The Work of Philip Abrams*, Cambridge: Cambridge University Press

Clark, H., Enevoldson, H., Lansley, J., and Smith, A. (1991), 'Helping Elderly Tenants of Housing Associations to Stay in Their Own Homes', *Applied Community Studies*, 1(1): 23–28

Cowgill, D. O. (1974), 'The Ageing of Populations and Societies', *Annals of the American Academy of Political and Social Science*, 415: 1–18

Cumming, E., and Henry, W. E. (1961), *Growing Old: The Process of Disengagement*, New York: Basic Books

Estes, C. (1979), *The Aging Enterprise*, San Francisco: Jossey Bass

Falkingham, J., and Victor, C. (1991), 'The Myth of the Woopie?: Incomes, the Elderly and Targeting Welfare', *Ageing and Society*, 11(4): 471–93

Fennell, G., Phillipson, C., and Evers, H. (1988), *The Sociology of Old Age*, Milton Keynes: Open University Press

Harper, S., and Laws, G. (1995), 'Rethinking the Geography of Ageing', *Progress in Human Geography*, 19(2): 199–221

Havighurst, R. J. (1963), 'Successful Ageing', in R. H. Williams, C. Tibbitts and W. Donahue (eds), *Processes of Ageing*, Vol. I, New York: Atherton

Jerrome, D. (1992), *Good Company*, Edinburgh: Edinburgh University Press

Karn, V. (1977), *Retiring to the Seaside*, London: Routledge and Kegan Paul

Laws, G. (1993), '"The Land of Old Age": Society's Changing Attitudes Toward Urban Built Environments for Elderly People', *Annals of the Association of American Geographers*, 83(4): 672–93

Meade, C. (1989), *The Thoughts of Betty Spital*, Harmondsworth: Penguin

Minkler, M., and Estes, C. (1991), *Critical Perspectives on Ageing: The Political and Moral Economy of Growing Old*, New York: Baywood

— (1998), *Critical Gerontology: Perspectives from Political and Moral Economy*, New York: Baywood

Palmore, E., and Manton, K. (1974), 'Modernisation and Status of the Aged', *Journal of Gerontology*, 29(2): 205–10

Palmore, E., and Whittington, F. (1971), 'Trends in the Relative Status of the Aged', *Social Forces*, 50: 84–91

Phillipson, C. (1982), *Capitalism and the Construction of Old Age*, London: Macmillan

— (1998), *Reconstructing Old Age*, London: Sage

Phillipson, C., Bernard, M., Phillips, J., and Ogg, J. (2000), *The Family and Community Life of Older People: Social Networks and Social Support in Three Urban Areas*, London: Routledge

Phillipson, C., and Walker, A. (1986), *Ageing and Social Policy: A Critical Assessment*, Aldershot: Gower

Rosser, C., and Harris, C. (1965), *The Family and Social Change*, London: Routledge and Kegan Paul

Rowles, G. (1986), 'The Geography of Ageing and the Aged: Towards an Integrated Perspective', *Progress in Human Geography*, 10: 511–39

Seebohm, F. (Chair) (1968), *Report of the Committee on Local Authority and Allied Personal Social Services* (Cmnd 3073), London: HMSO

Sixsmith, A. (1990), 'The Meaning and Experience of "Home" in Later Life', in B. Bytheway and J. Johnson (eds), *Welfare and the Ageing Experience*, Aldershot: Avebury

Smith, G. C. (1991), 'Grocery Shopping Patterns of the Ambulatory Elderly', *Environment and Behaviour*, 23(1): 86–114

Thompson, P., Itzin, C., and Abendstern, M. (1990), *I Don't Feel Old: The Experience of Later Life*, Oxford: Oxford University Press

Tout, K. (1989), *Ageing in Developing Countries*, Oxford: Oxford University Press

Townsend, P. (1957), *The Family Life of Old People*, London: Routledge and Kegan Paul

Vesperi, M. (1985), *City of Green Benches: Growing Old in a New Downtown*, Ithaca, NY: Cornell University Press

Vincent, J. (1999), *Politics, Power and Old Age*, Buckingham: Open University Press

Warnes, A. M. (1992), *Homes and Travel: Local Life in the Third Age* (Carnegie Enquiry into the Third Age, Research Paper 5), Dunfermline: Carnegie UK Trust

Walker, A. (1981), 'Towards a Political Economy of Old Age', *Ageing and Society*, 1: 73–94

Wenger, G. C. (1984), *The Supportive Network*, London: Allen & Unwin

— (1989), 'Support Networks in Old Age – Constructing a Typology', in M. Jefferys (ed.), *Ageing in the 20th Century*, London: Routledge

— (1990), 'Elderly Carers: The Need for Appropriate Interventions', *Ageing and Society*, 10: 197–219

— (1992), *Help in Old Age – Facing Up to Change*, Liverpool: Liverpool University Press for the Institute of Human Ageing

Wilson, G. (2000), *Understanding Old Age: Critical and Global Perspectives*, London: Sage

Part III: Transformation

9. Living in the City: Poverty and Social Exclusion

Tony Novak

The problem of the decline of poor working-class areas, and the possibilities for their regeneration, have been a key concern of urban policy for many years. More than many other cities, Liverpool has over this time been a focus of most of the initiatives – from the early Community Development Projects through to Objective One and the Single Regeneration Budget – that have attempted to deal with these problems. Their failure significantly to impact on poverty in the city says much about the systemic limitations of past and current regeneration strategies in the face of structural economic change and decline and widening inequality that cannot adequately be examined here. But they also reveal a high degree of continuity in the assumptions made about such neighbourhoods that need to be challenged.

Most regeneration initiatives have been based on a view, implicit or explicit, of poor communities as deficient and defective. It is an assumed lack of capacity – and hence the need to build it – that is seen as lying at the heart of the problem. Whether it is through apathy, the lack of education and skills, the absence of social and support networks, or the loosely defined threat of 'antisocial behaviour', the problems of poor communities, like the problem of poverty itself, are frequently seen as located within the individuals and communities who suffer from it.

This chapter sets out to challenge such assumptions. Based on a series of interviews in two working-class communities in Liverpool, Dingle and Speke (see Andersen et al., 1999), it attempts to give a voice to those who have been involved in community action and regeneration, some for many years, but whose views are often not heard or are simply ignored. What these interviews reveal are communities that, despite their obvious economic problems and lack of material resources, are in many other ways vibrant and resourceful. They show people who, despite numerous setbacks and a constant uphill struggle to get their voices heard, remain committed to their area and to their own role in its improvement. Above all they show communities that have the capacity, the skills and the knowledge to bring about substantial improvement and change, but whose aspirations are blocked by the implementation of regeneration strategies 'from above'.

Community participation is fast becoming a mantra in regeneration projects, but if urban regeneration is to have any hope of success it not only has to address the fundamental and structural economic decline of many communities; it also has to give the lead to communities themselves. Token participation and consultation are not enough. This may well bring an unwelcome message to the professionals and the so-called 'partners' who currently dominate regeneration initiatives. It also lays down the challenge of a real transfer of power from both local and central government. Whether the desire for urban regeneration is willing to go so far is another question, but without it current initiatives will only add to the long list of failed attempts in the past.

Living in a Slum?

Although both areas have more than their share of poverty and unemployment and the problems associated with these, the reality of life in Dingle and Speke appears far removed from the overwhelmingly negative images of the 'socially excluded'. Indeed, such images, frequently articulated by 'outsiders', rankle greatly with those who live there. As one resident recounted:

> Paddy Ashdown visited the estate last week and compared it to Sarajevo; he said that Speke was worse than Sarajevo! Some of the comments he made did a disservice to the people of Speke. Speke is not a Sarajevo; Speke is quite a nice estate. The only problem is that you have these people who come flying in from here, there and everywhere who don't live on the estate and can't see the good things that actually happen . . .

For many people who live in both Dingle and Speke the poverty of the areas produces a mixture of reactions. On the one hand, they are seen as neighbourhoods in decline, with little to offer in the way of employment, amenities or future prospects. As one resident put it: 'we're all living in a slum'. On the other hand, they are places that are fiercely defended – often by the same people.

Frequently, this polarised image is understood by drawing a distinction between the poor physical state and amenities of the area, and the qualities of the people who live there. According to one Speke resident, 'the people are great, but the houses are terrible on this estate'. The failure of outsiders to engage with the community, to get beneath the surface of physical decline and the stereotypes of the people who live there, was a frequent source of complaint.

It was the people of the area – the networks of friends and families and the support they offered – that for most people defined what was positive about where they lived: 'It's all down to the people . . . we've got a brilliant community'. These networks were above all else what made the neighbourhoods attractive and, in terms of coping with the problems they faced, helped people get through. This was especially apparent among older people, and older women in particular. As one group of older women we talked to saw it:

> You can always find someone who will help . . . Say the lights go off or you have a flood or something . . . or you get locked out . . . you'll always find somebody who will do something . . . And if you don't know somebody, then someone else will.

For one woman it was this circle of friends and neighbours – 'and it's not just a small group of us, there's a wide circle' – that made all the difference:

When I first came out of hospital, 10 years ago now, my doctor said to me that they were building some bungalows, and would I like a bungalow? He told me to think about it, and I did, and I thought 'No, I wouldn't'. Because I could stand at my door just getting fresh air and people would pass by and say 'I'm just going to the Parade; is there anything you want?' And I would miss that. You won't get that anywhere else, so there was no way I was leaving.

What is important in such networks and relationships is not just that 'it gives you a nice warm feeling to know that they care'. It is also the attention to detail, and the knowledge of what is needed in times of crisis or an emergency that comes from a shared experience. As one member of a housing co-operative in Dingle recounted:

We also have a little welfare fund in our co-op for when anyone is in hospital, to help with the taxis for the partner to go up or whatever, or if anyone dies we can help with the costs . . . I can set a prime example here. My son was seriously run over, 14 years ago now, and I just couldn't believe it. I knew I had good friends; I knew I had good neighbours, but on the odd occasion I just came home to change clothes (he was on a life support machine), I wouldn't even get to my back door before there would be people there with a car waiting to take me back to the hospital . . . You wouldn't believe the help and support we got . . . Even the day we brought him home, a couple of them had got my key and gone in and set a party up in our house, and there was a tea cooking and all the house was cleaned. It was unbelievable. It wasn't just money, it was everything . . . offers of child support, sweets for the other children because they thought they possibly weren't getting the attention that they usually got, cards going up, phone calls, offers of cups of tea . . . You know: 'Come in and have a chat; how are you feeling? We know your son is bad, but how are you?' I will never forget that, and that is just an example. It goes on with smaller things as well. Welfare wise there is a lot of help, even if it's just a chat and a cup of tea. It's the support.

It is, moreover, a support that is reciprocal. While the group of older women we talked to in Speke valued the support of those around them, so they also offered support to others:

There's a girl in our road who was left on her own just before Christmas. She had three children, with another one on the way. We're not blowing our trumpets or nothing – but this is the way it goes – we got them little things. We went to town, metaphorically, and even got money towards groceries, and we got beautiful cards from her thanking us, and saying that the children had never had a Christmas like it.

This sort of support is commonplace – 'this is the way it goes' – providing not only, or even mainly, material support but a level of emotional and social assistance that shows that other people care.

'Public' Services

In contrast, help and support from the statutory services were seen as less than forthcoming:

> If you go [to] the Social Services, to the people who are supposed to count, the response is that they haven't got any money, can't get any money, the grants have run out, you'll have to wait until next year until they get some money – so you just don't go there.

Over the 1980s and 1990s the relationship of the state in particular to poor communities has deteriorated markedly (Jones and Novak, 1999). Public services have been cut; some have disappeared altogether, while others have been pared back to a core of activities that have more to do with containing and controlling the consequences of poverty than with meeting the needs and welfare of the population they are meant to serve. As a result large parts of the so-called 'welfare state' are increasingly seen as part of the problem rather than part of the solution as the approach they adopt becomes more punitive and with less positive support to offer. In this context the reluctance to approach statutory services is not only a matter of lack of resources:

> We had a meeting about domestic violence, and we said that if people see you going into Social Services you get a bad name. They'll think there's something wrong with you: you're doing something to your kids; they're going to take your kids away. So people won't go there.

Other local authority services were similarly seen as having little to offer. The Housing Department in particular was a source of criticism; according to other women:

> I had a house and it flooded out three years ago. They never repaired it. I had to move in with my mum and dad because they wouldn't do the repairs.

> My electricity blew and I was left in the dark with a baby for two days because the electrician was off. For two days they left me in the dark to use candles.

As one woman put it, 'the Council don't really do a lot for us'. This came with a sense of resignation, but also disappointment. Little was expected of the council and its officials, but at the same time there was a sense of genuine dismay that the latter had little attachment to the areas they worked in:

> I went into the school office and I said 'Look, we've got a great house here, are there any of the teachers looking for a great house?' and the reaction I got was quite weird: you know, there's no way in which any teacher in a staff room like that would consider that they would live on the estate, and I think that this is one of the great shames . . . There are no social workers, there are no teachers, there are no police who both live and work on the estate, which I think is quite significant, we could do with that.

Working-class communities have a long history of ambivalence towards the state (Jones and Novak, 2000), one that has in some ways grown as the state has become ever more involved in people's lives. On the one hand, the state provides many of the things that people need, in the areas of health, education, housing or income; at the same time, these services and benefits are provided in ways that are often experienced as hostile, demeaning and unsympathetic. It has long been argued

(London Edinburgh Weekend Return Group, 1980) that those who work for the state, and who seek to use its powers for the benefit of poor communities, need to recognise this ambivalence. Above all it means that attention has to be paid to the quality of the relationships that those who depend on state services encounter. At heart, what this calls for is a fundamental level of respect on the part of welfare professionals and other state workers towards those they work with. In a society that is polarised and in which government continues the 'coercive tilt' of state services, it also calls for welfare workers increasingly to decide whose side they are on, and to make a commitment to the communities they serve. As Bob Holman has argued, some of the most successful community-based regeneration projects are those where the professionals who work in them have a commitment to the area. In his review of one such project in Bristol where he had worked he noted:

> The project became regarded as part of the neighbourhood. Not least, the staff grew up with families. It was easier to relate with some disruptive teenagers when they had been known since they were small. The essence was a neighbourhood approach developed by staff who lived long-term in the area. These features do not feature prominently in the publications of New Labour's youth justice board or Social Exclusion Unit. In favour now are short-term interventions aimed at targeted youngsters by professionals who commute in. (Holman, 2000: 7)

A Disappearing Infrastructure

While economic decline may begin with job losses, the resulting population loss and decline in spending power soon lead to the disappearance of other amenities crucial to community life. In both areas, residents complained of the lack of shopping facilities and public amenities – something that had been seen to decline significantly, in particular in Speke:

> We used to have a Kwik Save but that's gone. We had a fire service but that's gone. We had a water works but that's gone. We had Brown's clothes shop but that's gone. We had shoe shops but they've gone. The bank went, and when that went, well, the business was gone.

As in most poor areas, the flight of local shops, banks and other services means not only that access is more difficult, but also that the poor end up paying more. As one Dingle resident saw it:

> At one time you could buy anything at all. You can't now: you have to go to these supermarkets. Say if you want to buy a couple of screws, you have to buy a packet of about 20, and you might not have the money to buy 20, so you do without.

In Speke, isolated at the edge of the city, the lack of local shopping amenities was felt to be most acute. The closure of Kwik Save had left only two food shops on the estate: 'because they're the only ones in Speke they can charge whatever they want'. Shopping elsewhere means a bus ride, and if there are children to be taken along, the cost of fares is considerable. Trips into town also mean further expense:

> If you want to buy shoes for your kids you've got to drag them into town . . . and they
> start playing up as soon as you get there . . . McDonald's, that's the first thing they say . . .
> You go into town to get something specific and end up coming home without what you
> wanted, and the kids with a 'Happy Meal'.

Apart from the expense, the lack of public transport is also a problem, especially 'later on in the evening, there are very few buses coming into Speke . . . At rush hour times it's not too bad, and Saturdays are not too bad, but on Sunday you've got no chance'. Following the closure of the only bank in Speke, residents now have to make a trip to neighbouring Garston. This too creates its problems for the viability of the local economy: 'they'll draw their money out and they'll spend it in Garston, and so money is being drained away because of a simple thing like a bank closing'. And so the spiral of local decline continues.

Self-help

In many poor working-class communities there is now a sense of abandonment (Campbell, 1993). As the private sector has withdrawn, and public services have been cut, or become more constrained and punitive in what they offer, and has even adopted the same principles of the marketplace, people are left with a sense that they have been deserted, with only themselves left to rely on.

In the face of the consequences of such 'market forces' – 'we have no control over banks; their business is not social services; if they want to go, they'll go' – both communities had established credit unions. For some, the credit union was largely irrelevant – 'we never have any to save' – but for most of the people we talked to about them, they were a significant improvement:

> The Credit Union took over the bank for the people of Speke, to get rid of the loan sharks
> . . . They used to charge exorbitant interest rates. You could borrow £100 but you'd end
> up paying back £150. And some of them were taking the Family Allowance and every-
> thing. So we got rid of them by getting the Credit Union in.

What was more significant, however, was that this was seen as the product of local initiative: 'Nobody outside Speke did that. It was Speke that did that. It was ourselves that got the Credit Union'. The same was true of other grass-roots initiatives such as the Well Woman Clinic:

> The people got that going, again . . . We had nowhere; if the kids fell over or cut them-
> selves they had nowhere to go because they started cutting all the accident and emer-
> gency services. The nearest one is in town . . . So a group of mothers got together and
> said something would have to be done. They started the ball rolling, and more mothers
> got in touch, and it all started from there.

Such initiatives defined the communities' response to the problems of poverty and neglect they experienced – 'everything we've got we've fought for. We really have.' Like many other poor communities, both Dingle and Speke boasted countless examples of initiatives set up by local people, ranging from playgroups and youth clubs to centres for older people. Far from being disorganised communities, they are vibrant and full of ideas and aspirations. Often these initiatives are set up in the face of outside indifference and lack of support:

> We've all been in community groups that have had bits of money that we've raised and funded ourselves. But if you go to these big bosses they don't want to know you. Unless you have a big name behind, you're not on. So you've got to be able to say 'Sir' or 'Lord' someone is behind . . . It's who you know. If you're doing it yourself, they're not interested.

In Dingle, a housing cooperative had been formed in 1979, following the clearance of the old tenement blocks:

> The old blocks were getting scattered everywhere, so we decided to stay as a group and do something about it . . . They kind of tore the heart out of it. That's why we decided to stick together. The council wouldn't help so we had to do something ourselves.

Charged by a desire to take control over their own housing – 'we wanted to manage our own, build our own and design our own' – the group, one of a number of housing cooperatives set up in the area, went on to build and manage 36 houses. Here again was a model of grass-roots activism and success, and one again that was striking both in its ability to respond to the day-to-day realities of working-class life and in the evidence it offered of the capacities of working people to take control over their own situation. Their struggle had not been an easy one. Faced in its early days by a Militant-dominated city council, their hopes and plans had from the start been met with hostility and criticism:

> They didn't think we were capable of controlling all this money, they just didn't think we could do it . . . At the end of the day we were all working-class people and they were just laughing at us.

As Colin Ward (1990; 1991) has argued, there are immense reserves of creativity, imagination, skill and ability within most working-class neighbourhoods. Although these emerge in community initiatives and the thousand and one ways in which people organise their leisure activities and social lives,[1] for the most part they go untapped, stifled by the fear that those in power have of unleashing working-class potential.

Against the Odds

It is, of course, possible to romanticise and exaggerate 'community spirit' and the extent of community and family support. Families are not always what people want to turn to: 'It can be good in a way, but in other ways it's bad. It's good to have them there, but you can't move sometimes without your family knowing what you're

---

[1] For a good study of this in the USA, see Boyte, 1980.

doing.' Yet for the most part it was the networks of support and friendships and the activities they involved that defined above all else what was positive about the areas people lived in.

Although these support networks were seen as valuable, they were also viewed as in decline, with the space and time for community involvement squeezed by the pressures of getting by and making a living:

> People are moving too fast . . . A lot of people are out at work all day . . . when you go in through your front door now, your door shuts, and that's it.

At the same time, activists can often seem thin on the ground, and the wider community reluctant to get involved. But the decline of involvement of residents in community initiatives is often the product of disappointment:

> We're not as involved as we used to be years ago, because when we do try to get a new initiative going we hit a brick wall . . . We get ignored because there are bigger things going on. It's a hierarchy: they set out strategies, so the little people don't have the strength, they can't force anything through.

> The spirit has gone as well. We've been promised that much and been let down so many times, you lose hope and people don't trust the groups again. They don't listen to promises anymore, they just look at it with scepticism. Perhaps if the people said what they would like to see and it appeared then the next project that came along, they'd think 'Well, we got it last time' and then you'd see them coming out in force. But it's when the promises don't materialise. It's been going on for years now and people just sit back and say 'Yeah, I'll believe it when I see it' and that's it.

Despite this, evidence of and pride in the level of community activity and involvement remained widespread. This is not to say that residents saw such activities as capable of solving all their problems:

> We've got a whole range of voluntary groups and community groups . . . But what we still have not managed to cure is the economic deprivation of the area . . . We could spend £100 million on this estate, but in ten years time we would be back to where we are now, because we would still have major unemployment, and all the social problems that go with it. That's the problem: it's unemployment that's created most of the problems up here.

It is, however, not only unemployment that creates problems for such communities. Their ability to respond to these problems is also affected by the new jobs and the new more casual labour market that are promoted as the solution. The fact that those with jobs increasingly have to work long, unsociable hours, and that many need more than one low-paid job to make ends meet, adds to the pressures and tensions within families and the wider neighbourhood. In a country where those in employment work the longest hours in Europe, not only are people more tired, but they have less time for the social networks and activities that make up a community.

Concern for Young People

While unemployment remained a major problem, by far the greatest concern expressed by the people we talked to in both areas was for young people, and especially for those teenagers who fell between the provision made for younger children and the activities of adults:

> The kids today are in a no-win situation: they're too young for one thing, and they're too old for something else . . . Someone round here was chasing the kids away the other day, and they actually shouted back, 'Well, do something for us; there's nothing else for us to do, is there?'

In part the problems of young people were seen by some adults to reflect a general social neglect: 'I have known for a long, long time', said one, 'that in this country kids will come last. They will pull out all the stops for pop stars, royalty, anything you mention, but the kids will come last. We're a very coldhearted nation when it comes to children.' Of more immediate concern, however, was the bleak future that, in the context of the collapse of meaningful work, most young people from such communities now face:

> Over the last 20 or 30 years, the youth have changed, life has changed. Say 20 or 25 years ago when our parents left school, they walked into jobs. As they've grown up, everywhere has shut down, their mums and dads are made redundant, coming out of work, brought up in poverty. And all they say is, 'What's the point in having an education because there are no jobs to go to at the end?'

Added to these pressures were the stereotypes that young people were faced with. These were common in young people's encounters with the police:

> If there's a group of lads, the police will pass them by, they won't stop and search them. But you get one kid or two kids together, and they could be just going to the shop and they'll stop them and search them.

> My son came in from work one night, he had his tea and went down to his friends. He got halfway there and he was stopped and questioned and then made to empty his pockets and when they asked for identification he only had his work ID with him and when they found out that he worked for Barclays their attitude changed, just like that, because he was working. They don't expect them to have good jobs.

The problems of young people impacted on residents in two ways, neither of them supportive of the simple view expressed by the Prime Minister at the launch of the Social Exclusion Unit that disaffected young people are 'the scourge of many communities' (Blair, 1997). In the first place they were sons and daughters for whom the area seemed to have little or nothing to offer: 'I've got teenagers and they come in and say "I'm bored, what can I do?" They're teenagers, fourteen and fifteen, "What can I do? I'm bored, where can I go?"' This can also lead to conflict within families; as one mother put it: 'they're bored and they get at you, and you get at them, and it's not fair on them'. The lack of jobs and facilities for young people also meant that as a result the community was also seen to be fragmenting:

> A lot of the kids are moving out because there are no prospects here. They want better accommodation, better shops, jobs. It's what we all want really. But they don't have the ties, and they have the opportunity to move, so they do . . . They're being forced out really.

In the second place, young people were often the source of neighbourhood tensions, of mischief, vandalism and crime. Yet despite often being on the receiving end of young people's destructiveness, residents frequently understood the reasons for such a situation:

> I think when you talk about young people, you can't take away what has happened over the last 18 years. A generation has grown up with massive Government cuts in education and everything else together with lack of opportunity. That has an impact on those young people and it has an impact on young girls who wind up pregnant, because people need a hope for the future. We've largely got a generation who have been brought up in Speke and in other areas of the country, not just us, who have virtually grown up with very little hope of having anything to show for all the years they've spent at school . . . they're not all going to be gardeners or security guards, I mean, maybe that's part of the problem.

Despite the destruction and anger that young people can cause, and its potential to create a punitive backlash against the young, residents struggled to find more constructive solutions:

> What we should be saying to these young people is that they are a part of our community, and we want them to be a part of our community . . . not just saying 'Get out, we don't want you' . . . Some need a lot more support than others, but if they need that support, give it to them. Because if you don't what you've got is vandalism and kids who feel that they have no stake in the community . . . They're not beyond redemption, but by the time they're 16 or 17, and they've been called all the names under the sun for years, and told to get lost, because the schools don't want you, the community hate your guts, it's too late: the community has rejected them and they've rejected the community.

There is a genuine and deep concern for the future prospects of young people. The cumulative impact of over 20 years of high levels of youth unemployment and the failures of successive government 'youth opportunities' schemes, while at the same time young people's entitlements to welfare have been slashed, have all left their mark on young people. Fears of young people's disillusionment and disaffection are now increasingly dominated by the threat of hard drugs, as a means both of escape and of economic survival. Doing something about this calls for understanding, imagination and, of course, resources. It is not a situation that will be remedied, as current government measures propose, by curfews and 'antisocial behaviour' orders.

Regeneration and Improvement

The dismissal of the capabilities of ordinary working-class people to run and control their own lives is a constant feature of the way in which the poor are treated by those with power. It is also the thing that causes the greatest resentment about the numerous regeneration projects that both communities had experienced:

> They don't recognise the problems we have here . . . They think the people are lazy; they're not used to seeing poverty . . . We don't need an outsider coming in and telling us what a holy show it is. We know that. There are too many people in high places being paid vast amounts of money, expecting people to work voluntarily. And then they get called 'dole-ites' when they do it! There are an awful lot of voluntary workers giving up their precious time, but they get nothing for it: no thanks, nothing. It's those at the top who get all the praise, and get paid £100,000 a year for doing nothing . . . I don't need someone from outside Liverpool coming in and judging me.

This resentment was particularly reserved for the outside professionals and consultants brought in to design and run the projects: 'they may be from the Wirral, or somewhere like that: from their £250,000 houses, and they belittle you'. They were also seen as bringing with them their own agendas:

> We didn't need consultants to write strategies, we knew what we wanted, we told them what we wanted, they could have come to me and I could have written down what the people wanted. All the work that had been put in on the domestic violence projects, all the work had been put in on what we wanted from housing . . . on what we wanted from health . . . on what we wanted on community safety. We got a consultant who came along, God knows how much he was paid, to do a community safety document and there he was devoting all his stuff to probationary tenancies which we'd said we didn't want! . . . everything was put on council tenants.

Despite the much-vaunted talk of consultation and participation, for many it was at best tokenistic:

> Even though there is consultation, and there is massive consultation that has gone on in this estate, what people find is that nobody takes any notice of you . . . what actually happens is that you get the consultants who come in and have a big consultation exercise, they put up their plans and then they say, 'Well, here's five sets of plans, choose one', and that's what they did. They don't say to you, 'How would you like to see it develop?', they just say to you, 'There's five lots of plans there, please choose one'.

Regeneration projects, while appearing to offer much to the areas, were in practice thus viewed with considerable suspicion. It was not only that consultants and professionals were seen to be lining their own pockets at the community's expense, it was also that they were sometimes seen as replacing mainstream provision:

> [t]hey will fund an education project, but that sort of education project used to be there years before, funded by City Council money. You'll get SRB for example, that will fund a Youth Worker, but that used to be there beforehand, so in a way, you're thinking that

you're getting an extra £6 million invested in the area, but it's just subsidising the money and resources that we used to have beforehand but they took it off us and gave it another name.

That local communities now have to bid for such projects, and in doing so compete with other areas, was also a source of resentment. 'This funding business has made more enemies', said one respondent; previously, 'there was none of this bitterness and none of this back-stabbing, but now it seems like people are getting put into little pockets'.

Frequent criticisms were also raised about the lack of visibility in terms of where regeneration money was being spent. This was often seen as a consequence of the way in which regeneration money was concentrated on training initiatives, rather than on capital projects or improvements to the environment: 'A lot of the SRB money, that I see, is all for training, and it's a hell of a lot'. The concentration of many projects on training, to the neglect of improvements in the physical infrastructure and housing, meant that 'for the ordinary people in the street' little was seen as being done: 'People don't see any of the money that is being talked about. So you can't blame them for being disheartened.'

Where money was spent on capital buildings or other work, this feeling was exacerbated by the practice of contracting, in which whatever jobs became available were seen to be taken by people from outside the area:

If a new project gets under way – we'll use this new school for an example – it says that for the short term there will be so many contract jobs and then there will be so many cleaners' jobs, etc. We all know that there won't be one of our men or women or anyone employed labouring or cleaning or anything. It's always an outside contractor.

Most of the people are saying that all they can see is that the money, instead of being spent in the area and being regenerated in the area, has actually been taken out. If you have a look at the companies that have come in to do the work, they're not actually local companies, they're not even from Liverpool.

In Dingle, one man recounted how he had applied for work at the Garden Festival, created close to the area with government money following the Toxteth riots:

We went over there looking for a job but got no joy. And then one evening we were standing on the corner having a chat and five Irish fellas came up looking for digs. They'd been hired to do the work in Dublin, and we were overlooking the place and couldn't get a job! If they're offering the jobs in Dublin, what can you do?

The scepticism also extended to the longer term future:

The danger if these professionals come in is that they make us dependent upon them; and then when they go we can get stuffed . . . I think that one of the biggest problems that we have is that there has been that much dependence on the likes of the Single Regeneration Budget, the English Partnerships, the Speke and Garston Partnership, that when they go it will be the likes of ourselves that will be left to pick up the pieces.

It is in the face of such experiences that people struggle on. Their expectations are not wild or unrealistic. On the contrary, to many they may appear extremely modest:

> We want to be recognised, to have the same things as other people. To be equal with the others. That's not asking a lot. We want our own shops, we want things to entertain the children rather than making a mess out of everything. We want councillors who will work for us, rather than against us.

Of course, people's expectations can be very radical, depending on the context. As one woman put it, 'I think there are things we should be entitled to, like work-place and community-based nurseries . . . It shouldn't be a radical concept, it should be an entitlement.' In a society where notions of duty and responsibility are, at least in government parlance, fast replacing those of rights, such demands may entail more than their modest content suggests.

Conclusion

In the meantime, in communities such as Dingle and Speke, people continue to see themselves as to some extent separate and apart from the rest of society. This is not 'social exclusion' as it is conventionally understood. It is, rather, part of that long historical sense within poor working-class communities described by Richard Hoggart and others of having different interests in a divided society. For one Speke resident this was evident in the contrast with other parts of the city: 'I always thought that if this were a private estate, if this was not a Council estate, it would be a lovely little garden suburb'. When pressed on this, his explanation revealed a sense of people living in a society that wanted them to be kept in their place:

> It wouldn't be full of poverty, would it, if it wasn't a Council estate . . . I think govern-ments prefer to keep us economically deprived; we're not very powerful if we're eco-nomically deprived, are we?

In Dingle, too, this sense of powerlessness in the face of authority, of an inabil-ity to affect decisions that had a major impact on people's lives, was strong. It was not a powerlessness that resulted from a lack of determination, or knowledge of what needed to be done, or lack of ability to do it. On the contrary, 'they tell us we need professionals to come and sort us out. No we don't. We want the money so we can do it ourselves'. Yet,

> If money ever comes into the area, say via the City Council or other organisations, there are restrictions on it. It's like they're giving the money so they can dictate to us. You know, they have the money and they have the power. We never have the power.

Poverty is partly about lack of money. But it is also crucially about lack of power. Coping with, and confronting, this situation, then, is also about how this power is experienced, and the types of relationships it produces. It is also about establish-ing other forms of relationships, and other sources of power.

In the end, 'the only way the estate will change is by the people inside doing it'. Residents have struggled, some of them for many years, to achieve this, and faced countless setbacks and frustrations. It would not be surprising if this led to apathy and resignation, to a belief that nothing could be changed: 'but, in all honesty, if we really believed that, none of us would be here now, you wouldn't be involved . . . but deep down we still believe that something can be done'.

References

Andersen, H., Munck, R., et al. (1999), *Neighbourhood Images in Liverpool: 'It's All Down to the People'*, York: Joseph Rowntree Foundation

Blair, T. (1997), Speech at the Aylesbury estate, Southwark, 2 June, http://www.open.gov.uk/co/seu.more.html/speech

Boyte, H. (1980), *The Backyard Revolution: Understanding the New Citizen Movement*, Philadelphia: Temple University Press

Campbell, B. (1993), *Goliath: Britain's Dangerous Places*, London: Methuen

Holman, B. (2000), 'Pride of Place', *The Guardian*, 9 February

Jones, C., and Novak, T. (1999), *Poverty, Welfare and the Disciplinary State*, London: Routledge

— (2000), 'Class Struggle, Self Help and Popular Welfare', in M. Lavalette and G. Mooney (eds), *Class Struggle and Social Welfare*, London: Routledge

London Edinburgh Weekend Return Group (1980), *In and Against the State*, London: Pluto Press

Ward, C. (1990), *Talking Houses*, London: Freedom Press

— (1991), *Influences: Voices of Creative Dissent*, Bideford: Green Books

10. Images of the City

David Hall

Analysing the City

Cities are seen as places of contrast, contradiction and crisis (Pile et al., 1999; Loney and Allen, 1979). Even the attempt at defining what is unique about cities is a difficult undertaking. Should one concentrate on the physical aspects of scale and the unique built environment or focus on more human aspects of social interaction mediated through population density and heterogeneity? Is the city a place defined by boundaries, or is it rather a state of mind, a way of life (Pile, 1999)?

The challenges of cities were apparent well before the dawn of the twentieth century, when for the first time the majority of the population of Britain was urban rather than rural. Weber (1958: 94) quotes the proverb, 'City air makes man free', while Engels (1844) had previously drawn attention to the less desirable features of industrial Manchester. Freedom from the social controls and stifling parochialism of the rural life was countered to some extent by the worst excesses of relatively unconstrained capitalist growth in the slums of the city.

Yet still people poured into the city from the country, looking for work, for opportunity, for freedom. For all its unplanned growth, the city seemed to display an organisation all of its own, as districts emerged with different activities, different social compositions. To the theorists of the Chicago school, this seemed to speak of a social ecology, and of a process of change and transition as new resources are swept into the urban mass and filter outwards in ever increasing circles.

Yet when this broad picture is questioned, the facts appear stubbornly resistant. Instead of a series of concentric zones, there is a more diverse and segregated pattern, and underneath the new order of the city can be seen smaller 'villages' which have outlasted the urban growth while being consumed and transformed by it. So the 'ecological perspective' (Pacione, 1997) has been largely replaced by political economy approaches in which processes outside the city are seen to impact on its development. For example, Pacione (1997: 7) views urban deprivation as part of the patterning imposed on spatial locations by global capitalism:

> Uneven development is an inherent characteristic of capitalism which stems from the propensity of capital to flow to locations that offer the greatest potential return. The differential use of space by capital in pursuit of profit creates a mosaic of inequality at all geographic levels from global to local. Consequently, at any one time certain countries,

191

regions, cities and localities will be in the throes of decline, as a result of the retreat of capital investment, while others will be experiencing the impact of capital inflows. At the metropolitan scale, the outcome of the uneven development process is manifested in the poverty, powerlessness and polarization of disadvantaged residents.

It has become a commonplace that the city has moved from being a centre of production to one of consumption. The wreck of industrial factories, and their transformation to shopping malls, bear witness to that, though we should also note the emergence of new 'high-tech' industries, and the continuation, on a less secure and much less labour-intensive scale, of some of the traditional forms.

An underlying feature of the city is that it has become more spatially polarised and socially divided (Byrne, 1999: 109). There is the suggestion that the cleavages of class were covered to some extent by the creation of community, but that this remedy is no longer available as areas lose their stability and become more heterogeneous. Spatial mobility and access to (usually private) means of transport release people from the necessity to live close to workplaces, and mirror social mobility as those who are able move away from less favoured areas and into areas where the local infrastructure of schools, leisure and security are important aspects of their desired life courses.

Pacione argues (1997: 39) that the problems of poverty and deprivation increased in the 1980s and 1990s for those marginal to capitalistic development, and in particular those living in cities, which have experienced de-industrialisation through economic restructuring. This urban crisis involves a concentration of multiple forms of deprivation, in which poverty is a key factor (Pacione, 1997: 42). Deprivation is often concentrated on council estates in the inner and outer cities (Lovering, 1997: 67). The zones of inner urban stress, with nineteenth-century working-class housing, have been added to by post-war estates on the urban fringes of many British cities, which in turn have become problem areas (see Mooney, 1999).

Narratives of the Inner City

But how are these problems explained? Lovering develops a narrative of 'The Simple Story' (1997: 68–70) which 'has become almost as much a part of popular political culture as it has become an academic and political orthodoxy'. The simple story is one of the decline of traditional industry, and the replacement of production by consumption. In this new economy, the old skills are no longer in demand, and new employment favours those with more skills (the more educated) or those with a weaker position in the labour force (especially women). Joblessness tends to become pathological, leading to an unemployable underclass. A cycle of deprivation sets in which drives potential employers away. There is 'little that can be done'.

The result is to create areas of social exclusion, where the poor are separated off (Byrne, 1999: 110). Urban regeneration intensifies the process by gentrifying some inner-city urban spaces and displacing the poor to increasingly monochrome areas of social housing. Byrne concludes that the evidence from cities across the world is that social polarisation and exclusion are increasing.

Curiously, the attempts at redevelopment have increased the marked differentials between closely contiguous areas within the city. As Fainstein demonstrates, 'Redevelopment took the form of islands of shiny new structures in the midst of decayed public facilities and deterioration in the living conditions for the poor (cited in Imrie, 1997: 99). As I shall show, this process is well established in Liverpool, where the development of the old airport site at Speke, with its listed buildings to be turned into hotel and leisure developments for the affluent, contrasts sharply with the housing estate nearby.

The explanations on offer suggest different and conflicting processes towards polarisation. Fainstein and Harloe explain that

> For some it entails the loss of middle-income groups from the social structure. Others stress the growth of an affluent middle class alongside an impoverished, marginalized group. But what both conceptions share is the belief that economic restructuring and social change result in the creation of an increasingly isolated mass of impoverished people, whose chances of upward social and economic mobility are minimal. (Fainstein and Harloe, 1992: 9)

Yet they also argue that 'the hard evidence for such a sweeping and general conclusion regarding the outcome of economic restructuring and urban change is, at best, patchy and ambiguous' (Fainstein and Harloe, 1992: 13) and thus reject the simplistic versions of the underclass thesis. Logan et al. (1992: 146) show instead that polarisation is not sufficient to explain the experience of residents on inner-city estates, where 'the term most commonly used to describe the estate by those who live there is "mixed"'. They point to 'chronic insecurity' as a feature of residents' lives, but also to the efforts to maintain a 'nice home'.

Westwood and Williams, in their volume *Imagining Cities* (1997), suggest three moments in which sociological accounts of the city have been recast in recent times. These they call 'decentring of the social', in which an overall picture of urbanism is replaced by overlapping and fragmentary relationships as a multiplicity of different actions and engagements are played out on the ground; 'reintegration of the social and the spatial' in accounts of social relations, where power is played out in specific locales and the ethnographer provides narratives of people situated within rather than from the city; and the 'encoding of urban practices into social/spatial relations of time' (Westwood and Williams, 1997: 5) whereby the historical frame lends impetus to the different perceptions (or indeed invisibility) of areas within the city.

Whereas in the past cities could be seen as the grounds for identification and civic pride, now there is a view of the decentred subject, without the possibility of identity through the city, as the urban spaces themselves become decentred in the 'multiple discourses of urban spatiality' (Keith, 1993: 208).

The city has a history – a history that can be read in the buildings, in the names of localities, in the street plan and the many ways in which people have left their mark on the physical space. Yet that history is also partial and multifaceted, a sign to some, a mystery to others. And through nostalgia, even that history is reconstructed by the present to emphasise some aspects and downplay or ignore other aspects of the past.

Representation of the City in Images

The processes of polarisation and conflict described above are abstract generalisations derived ultimately from people's experiences of life in the city, and it is to those experiences that the argument now turns. As we have seen above, the views that people generate about the city can have both positive and negative evaluations, depending on their stance and their interpretation of the city that they see. Interpretations can of course change over time: in the nineteenth century the smoke of industrial cities was understood as a positive feature of the wealth-creating manufacturing; in the second half of the twentieth century the smog of the city was recognised as a major killer, and clean air acts changed the appearance of the city. In this example, the visual image of smoke from chimneys is a sign which is then given meaning by being related to a concept within a system of meaning. The sign is in itself ambiguous, until interpreted within a framework of 'production' or 'health'.

For McQuire (1998) the unique identifying characteristic of the city is its modernity, understood as concentration of technological innovation and a built environment profoundly different from the rural, whose memory it nevertheless seeks to replicate in botanical gardens, zoos and public parks. The skyscraper is an element in the shifting of the axis of development from the horizontal to the vertical; while the collapsing of space through new forms of transport brings ever more distant environs into the orbit of the city. Speed becomes a definer of city life, and it is argued that consequently there is a degradation in people's experiences of continuity as they dash through traffic from one stopping place to the next.

If the Eiffel Tower is the 'establishing shot' of Paris, and the Manhattan skyline that of New York (McQuire, 1998: 208), then that of Liverpool is the Liver Building and the Pier Head (Lane, 1997: 1; and as currently used by Liverpool City Council in its recruitment advertising). From this view across the Mersey, pan right to take in the Albert Dock, brought back into use as a leisure site after the demise of its industrial purpose, and zoom up to the Anglican cathedral, perched on a rise where its immense bulk is visible for miles around, and in close-up possessing a size and scale that cannot be comprehended in a single glance.

Our research (Andersen et al., 1999), however, is concerned not with the well-known and highly visible areas of the riverfront, but with the less visible areas of social exclusion, Dingle and Speke. Yet Dingle is close enough to the River Mersey and the city centre to be overshadowed by the cathedral at its northern edge, and Speke may be familiar as the location of Liverpool Airport – at the far edge of the city – where it owes its existence to transport making new areas accessible, and the constant flow of population outwards, as plans were made to tackle inner-city housing problems by building the outer estates.

For these areas, other images will have to serve as identifiers. Such images are interpreted by a kind of discourse that provides meaning to the sights. For the inner city/outer estates this is a discourse of 'problems', contrasting with the view of leafy suburbs, and writing a script of 'dereliction' and 'danger'. It is not difficult to find evidence for such a discourse, by a cursory glance at, for example, broken down and burned-out buildings. Yet it has to be questioned how far residents themselves use this discourse, or whether it is one provided by those in power both to justify their actions in regeneration and also to justify their inability to transform the landscape.

How do people think about their areas of the city? What kinds of images are important to them? These were some of the questions that were asked in the study of attitudes and aspirations in areas of social exclusion in Liverpool (Andersen et al., 1999), funded by the Joseph Rowntree Foundation as part of its urban programme looking at cities fighting deprivation. The research involved focus group studies with selected groups of residents, together with interviews with key informants, and extracts from some of these are quoted below.

As the researchers covered the ground in which the residents lived, so they could also capture photographically images of the environment, which spoke to them of characteristics of the area – but did they have the same meanings to residents, and what did the residents' imagery add to the conceptual understanding of the area? Sociologists have argued that visual images, such as photographs, have largely become excluded from sociological attempts at explanation, which prefer the verbal form to deal with abstract concepts. But Chaplin proposes that there is a place for photography in portraying the particular: 'While generalising about the social world is perhaps best accomplished with words, arrays of photographic images emphasise particular differences – and particularising is increasingly valued in both critical and empirical paradigms' (Chaplin, 1994: 277). So there has been a small but significant countermove in recent times to visual sociology (Harper, 1998a; 1998b). However, the documentary style, as a simple provider of visual information, is no longer tenable as a view of 'reality', as one comes to understand that photographs are 'made' not 'taken', and that the viewer also constructs meaning from the visual image. As Chaplin remarks, 'The relationship between photographs, information and empirical social science is particularly hard to state, and fraught with pitfalls' (Chaplin, 1994: 206).

New techniques are then sought to break down the privileged power relationship between photographer and subject, and to open the image to different interpretations. One method is the photo elicitation technique (Harper, 1998a: 144), which uses photographs as the stimulus for open-ended interviews with those depicted in the photos. Another is to restrict the freedom of the photographer by setting rules about time and subject – a form of sampling, which Chaplin (1994: 224–29) used to construct a 'visual diary'. A third is to reverse the photographer/subject relationship by giving people their own cameras to photograph their view of what is important to them.

This is what happened with the 'Streetscenes' project (Hall et al., 1999). As an offshoot from the research study on Dingle and Speke, we were interested in getting people from these areas to take photographs of things that were meaningful to them, in order to present an insider's view of these neighbourhoods. Artskills was a voluntary sector agency providing training in a variety of arts to young people in both these areas, and it was agreed that the photographic project would fit into part of their training programme. Artskills already used digital cameras for trainees to take visual images and output them on computer, so the young people were asked if they would take on an assignment to photograph the places and sights of the neighbourhood that were familiar to them. The project was a success in the sense that over 3,000 digital images were taken by the young people in Dingle and Speke, and a selection has been published from this work, which includes the young people's comments – generally negative – on the areas, and their captions to the photographs (Hall et al., 1999). Chaplin (1994: 212) notes that

> It is traditional not to let the subject play any other role than to be observed [. . .] The massed images, in sequence and juxtaposition, create a micro-world whose visual coherence is such that we acquire an understanding of that society and its ethos which is not straightforwardly a function of verbal conventions, and verbal social science.

So it is perhaps unwise to attempt any verbal summary of this material. However, to give a flavour of the project, Streetscenes brings into focus the world of the young people, emphasising the peer group, local food stores, convenience shops and hairdressers, and other landmarks such as pubs, betting shops, and so forth. Family and pets also feature. In the inner city, the houses are not all old, but contain a fair mixture of new properties. The captions suggest aspirations, as is shown by the photo of a white sports car with the comment 'beast of a car'.

The Study Areas of Dingle and Speke

The areas focused on in this study are two contrasting areas in Liverpool. Dingle is an inner-city district within the L8 postcode, just south of the city centre and close to the river Mersey, and traditionally associated with the docks and dock industries, though most of these have now gone. The extent to which Liverpool was based on the port and related industry, and how this has massively declined since the 1960s with the growth of containerisation and the rise of east coast ports, is graphically described by Lane (1997). Speke, by contrast, is six miles further along the main road leading south. It is a large housing estate at the margins of the city (indeed the land was purchased by Liverpool from the neighbouring council for development during the inter-war years [Meegan, 1989]), close to the airport, and bounded to one side by the arterial road south and on the other by the river Mersey a little before the first bridge crossing at Runcorn. Both could be said to be areas of social deprivation; the education statistics tell a tale of low achievement; the casual observer notes the large numbers of derelict houses and other buildings; and the census reveals above-average levels of unemployment even within a region of high unemployment.

For Speke, as for other outer-city estates, Meegan (1989) reveals a changing

socio-economic history, with an initial post-war growth period of industrial manufacturing, significantly in chemicals and the car industry, supported by a large
housing estate mainly developed in the 1950s and 1960s from a late 1930s beginning. Speke was but one part of the dispersal of 'overspill' population from the inner
city to 'an outer ring of municipally owned housing estates' (Meegan, 1989: 200).

The influence of the planners on the design and layout of this new estate can be
read in the street layout, with a central shopping and service area, a grid plan, and
main cross-thoroughfares (Eastern and Western Avenues). The ideals of the garden
city can be inferred from the design: a central core, a ring of housing, and an outer
ring of industry for the local population. Early proposals also show the central
avenue extending towards the river, with access for the residents to the river bank
for recreation, though the development of the airport has blocked this direction of
expansion.

The 1970s and 1980s, however, were times of job loss, of factory closures, and of
economic restructuring. Meegan (1989: 208) gives a table showing the extent of
redundancies in the outer estates of Speke, Kirkby and Halewood in the decade
1978–87. It amounts to eight major factory closures, and significant job losses at
another six establishments. The closure of industrial manufacturing was also mir-
rored in the closure of retailing. Although there had never been major retailers at
Speke, the services of banks and chain stores retrenched also. The residents found
that the raison d'être of the new estate – land outside the built-up city area – now
became a barrier to their access to retail, leisure and employment. Speke was cut
off and isolated. Thus one can speak of marginalisation of the economic and social
life of those in the estate.

Yet also there is another side to the picture, which Meegan terms 'resilience' and
'resistance' (Meegan, 1989: 226). This is the story of the response by people in the
area to adverse situations, drawing on the strength of cooperation and bloody-
mindedness that may be characteristic of working-class communities under threat
(see Lane, 1997). Beneath the surface, there is also a fairly strong tradition of
mutual self-help and of voluntary endeavour.

Dingle too shows an original grid plan of rows of Victorian terraces squeezed in
between the main longitudinal thoroughfares, now broken by areas of waste land
following demolition, and a newer and more sinuous pattern of patches of redevelopment in flats and, more recently, houses. Its northern and southern limits are
Parliament Street, under the shadow of the Anglican cathedral, and Dingle Lane
leading down towards the site of the former Garden Festival. Its identity seems to
derive not so much from an overall unity, but rather from the streets that thread
through the sector – Mill Street and Park Road longitudinally, Warwick Street,
Northumberland Street and High Park Street laterally, enclosing blocks of themat-
ically named Victorian streets: the 'Dickensian' streets, the 'Holy Land', the 'Groves'
(and, of TV fame, the 'Bread' block). The south docks are closed, and have been
turned over to a marina, expensive housing and small businesses. Redevelopment
of the docks is in any case made remote from Dingle because of the closing of access
roads to the dock road. Of the old port industries, a flour mill survives.

Whereas in Speke the boundaries are fixed by the physical perimeter, in Dingle there is a lively debate among residents as to where the boundaries lie. This is shown, for example, in the report of the Toxteth Community Council (McKeown, 1994), where the 'area of benefit' covers parts of three different council wards (Abercromby, Dingle and Granby) and although this is known as the Dingle, it is not coterminous with Dingle ward.

'Toxteth' (and its synonym, 'Liverpool 8') is for many a misnomer: only 25 per cent of residents in the 1994 survey used it as a description of the area, compared with 55 per cent using 'Dingle'. The report notes

> resentment of the name 'Toxteth', which many residents insisted describes the adjacent Granby ward. Residents identify more positively with the names Dingle or the South End. It would seem that much of this has been a media-led attitude in the wake of the disturbances of 1981 that primarily occurred in the Granby ward. (McKeown, 1994: 32)

There are parallels here with Farrar's examination of the Chapeltown area of Leeds, containing the majority of the city's black residents. It is claimed that this area is only defined by local knowledge, rather than a place name on a map. It is both visible and invisible: 'While cartographers make Chapeltown invisible, the myth-makers insist on representing the black residents of the territory everyone in Leeds knows as Chapeltown' (Farrar, 1997: 105). Farrar quotes Shields (1991) on the cultural codings of spatial territories, such that 'sites become symbols of good and evil and states of mind, "zones of the social imaginary"' (Farrar, 1997: 108).

Our research confirmed this concern over identity. 'We are Dingle, it's not Toxteth' is what many residents say in defining their territory. Toxteth in this sense is the other (eastern) side of a dividing line running along Park Road, though others put the boundary along the next north–south thoroughfare of Windsor Street/Admiral Street, which is how Dingle is defined by the area of the SRB.

Both Dingle and Speke are recognised as areas of social exclusion, and both are the subject of regeneration partnerships. But what about the views of residents? Contrasting with the picture of polarisation, the view on the ground from the micro-studies of social exclusion reveals considerable variation and differentiation.

Speke: Residents' Views and Images

People refer to Speke, large as it is, as 'the estate', and further distinguish it in terms of 'ends', west and east, as well as the 'Dymchurch' (after Dymchurch Avenue) whose reputation has been somewhat worse than that of the rest (though it is currently subject to rebuilding and transformation). They are keenly aware that the reputation of Speke as a whole among outsiders is bad – as bad as that of the other outer-city estate of Kirkby.

The outsider is readily aware of the many empty, boarded-up and vandalised properties, some in blocks obviously due for demolition or refurbishment, others as odd ones in otherwise apparently well-kept terraces. Residents count the

Speke: empty and boarded-up housing

number in the hundreds, as one focus group reported: 'If you walk around Speke, there are about 500 empty houses'.

Images such as these call for explanation, though the image itself is ambiguous. As I noted above, the photograph has a superficial claim to veracity, to portraying things and people 'as they are', and this is recognised in such practices as using photographs for identification purposes. Even the capacity of the photographer to 'lie' by retouching images (made even easier with the advent of digital imaging) presupposes that the faked image can be accepted as true. So documentary images have been used to expose the generally hidden side of society to public view, and to demand a public response.

Yet the role of the photograph and the photographer as researcher is under dispute, especially when claims to 'documentary truthfulness' are made (Harper, 1998b: 32). Photographs are now understood much less as objective records but rather as images requiring the interpretation of the observer to sustain the claim of authenticity (Winston, 1998: 67). Such authenticity involves the ability of the observer to narrativise the image, that is to say, to construct a meaning or context in which the image is interpretable. The meaning is not resident in the image itself, but (under the constructivist view), derives from the interpretation placed on it by the observer. Nevertheless, this is not solely an individualistic interpretation, because the image may draw on cultural associations to derive a shared meaning, or the interpretation may become shared through repeated use of and discussion of the images.

A commonly found interpretation of the areas of dereliction in Speke used the metaphor of civil war:

> If you mention to someone outside Speke the word 'Speke', they automatically think, well, 'Beirut – I wouldn't live there'.

> Even taxis. If you get a taxi from town and say 'I want to go to Speke', half of them won't take you or they'll say 'Oh, I'll have to watch my car'.

'Beirut' has become a shorthand term to refer to the physical damage to the housing stock and as well to a presumed correlation with social breakdown. Paddy Ashdown on his visit of 13 June 1998 produced an updating of the same civil war image by likening Speke to Sarajevo (*Liverpool Echo*, June 1998).

This is inevitably an exaggeration; we are not dealing with war-torn streets here, but the term graphically portrays the outsider's astonishment at the high level of dereliction of housing in the area, compared with other more favoured parts of the country. There is also the residents' grim appropriation of the description as a way of making the point that their situation is unusual even by local standards, and further, that it creates a division between themselves and other residents of the city:

> It's OK with the people who live in Speke, but those who live outside Speke are terrible. Yes, they think it's Beirut.

Yet there is also rejection of this image, seen as a media creation that fails to recognise the examples of community spirit among long-term residents:

> There's a poor image being portrayed by the media of Speke, if you have a look at it, it has been classed as Beirut, Sarajevo, houses from Hell.

> Speke is not a Sarajevo; Speke is quite a nice estate. The only problem is that you have these people who come flying in from here, there and everywhere who actually don't live on the estate and can't see the good things that actually happen on the estate, nor can they see the potential of what is going to happen over the next few years.

Another example of different interpretations comes from the Dymchurch estate at the western edge of Speke, close to the airport. The housing stock here is noticeably different from the main part of Speke, with squat, lower-pitched roofs, and in 1998 there were appreciably more empty and boarded-up properties in the Dymchurch estate than in other areas. The area had a poor reputation locally, being thought of as the least desirable area on the estate. The policy document on redevelopment lists the tenants' and residents' associations, the police and the development partnership as all recognising it as the 'worst' estate in the district.

The outsider has only the previously expressed meaning of physical dereliction and social breakdown with which to narrativise and interpret the scene. However, an alternative is supplied through knowledge of the historical development of the area. According to Liverpool Housing Trust (LHT – which took over responsibility for the regeneration of this estate), the Dymchurch estate was built between 1997 and 1998 to house predominantly older people from west Speke. LHT identifies a number of design faults with the buildings: they were built with a 'Radburn'

Dymchurch: renovated housing

layout, fronting onto courts with no vehicular access, and the low-pitched roofs were designed because of the proximity of the airport. Social factors then intervened. Because of unexpectedly low demand from elderly people, the one- and two-bed flats were let to young single people, and 'the estate became populated by a transitory section of the overall population and the flats became notorious for drug abuse and giro drops' (http://www.lht.co.uk/dymchurch.htm)

Remedial action involved changes in the letting policy, and demolition of large numbers of flats between 1993 and 1995, leaving the land vacant and prey to tipping. Following a vote by residents, the estate was transferred to LHT, and redevelopment put in place, which meant some demolition of the hard-to-let flats, building new houses on the vacant land, and refurbishing existing properties by reversing the layout and fitting conventional pitched roofs.

So the picture is far from a static one: houses that were abandoned and derelict during the research period (1998) have now been completely demolished. As on the Dymchurch estate, a programme of selective demolition and refurbishment of existing properties is changing the physical appearance of the estate, and may do much to change the social image under which it laboured.

But change needs to be more than cosmetic. The strongest criticisms from residents were reserved for changes that seemed to be about presentation rather than tackling what were perceived to be the real issues of housing repairs and social isolation. For example, the most immediate evidence of the physical changes brought about by the regeneration agency, Speke–Garston Partnership, was viewed by residents as cosmetic. This included the planting of trees along the dual carriageway separating the residential area from the industrial area. While this can be seen as an 'improvement' to the area, most people's responses used a different frame of reference.

Interviews with local residents showed overwhelmingly that the people of Speke felt cut off from the rest of the city. We have already seen how the area was developed on land outside the original city boundaries, approximately seven miles south of the city centre, purchased in the 1930s. This feeling of isolation was compounded by the fact that the main arterial road south passed one boundary of the estate, and as one resident explained, when coming from the city centre, 'You have to turn right at Speke, otherwise you miss it'.

Even the amenities and facilities that people outside the area took for granted, such as the airport and the National Trust property, Speke Hall, lie outside the boundary roads of the estate. Residents expressed this sense of isolation in terms of Speke being an 'island', that is, an enclave entirely surrounded by the barrier of roads, fields, the airport runway and the River Mersey:

> We have got a very narrow perception of distance because we are an island. Just the geo-graphical nature of Speke, it takes a good 45 minutes from town, that distance in our minds because of where we come from is a huge distance.

So when trees were planted along the dual carriageway, already seen as a barrier to entrance, the feeling was generated that here was another attempt to disguise the area, and to hide it away from public view and public concern:

> They're spending £1 million up the road putting trees and plants in, it looks lovely, well, it will do when it's finished.

> Why don't they come into Speke and spend some money here instead of stuck up on to the top road, as people go past saying, 'Speke's great, it looks lovely', but Speke isn't great.

The essential element in perception of change is time. Visual images such as photographs are by definition 'snapshots' which are divorced from a time context. In interpreting such images, people tend to attempt to fill in the details, to construct a narrative around the images. So when looking at people's mental images of their areas, time is a crucial dimension in the accounts and the explanations that people offer.

As we have seen above, for Speke there was a major change in socio-economic circumstances in the 1970s, and this coincides with residents' views of a more idyllic past compared with the problems of the present. The most frequent image is that of loss, and the difference from times gone by that people still remember:

> It used to be a lovely place to live.

> Yes, about ten or fifteen years ago.

> All the shops in the Parade are closing down.

> We used to have tennis courts and everything – bowling greens.

Speke Boulevard: regeneration sign and new planting

A lot of men are retired now, but the firms they worked in have gone. Dunlops, the bottle works, and the Standard Triumph, it was a good area for employment when I was younger and now there is nothing.

We used to have a Kwik Save but that's gone. We had a fire service but that's gone. We had a water works but that's gone. We had a Brown's clothes shop but that's gone. We had shoe shops but they've gone. The bank went, and when that went, well, the business was gone. It's alright for us, like, because we've got passes for the buses, but for the others, well . . .

[T]hings that close down temporarily here stay closed down.

All that's left up there now are a couple of big shops and the rest are rubbish, and I mean it.

The frequency and intensity with which the sense of loss was reported, together with a feeling of impotence, an inability to affect what was happening, and blame directed at 'them', the faceless officials and managers who had made the decisions to leave, suggest something stronger than mere loss. It would be little exaggeration to say that here is an expression of grief (Marris, 1974).

Chief among the culprits for many was the local council, in its role as housing provider and because of its perceived failure to deal with either housing repairs or vacant tenancies. Stories of waiting ages for repairs were common, and of houses being left vacant and then vandalised. The park is a case in point: where there were once tennis courts and bowling greens, the council (in the 1980s Militant era) closed them down and landscaped the area, so that people became afraid to use the park in the evening.

> I lived by the Park when I was younger and it was a lovely park. There were bowling greens, tennis courts, the lads could play football. And suddenly they moved in and there were these hills being built . . . Nobody goes there now, only some people walking their dogs.

Loss of physical plant, the shops and factories, was also traced through to a weakening of the social fabric. Again there is the contrast between the good times of close community, and the present:

> There was good employment and everything else, and now we seem to be the forgotten people.

> I think it's the newer ones who are coming in who are causing the problem. As the old ones move out, it's who they're putting in the houses.

> They also have a thing where everyone sort of knew everyone in Speke, but lately it seems to be divided between those who live at that end, those in the middle, and those at this end. You just sort of stay in an area. At one time, socially, everyone went around all the different places and got together . . . I think a lot of it is to do with the factories closing, people knew each other from work . . . and you used to go and visit people, it's now as though people just stay in their own little place now.

The overwhelming feeling was therefore one of being passed by, of being cut off, of invisibility, and of token improvements that did not address what the residents perceived to be the realities of the situation. Physical changes were happening, and the transfer of council-owned housing stock to a separate social landlord, following a vote of residents, promised improvements. Yet the image held of the area by outsiders was likely to remain stubbornly resistant to change.

Dingle

Like Speke, Dingle is also an area with a poor press. For residents this means that the image of Toxteth as 'trouble' reaches out to taint the Dingle in the eyes of other citizens of Liverpool:

> [E]ven with your work in town and that, I say 'Dingle' and you can see them going like that . . .
> I get annoyed when people call it Toxteth.

> If you tell people you're from Toxteth, that's it, you're wiped off.
> Liverpool 8.
> They don't give you a reason though. All you have to say is Liverpool 8 and that's it, their attitude changes.
> People are afraid of the area, they don't know it though.

Young people too feel the stigma attached to Toxteth from others they meet at school: 'Half the girls in our school are dead posh and they skit you about the way that you talk, don't they? They say, "Oh no, Tockyites!"'.

Although some activists prefer 'Liverpool 8' and 'Toxteth' as identifiers for community activity, because 'Dingle' carries a much narrower association, others regard 'Toxteth' as a modern invention:

> It was never known as Toxteth, it was always the Dingle.

> Always when we were growing up, once you got past Parliament Street it was Dingle.

The alternative view of Dingle is the southern end of this sector (15 per cent of the 1994 survey respondents preferred the term 'South End'), around the end of Park Road, which has in the past been associated with a white, Protestant, close-knit community with the reputation of being racist. This is recognised by some respondents:

> Although Dingle is Liverpool 8, there is a racial boundary. The side of Dickens Street going down is predominantly white, going down from the part of Windsor Street which is the right hand side of Windsor Street reaching down to Cockburn Street.

> It is interesting to see how gradually the Yemenis and Somalis have moved across the road having established their base in Granby, and are now filtering out into what has traditionally been the Dingle area. They haven't gone much further than Admiral Street which is two roads away from Granby.

Within Dingle, however defined, the sense of belonging and the feeling of community are reportedly strong, but tend to be restricted to a group of streets, a small neighbourhood, or a block of houses. People can point to the past, when dock work was a major identifier, or to the tenement blocks, now demolished, which also created a sense of neighbourhood: 'There was a strong sense of community because we'd lived and worked here all our lives'. Yet the area still holds that community strength in the number of housing cooperatives that have followed on redevelopment: the Holy Land housing cooperative, the Dingle Residents' housing cooperative, and others, for which the residents had to battle with determination against council opposition at the time:

> The Labour man who was there at the time actually shouted and called us for anything outside the Town Hall when we were all waiting to go in. We wanted our own houses, you see, and the Labour Party wanted to take our houses and rent them to us, and we said, no, after we'd done all the work. They wanted to take them from us and for us to just rent them like the Council.

One of the perceptions of the area now is that of new houses springing up – yet the main facilities such as shopping centres are on the decline. Again it is the story of major retailers such as the Co-op being replaced by, in the case of Dingle, Mecca bingo. For those with access to transport, the city centre is nearby, but for those without, the bus service is seen as infrequent and the area perceived as isolated, while ironically the traffic improvements caused by closing off Mill Street make the main thoroughfare of Park Road too busy to cross.

People are aware of both the strength and limitations of such small-scale community feeling: 'close-knit' and 'closed' are used together, hinting again at a

The 'Florrie'

sectarianism that was once quite strong and lives on in patches, such that Dingle can be seen as a series of small neighbourhoods. To some extent this applies to community organisations – there is evidence of a mass of different community organisations within the area, yet a perception of the difficulty of getting them to work together.

Take for instance the 'Florrie', the Florence Institute, once a renowned youth club, now a building in much need of redevelopment. The building

> has had four surveys done on it in my lifetime, it never gets any further than that . . . we hear so much that the Florrie's coming back and it raises expectations, but it never actually formulates into anything . . . it is a three storey building which would need a lift installing, and you are talking megabucks.

The 1994 Toxteth Community Council report noted several responses concerning the then disused Florence Institute, and the 'potential uses of derelict/disused buildings as a solution to the area's problems' (McKeown, 1994: 37). Residents recalled its use as a youth club and community centre; its location in the south end was convenient for many:

> The Florence Institute had the facilities, had the halls, no messing. Upstairs and downstairs.
> And it was in the heart of the Dingle.

During the course of the research team's evaluation of the environmental health initiative for Dingle SRB (Globalisation and Social Exclusion Unit, 2000), the disused Florrie suffered fire damage, and the SRB instituted a survey of works needed to make it safe. However, a public meeting called to establish the 'Friends of the Florrie' to campaign for funds to restore it to use, in December 1999, failed to make progress – there was uncertainty about current ownership as the last owners could not be traced, and council cutbacks on youth service provision stirred up old resentments about funding.

In part this may be to do with a sense of loss of community, as the focus group interviews revealed:

> It's just been splattered, it's a shame really because it was very homely.
> When you say it's been splattered, what do you mean by that?
> Oh, it's far and wide – there's Speke, Halewood and all that.
> They kind of tore the heart out of it.

As with Speke, there was a felt contrast with the past, and a recognition of the loss of amenities:

> There used to be a community spirit but I think that the reason why it isn't the same now is that people are more fearful and they won't trust people the way they used to.

> The shops have just declined, they've just gone, there's nothing.
> We haven't even got a bus.
> No, not down Mill Street.

Yet these images of decline do not represent the whole truth about the area. For, as we have seen, it is (and has been) the subject of attempts at improvement. The latest has been Dingle Pride; evaluation (Globalisation and Social Exclusion Unit, 2000: 28) showed that when services, such as those mediated through the Environmental Health Department, were made responsive to people's immediate needs, there was evidence of 'some positive impact on local residents' feelings that they can become involved in local decision making'.

Improvements that did have an effect on both the physical layout and feelings of well-being included the 'alley-gate' scheme for some of the older terraced blocks, designed to prevent unauthorised access to or dumping in the back alleys. A problem has been that the works have been delayed for several months, with a consequent effect on residents' patience. The delays result from the fact that the alleys are technically thoroughfares, and therefore blocking them with gates to which only the residents of the street have keys requires a hearing in the Magistrates Court, for which there is a long waiting list (Globalisation and Social Exclusion Unit, 2000: 16).

Together with improved lighting, attempts have been made to respond to residents' concerns and make the environment safer. How this will impact on the residents' own image of the area it is still too early to say. Like many programmes to which the area has been subject, Dingle Pride has been an innovation limited by time and by budget. Many of the problems (for example, derelict buildings) that give rise to the visual image of the area are more resistant to quick and easy solutions.

New alley-gate at the end of a terrace

Conclusion

This chapter has looked at some of the images associated with the city, and with the inner city in particular. These images derive from many different sources, from theorising about the city in late capitalism, and the polarising effect on city areas; from the outsider's snapshots of urban decay and partial regeneration; from the media reporting; from young residents' views of what is important to them; and from the words of older residents, men and women, who experience these areas with a sense of loss, and yet still with a sense of attachment. It is a complex set of pictures, which both overlap and diverge. There are commonalities in people's experiences, though each area is distinct. And it is on the residents' own images that hopes and plans for improvement and regeneration will rest.

References

Andersen, H., Munck, R., et al. (1999), *Neighbourhood Images in Liverpool: 'It's All Down to the People'*, York: Joseph Rowntree Foundation

Byrne, D. (1999), *Social Exclusion*, Buckingham: Open University Press

Chaplin, E. (1994), *Sociology and Visual Representation*, London: Routledge

Engels, F. (1987) [1844], *The Condition of the Working Class in England*, Harmondsworth: Penguin

Fainstein, S. (1995), 'Urban Redevelopment and Public Policy in London and New York', in P. Healey, S. Cameron, S. Davoudi, S. Graham and A. Mandanipour (eds), *Managing Cities: The New Urban Context*, London: John Wiley

Fainstein, S., and Harloe, M. (1992), 'Introduction: London and New York in the Contemporary World', in S. Fainstein, I. Gordon and M. Harloe (eds), *Divided Cities: New York and London in the Contemporary World*, Oxford: Blackwell

Farrar, M. (1997), 'Migrant Spaces and Settlers' Time: Forming and Deforming an Inner City', in Westwood and Williams (eds)

Globalisation and Social Exclusion Unit (2000), *Dingle Pride: An Evaluation*, Department of Sociology, Social Policy and Social Work Studies, University of Liverpool

Hall, D., McDonald, J., and Andersen, H. (1999), *Streetscenes: Photoviews by Young People of Dingle and Speke/Garston*, Department of Sociology, Social Policy and Social Work Studies, University of Liverpool

Harper, D. (1998a), 'On the Authority of the Image: Visual Methods at the Crossroads', in N. Denzin and Y. Lincoln (eds), *Collecting and Interpreting Qualitative Materials*, Thousand Oaks: Sage

— (1998b), 'An Argument for Visual Sociology', in J. Prosser (ed.), *Image-Based Research*, London: Falmer Press

Imrie, R. (1997), 'National Economic Policy in the United Kingdom', in Pacione (ed.)

Keith, M. (1993), 'From Punishment to Discipline', in M. Cross and M. Keith (eds), *Racism, the City and the State*, London: Routledge

Lane, T. (1997), *Liverpool: City of the Sea*, Liverpool: Liverpool University Press

Logan, J., Taylor-Gooby, P., and Reuter, M. (1992), 'Poverty and Income Inequality', in S. Fainstein, I. Gordon and M. Harloe (eds), *Divided Cities: New York and London in the Contemporary World*, Oxford: Blackwell

Loney, M., and Allen, M. (1979), *The Crisis of the Inner City*, London: Macmillan

Lovering, J. (1997), 'Global Restructuring and Local Impact', in Pacione (ed.)

Marris, P. (1974), *Loss and Change*, London: Routledge and Kegan Paul

McKeown, P. (1994), Independent Research Report, Toxteth Community Council, Liverpool

McQuire, S. (1988), *Visions of Modernity: Representation, Memory, Time and Space in the Age of the Camera*, London: Sage

Meegan, R. (1989), 'Paradise Postponed: The Growth and Decline of Merseyside's Outer Estates', in P. Cooke (ed.), *Localities: The Changing Face of Urban Britain*, London: Unwin Hyman

Mooney, G. (1999), 'Urban Disorders', in Pile et al. (eds)

Pacione, M. (ed.) (1997), *Britain's Cities*, London: Routledge

Pile, S. (1999), 'What is a City?', in D. Massey, J. Allen and S. Pile (eds), *City Worlds*, London: Routledge

Pile, S., Brook, C., and Mooney, G. (eds) (1999), *Unruly Cities?*, London: Routledge

Shields, R. (1991), *Places on the Margin: Alternative Geographies of Modernity*, London: Routledge

Weber, M. (1958), *The City*, New York: Free Press

Westwood, S., and Williams, J. (eds) (1997), *Imagining Cities: Scripts, Signs, Memory*, London: Routledge

Winston, B. (1998), '"The Camera Never Lies": The Partiality of Photographic Evidence', in J. Prosser (ed.), *Image-Based Research*, London: Falmer Press

11. Community Development: Rhetoric or Reality?

Barney Rooney

Liverpool has more than a fair measure of poverty and it has a strong community identity and traditions of political and social organisation. If the tenets of community development are going to find fertile ground anywhere, this looks like the place. The city also has an extraordinary level of experience of attempts to deal with its poverty and the inevitable social problems that result – a level and variety of experience that might, one would think, have distilled into a confident local wisdom as to how these things should be done. In a seven-year period in the 1950s Liverpool City Council built Kirkby in Lancashire and populated it with 50,000 residents to relieve pressure on its housing list. From the late 1960s Liverpool was designated an Educational Priority Area (1968–72), with an intensive programme of positive discrimination to address the poor educational performance of children; then the Shelter Neighbourhood Action Project in the Granby area (1969–72) set out to involve local people in the development of imaginative responses to local housing need; then the Vauxhall Community Development Project (CDP) (1970–75) piloted the use of community development to find new ways of meeting local needs in areas of high social deprivation. At the same time as the Vauxhall CDP the Brunswick Neighbourhood Scheme (1971–73), on the other side of the city centre, was experimenting with the development of local amenities and environmental improvements, though without the engagement of local residents which was central in Vauxhall. Next came analysis, with the Inner Area Study (1973–76) attempting to understand the nature of inner-city problems from resident perspectives and making measured attempts to forge a corporate management response involving statutory, community and voluntary sectors. Then came the Urban Aid programme, fusing into the Partnership programme providing targeted support to meet central government-defined priority themes but available for statutory and voluntary agencies. And in between was the Third European Poverty programme in Granby Toxteth, and City Challenge, followed by SRB, ESF, health action zones, regional development funds, education action zones, development companies, and other EU programmes as well as the myriad funding streams within local authority and health departments – in short, a bewildering cornucopia of funding. And now it is Partnerships and Neighbourhood Renewal with Liverpool Council for Voluntary Services commissioned to manage the local administration of the Community Empowerment Fund, which will

211

develop the network of community organisation that will give the people a seat at the table alongside the professional social entrepreneurs and provide the 'joined-up' governance that a modern city needs.

So, there has been plenty of opportunity to learn and sharpen the skills necessary for community development. The city council itself has not only had a close involvement in all the above but also has its own programme of grant support to community groups and voluntary sector organisations. In 1971 it disbursed £100,000: in 2001 this had grown to over £3 million of discretionary grants. The full grant programme (amounting to over £15m) was reviewed in the late 1990s by external consultants to see if it could give more directive encouragement to groups to make the transition to non-grant income. Oddly, the review and the resulting 'corporate grant aid strategy' provided no analysis of the strategic impact of present arrangements for grant distribution but led to what is essentially an administrative overhaul titled 'The Investment Strategy' (Liverpool City Council, 2000). The Investment Strategy committed the council to 'empower local communities to identify, represent and meet the aspirations of Liverpool's communities', and it identifies 19 categories of citizens who are intended to benefit from its grant programme. These are children; young people; older people; disabled people (physical, learning, mental illness, long-term illness); black and ethnic minority groups; jobless and unemployed; carers; people with HIV/Aids; lesbians and gay men; refugees/asylum seekers; victims of crime; ex-offenders; one-parent families; substance abusers; young people in, and leaving, care; women; vulnerable young men; faith communities; and travellers – a pretty inclusive list of beneficiaries.

Positive Portents

The idea of 'community development' is closely associated with interventions to deal with social problems. It carries a faith in people, in their capacity to act together against the odds in a collective interest. It presumes that the 'problems' are shared and that the community, whether it is based in an area or on some shared identity or experience (such as ethnicity), does not have access to the resources to resolve them.

The Combat Poverty Agency in Ireland has defined community development as follows:

> Community development is about change in society in favour of those who benefit least. However, it is not just about making concrete changes in the quality of people's lives, it is also about how this is done.
>
> It is about involving people, most especially the disadvantaged, in making changes that they identify to be important and which use and develop their own skills, knowledge and experience.
>
> Community development seeks to challenge the causes of disadvantage/poverty and to offer new opportunities for those lacking choice, power and resources. (Department of Social Welfare, Dublin, 1995)

This alignment with explicit political objectives is much softened within the language used by the UK's Community Development Foundation (CDF), demonstrating the speed of disintegration of ideas of mutuality within social action. Their 'modernised' definition states:

> Community development is a proven technique for fostering more and more effective community activity. The professional practice of community development over many years has aspired to empower people, to overcome exclusion and to enable people to control their local conditions. However, limited funding has often meant that professional community development has been involved in short term projects or low-status auxiliary services. A modernised community development approach, better resources through regeneration programmes and local government reform, links empowerment with building civil society and social capital, and complements, through people's autonomous activities, a range of public service and development initiatives. (CDF, 2002)

There are important distinctions between these sets of definitions but, taken together, it is difficult to think of a time in recent history when the language of national and local politics has sounded so favourable to both the ethic and the practice of supporting poor communities' taking an active part in governance. Local politics look favourable. The Liberal Democrats are now in full control of Liverpool City Council, seemingly without any real prospect of opposition. They have created a brand image of responsiveness to the ordinary people – not populist, but conveying a sense that they care, would 'do the business' and would do it impartially.

The portents also look good in the whole equality/quality agenda, which has attempted to bring fairness and equity to the administration of public services. From the 1970s the lead in these issues had consistently come from self-representation groups, often most effective at a local level, and a common complaint has been the difficulty of any real progress without real political will. This is apparently no longer the case. The government's agenda for the reform of local government (DETR, 1998) seeks a new form of local government which combines efficiency with accountability and carries a clear ethical message; European Human Rights legislation sets new standards for the exercise of the state's responsibility to its citizens; the ripples from the Macpherson Report (HMSO, 1999) have entered the reporting formats of all public services.

Equality issues have also been around long enough for the usable activists to have been incorporated. Public agencies have engaged. The equality agenda is now institutionalised within the bureaucracy of government as an essential indicator of *quality* of service. Authorities cannot avoid setting out their plans within the increasingly codified documentation submitted by local to central government. This can be taken as a fairly reliable sign that one way or another the sting of confrontation has been removed; but there is also no doubt that the *idea* of an ethic concerned with the equality of citizens, their right to be heard and their right to information, is alive and well. Liverpool is listening. You can email the Chief

Executive directly, though it may take a little longer to hold on the phone for an answer from the city's overstretched call centre, Liverpool Direct.

At national level the Social Exclusion Unit, set up in December 1997, has a remit to help reduce social exclusion by producing 'joined-up solutions to joined-up problems'. Its major consultative policy report on neighbourhood renewal in September 1998 made recommendations for community involvement around the following themes:

> *helping residents tackle problems that threaten to undermine the community*, by bearing down on anti-social behaviour; using neighbourhood warden schemes to reduce crime and fear of crime; improving housing lettings policies; and tackling neighbourhood abandonment;

> *stimulating community activity*, by promoting arts and sport in deprived neighbourhoods; and encouraging more meeting places and opportunities, such as shops, community facilities or community activities; and

> *helping residents get involved in turning round their neighbourhoods*, by building community capacity and leadership; making it easier for community and voluntary organisations to get funding; and encouraging local involvement in service delivery. (Social Exclusion Unit, 1998)

This has now materialised in the Neighbourhood Renewal programme's Community Empowerment Fund.

So the portents for the involvement of the people and communities in the resolution of problems look very good indeed – and the problems are certainly there. Four of Liverpool's five parliamentary constituencies rank in the top 50 in the UK unemployment league (January 1999). Riverside ranks second and its 15.5 per cent unemployment rate masks the harsher statistic that over 50 per cent of residents of working age are without full-time employment (October 2000). Ill-health and poor educational performance follow in proportion. Indeed, it is the confidence with which these statistics of deprivation can be presented that brings in the initiatives, programmes and projects, and their grants. Poverty is an important experience within Liverpool's communities, but it is also a very important economic resource for the city.

The Past has Passed

Not that it would be put quite that way by the city's image builders. We are told that that's the old image, and it's time to forget it. It is in the past. The city has confronted and banished the demons. It is now modern, vital, cultured, ambitious and inventive. But what about community development? Look at the Eldonian Village, once a derelict area with a dispirited community which picked itself up and has transformed itself into a model urban village within a stone's throw of the city centre, with its own sports centre, businesses and old people's home. Walk up to London Road, transformed from a run-down shopping backwater just off the city centre to a vibrant retail area. Or take a look at the Furniture Resource Centre: two lads in an old stable block recycling unwanted furniture and now employing 160 people; a national model of how social businesses should be run, giving long-term unemployed the training to make the furniture that enables social landlords all over the country to furnish unwanted flats and let them to the homeless. Yesterday is history and we are a regenerated people.

The much admired Eldonian Village sits at the point where the triangle of the Vauxhall ward meets the city centre. The ward was the chosen area for the Vauxhall CDP. The CDP set up community groups, campaigned on local issues, brought arts and education to the area and attempted to sharpen up the quality of service provision by the local authority. By its own criteria, and the expectations of those who worked in it, the project was no great success. Within its tenure the major local employer, Tate and Lyle, closed down and relocated. Vauxhall was not turned around economically or socially and still remains a very poor district. The project also failed to improve the fragmented way in which local authority services managed their business. Local government proved incapable of engaging with the CDP in finding a workable model of area management. The CDP was adjudged a failure.

But end-of-term reports can come too early to judge a project that gave local residents unprecedented opportunities to study, to organise and to broaden their cultural and political experience. There has been no retrospective evaluation of the long-term impact of the Vauxhall CDP. Physically the whole area has now lost its scars – the derelict waterway, the rancid smells of rendering animal carcasses and tanning, the tenement blocks – and it is tempting to speculate that there is some influential link between these changes, the CDP and the Eldonian Village which followed some years later. Making the link might need some creativity. The CDP is deemed to have failed, whereas the Eldonians succeeded. The CDP was a professional incursion into the area which struggled for some time before it really got community activity moving; the Eldonian Village is presented as a triumph of active citizenship. The CDP was a limited attempt to challenge the inefficiencies of local government bureaucracy by developing resident organisation; the Eldonians perhaps resulted from an intervention by central government designed to hurt a dissident council by fomenting community division through uncustomary largesse.

Yet there is no point in speculating, as the CDP is lost to history. A review of all the past interventions will show that not only were they of limited success, they were also of their time. They reflected the political ideologies and interests of a different era. We have moved on. Indeed, but has any wisdom been gleaned from the experience? Are current policies towards poverty and community, and the perceived role of community development in those policies, informed by the past? The two definitions of community development quoted above give pointers: one already sounds dated and resigned to the structural stability of the conditions that cause poverty and disadvantage; the second acknowledges the limitations of the past but glows with optimism that things are looking better.

The Social Exclusion Unit might agree with the latter. 'Neighbourhood management is a new idea about how to help local outcomes by helping local services to join up and respond to local needs' (SEU, 2000). The notion of 'joined-up solutions to joined-up problems' is neat but in the world of social policy it is not new. The Shelter Neighbourhood Action Project in 1970 called it 'total approach'; the CDP tried to get all providers of local services working together within one building and with a shared structure of policy development and administration, as 'joined-up' as any of the contemporary Partnerships. The catchphrase nonetheless reminds us that social problems exist within a complex web of experiences, needs, resources, relationships, choices and opportunities, and that the same applies to responses to those problems. But it doesn't say a great deal about the processes by which different partners understand how presenting problems are defined and understood, or the parameters set on the options for responding to them, limited as they will be by ideology, financial ceilings, skill, political imperatives or imagination. The cleverness of the phrase, however, is that it implies that they are all on the agenda. It is a neat marketing slogan which disarms by implying that the complexities and contradictions have been considered, addressed and reconciled.

The Social Exclusion Unit's Report on Neighbourhood Renewal acknowledges the 'concentration in poor neighbourhoods of a range of interlocking problems such as high levels of unemployment, crime and ill-health, and poor education', and 'how the gap with the rest of the country [has] widened' in turn-of-the-century Britain. This is welcome regained ground. In the early 1990s there was considerable government resistance to the use of the word 'poverty' alongside a questioning of the existence of 'society'. But a fair amount of that ideological legacy is still around. The face is kinder and the words warmer but the mistrust of unreformed or un-'modernised' local government is still there. There are mixed messages in the political commitment to remove dependence on the state and transfer it back to individuals, their families or their communities. The present government is clearly committed to trying to maintain the level of public expenditure that is commensurate with its particular economic and social values, to a mixed economy in the provision of social services, to business models of efficiency and to no significant redistribution of wealth. The gap between the poor and the wealthy, which has stretched and widened over the past 20 years, and the consolidation of the poor into what are seen as problem neighbourhoods continue to be paralleled by the related withdrawal of services to poor areas. Since 2000 the modernising axe has again been swinging within Liverpool Social Services Department, each stroke telling someone emphatically that they have wasted their life in the service of the public. The city council has recently shed another 1,500 jobs, while claiming implausibly that there is no detriment to service.

The portents were looking reasonably good for an investment in community, but what then of the practice?

How to Socially Include

Nobody would let it appear that he could see nothing, for then he would not be fit for his post, or else he was a fool . . .

(Hans Christian Andersen, 'The Emperor's New Clothes', c.1870)

The diversification of funding streams and the extension of the culture of competition to social programmes have sharpened the descriptive skills of those who draft the bids, but it is hard to avoid an impression that somehow the confident and assertive analysis of local poverty, the empathy with its manifestations, and the articulate descriptions of the relationships between people, issues and places that preface funding bids become more elusive as the money is procured and wends its way through the programmes and projects to whatever place of rest money arrives at when the multiplier has given its last gasp.

It is now common practice to invite tenders to produce a study of projects that could be used to demonstrate good practice in social inclusion and, on the basis of the study, produce a 'tool kit' that could be used by businesses wanting to 'do social inclusion'. The idea of a Haynes Manual on Social Inclusion (with pull-out charts on, say, how to co-opt a long-term drug user onto your board, or how to give good pay and working conditions to part-time workers without affecting your profit margins) suggests a certain dislocation from the practicalities of addressing questions of social inclusion at an organisational or community level. We know that this work is very difficult indeed. The acknowledgement of that difficulty does not diminish the task; this is not the world of self-improvement, where admitting the problem is the first step in recovery. The idea of a tool kit reflects that mood of dilettantism that can enter approaches to inclusion and community when creative people with no experiential stake find themselves with free money to allocate. If social exclusion is seen to be an outcome of the exercise of mainstream interests and processes in society, a tool kit seems a slight and inadequate weapon to point towards those interests and processes. If it is seen as the outcome of the elective choices of the small number of people whose activities might be better managed, a tool kit can have appeal.

That this simplistic view exists, and it does, reflects a polarisation of experience between communities and service providers and a distorted perception of life within communities. The processes that have encouraged this are straightforward enough. There has been a loss of confidence within the Labour movement that core socialist principles can be reinterpreted rather than rendered irrelevant by 'modernisation', and we are seeing the effects of that modernisation on internal practice within providers of social services (in the broad sense). Decreased resources have led to fewer people spending more of their time dealing with more intractable problems, and social services have been reduced to involvement with only extreme problems or behaviour, sharpening the distinction between the lives of these people and 'ordinary' life; the same process brings about a normalisation of higher levels of unsupported problems in poor communities. A distancing between professionals and people has been consolidated by other changes taking place within the providers as they have transformed their organisational culture to adopt practices, codes and belief systems more in keeping with a business ethic. Other factors include over-optimism, the need for success, short-term programmes that never stay around to test the effectiveness of their ideas, a frenetic mobility in the employment market, a paranoia about demonstrating personal or professional weakness, ritual compliance, a lack of courage and a certain social distance from the reality of poverty and related social problems. There was a time when social sector professionals in poor areas would try not to look too out-of-place within the community where they worked (albeit with no great success) as a slight gesture of identification with residents; they are now reshaped into the distinctive, office-based role of social managers and seem happy to look the part.

With this increased distance, the interpretation of the conditions in poor communities then comes either from statistical compassion based on the consistent messages in data about health, youth justice, early pregnancy or school performance, or from the balance sheets of service costs. Or it comes from the stressed and overstretched service providers dealing with the most problematic individuals or households in the community. Or it is interpreted through the blinkered vision of moralising self-interest, so that problem-makers must first defer to the authority of the regenerators, must be brought into line and made to stop 'spoiling the party'.

There would be common agreement that members of communities should have a major say in defining their own experiences, needs and interests, but regeneration programmes past and present have often struggled to win the confidence of local people and to construct opportunities for their involvement (Anastacio et al., 2000). In Liverpool, although there are mechanisms for consultation, involvement and participation in management, there is no sense of a real engagement with communities, either through existing structures of representation or in new arrangements, even though that would have been claimed for the local Pathways structure. A distinct scepticism about the effectiveness of local government was noted by the Liverpool Democracy Commission:

> Local democracy has lost the trust and confidence of people because of the failure to provide effective leadership, its inability to engage with citizens and, perhaps most importantly of all, because of its failure to deliver consistently reliable and cost effective services. (Liverpool Democracy Commission, 1999)

This would also seem to apply to the administration and management of regeneration (Forrest and Kearns, 1999).

Pointing the finger at any single cause would miss the point that the conditions that determine effectiveness in implementing any area of social policy are complex. But, given that the traditional public sector has been so comprehensively stripped of any sense of its value and been righteously ground into the dust, I would like to have a tilt at the idea that the private sector holds the answer.

Business is Business

Business per se has to carry the weight of expectation that it will inevitably introduce flair, inventiveness, pragmatism, and above all efficiency, the portfolio of qualities that is now deemed to have been wholly absent from the fusty old bureaucracies of local government. There are obvious flaws in this expectation, and not just the common-sense ones that would be inferred from insolvency statistics. Three such flaws are as follows:

1. Business has significant deficiencies of skill and knowledge, and it has its own social values. Its culture can contribute to a reintroduction of values that had otherwise long been discarded. Post-war social scientists have scorned the Victorian concept of 'lesser eligibility', the idea of a hierarchy of worth and worthiness among the poor, as being mean-spirited, antisocial, moralistic and based on a simplistic understanding of the structural determinants of inequality. Since the 1990s it looks disturbingly unproblematic as the influence of the charitable traditions of Rotarians, Masons and celebrities finds an outlet in worthy and appealing causes. Compassion can have a narrow, prescribed and none too altruistic role within the business ethic.

2. It isn't only efficient businesses that will be attracted to the social sector. In the attempts to lure businesses into social partnerships it seems likely that the more efficient and successful will take greater care to ensure that the time they spend on any project, social or otherwise, guarantees a good return on their investment. If the returns are not good, the tendency may be to attract the mediocre.

3. Business is part of the problem and contributes to the experience of poverty through the higher costs of fuel and food, the absence of access to cheap credit or the withdrawal of utilities. This process is described by Speak and Graham (2000), who note the need for 'a greater recognition within regeneration policy of the importance of private sector services in the process of area decline and of the likely compound effects on residents'.

Notwithstanding these quibbles, any business with an eye on the market will have noticed the amount of money coming into Liverpool for disbursement through more flexible arrangements than in the past, and the opening up of, and encouragement to enter, the social market. A local illustration of a resulting marriage of community need and business flair would be Liverpool Primary STEP.

Liverpool Primary STEP

Sound education is considered a prerequisite of a sound economy and is therefore a priority within central government's social and economic project. Liverpool's educational system was heavily criticised in an Ofsted report in 1999, which showed consistent low scoring from schools in performance tables (Ofsted, 1999). The statistics are borne out in anecdotal experience, with very poor literacy and numeracy among many young people in poor areas.

Liverpool Primary STEP was a project to address literacy and numeracy in 35 primary schools in poor areas. It ran for four years from 1998 and had a budget of over £6 million. Its specific aim was to introduce computer-based education to improve the performance of children in the period before they moved on to secondary education, improving their chances of integrating into the secondary system. It set itself more far-sighted objectives than simple improvement in performance, aiming to 'support strategies challenging disaffection, poor motivation and truancy, further develop the core skills of parents and the local community and empower them to support family/community learning initiatives' (Background Information, Primary STEP Project). Its bid for SRB funding included the following statements:

> The bid has at its heart the aim of raising achievement but it also has wider objectives of breaking the cycle of de-motivation and underachievement, of reducing crime and improving community safety, and of addressing related quality of life issues and so producing social and economic inclusion [. . .]

> [. . .] the cycle of de-motivation and underachievement [is] much in evidence in each of the target Pathways areas yet poorly articulated and rarely addressed in its widest sense. This is in spite of the number and cost of numerous 'second chance' initiatives and other interventions by the LEA, Social Services, Police and juvenile justice services and other agencies to mitigate the results of failure. Primary STEP will break this cycle at source within the Pathways areas, widen opportunities and reduce the need for later intervention. (Liverpool Primary STEP, Application to SRB: 12)

STEP is in fact the creation of ICL, a multinational producer of computers and business software owned by Fujitsu, which is now a major player in IT within the education sector. This company set up an 'at risk' commercial venture in Bristol with British Telecom at the end of 1995 where it entered into a contract with a number of schools, without the agreement of the Local Education Authority, and provided computers, training and curriculum materials. A superficial evaluation was carried out through one of its collaborators, the Department of Education at the University of Exeter, which claimed that the venture was an educational success (Still and Sharp, 1997). It had subsequent contact with Liverpool Local Education Authority and negotiated provisional agreement to run a similar project in Liverpool. ICL worked with the LEA to design a specification targeted at SRB funding. This became Liverpool Primary STEP, a partnership between the public and private sectors.

The partnership offered the LEA the opportunity to bring in equipment and skills to financially hard-pressed schools and allowed ICL to develop its market, not only for the computers themselves but also for the related training and software. To secure funding the partnership had to engage a third sector, the community, and bring on board the local Pathways partnerships which formally represented a community interest within regeneration activity. This was done by the choice of schools to be involved, the emphasis on community benefits, involvement of the Pathways partnerships on a management board, and the promise of four community computer centres. Having helped to design the brief for the scheme, ICL then withdrew from the process to sever its interest, submitted a tender and was appointed as prime contractor. It is currently implementing the project elements related to provision of computers, engagement of schools and teaching staff. A neat and successful commercial venture.

And what about the promised contract with 'the community', or the Education Directorate's ambitions for far-reaching effects at the individual, family and community levels to be closely monitored by the 'evaluation' that was one of the central principles of the proposal? As far as ICL was concerned, the community element (working with parents and setting up community computer centres) was acknowledged as being outside its skill and expertise. Although it was an essential part of the bid and absolutely central to the worthy social objectives of the project, it was excluded from the contracted outputs, and ICL was relieved of the task, without alternative arrangements being made. Three years into the project no independent arrangements for evaluation were in place. And as is often the way with 'easy money', the relevance of community benefits had receded: the project was doing what ICL wanted, the Education Directorate was involved in another process of change, in short the action had moved on.

If the language of the bid is to be taken at face value (and not to do so is to accuse the bidders of deception) this de-prioritisation could be seen as an exploitative invocation of community needs for commercial gain. Whether or not it is exploitative may depend on one's point of view. From a business perspective it looks fair enough. The first priority for business involvement is commercial viability: a project must cover its outlay and meet or exceed its planned profit margins. The second priority is that the involvement can be presented as a success in terms that will enhance the company's reputation and future commercial opportunities. The stated objectives of the project diminish in importance. They are the means to the end of getting the funding and are important only in so far as they remain the active criteria by which the business itself will be judged, professionally or commercially.

Within the business sector there are undoubted skills and techniques in the areas of audit, planning, project management, notions of cost and the value of time. These can be much sharper than in the traditional public sector. But assessing the effectiveness of social outputs is much more challenging. There is plenty of loose talk around about concepts such as 'social capital', but few social businesses have developed methods of auditing their social output that are as accurate or useful as their systems of financial audit. Assessing effectiveness is therefore either wholly reduced to conventional finance-based criteria, or it is taken out of the sphere of audit and becomes an issue of marketing. As such, objective fact is not what matters; management of image is what really counts. How effective the business is in applying its skills to social objectives is less important than projecting the image that it is effective.

Talk It Up

Marketing is now important in the social sector and the talk is of strategy, SMART objectives and measurable outputs, expertise, really efficient management and a hard-headed rationality, in marked contrast to the old days of bickering politicians and councils perceived to be overstaffed and bureaucratic. Ofsted, the Audit Commission and HM Inspector of Prisons may generate a comprehensive form of critical scrutiny that can be institutionalised in other sectors, but at present their degree of rigour is not common. The transitory nature of projects and programmes makes arrangements for real accountability cumbersome; methods for auditing social outcomes are crude and extremely underdeveloped. Long-standing dependence on funding via grant-based programmes doesn't help. The terms change and the flow is not predictable. The creative art is in getting the funding approved, particularly with competitive programmes; disbursing it can then be a tedious, administrative hassle in which the question of effectiveness may become sidelined. Given the emphasis on projecting a market image of buoyant success, it becomes very difficult indeed to be confident that the projects and schemes that claim success, or have success claimed on their behalf, would stand up to objective scrutiny.

The grants come with their own conditions and objectives spilling into one another so that one project may be getting funding from four or five different programmes. The idea of a *Single* Regeneration Budget has been overwhelmed in an impatient flurry of funding streams. This funding regime draws people into the illusion that each phase is *the* real opportunity to turn a particular place around rather than the more realistic view that this is an unsatisfactory method of cyclical top-up for a persistently underfunded area. Some sort of accumulated wisdom coming out of this would be useful but unlikely.

However, optimism, confidence and the image of success are important for the city. The carping, dissenting voices are unwelcome. There are few of them anyway as the net of patronage and partnership spreads wide. The message is that regeneration will create vibrant local areas with jobs and resolve social problems. Consultation and participation are acknowledged as essential parts of a multi-dimensional approach, but the plan comes first. People are mobile. If the plan requires it they can relocate. Kirkby, Halewood, Speke and Scotland Road were regenerated 30 years ago, the Falkner Estate 15 years ago, London Road five years ago. Communities can adapt to change. The planned expansion of students coming to the city (perhaps the most successful part of Liverpool's regeneration programme) illustrates that strong, quiet leadership works well. This key decision, which has brought a large influx of fairly homogeneous new residents to the city, has had real impact on streets, areas and people but was not based on consultation. Leadership is part of the message and people are a commodity along with the lie of the land, proximity to feeder resources and buildings – there to be considered in the re-packaging to create the image or prospect that looks attractive to funders.

Negative Portents

The techniques of community development lend themselves to strategic interventions to deal with specific issues affecting a community, or, more subtly, to help stabilise communities by providing an infrastructure of relationship and inculcating a culture of system and conformity to channel energies into structures that can then be politically engaged. In this latter approach what type of activity takes place is less important than the fact that it is taking place. This approach is evident in the political management of conflict in Northern Ireland, and the 'modernised' community development advocated in the definition of the CDF (2002, cited above) comes pretty close to it. In practice, neither of these options seems to be under consideration in Liverpool. Forrest and Kearns' (1999) study of social cohesion and neighbourhood regeneration argued that there was a real need for community development at a level more substantial than current commitments to community participation. But there is a difficulty in confidently identifying the conditions in which such development would easily fit with current approaches to regeneration activity. It is not conceptually difficult to find a role, since everyone agrees with the development of community, but in practice the climate of increasingly centralised decision making, a council now reorganised, talk of an elected mayor and strong leadership, business ethics and opportunities, makes it hard to see who even thinks in terms of real participation or has the vision and authority to make the investment over the sort of timescale that would be involved.

Equally, it is difficult to see where within the regeneration community there is an understanding of the nature and causation of social problems that could accommodate anything as unspecific as 'community development' when other methods are seen to provide more effective management. The links between social need and social problems are unexplored and rarely articulated, leaving a regeneration agenda in denial of its roots. Crime is seen to be under control, 'race' is confined to a small part of the city and drugs can be seen as part of the informal economy. And there is enough lottery, HAZ and other grant funding sprinkled over every other 'welfare' variety of social problem to assure us that everything's OK, someone is looking after it.

It is just as difficult to see how the commonality of experience within a community can be readily formed into a local and consensual agenda, given the fragmentation of those groupings which have in the past drawn experiences of social inequality and social injustice into a common explaining political philosophy. The idea that people in disadvantaged communities have bonds of experience that transcend their differences seems outdated. Dingle, in the south end of Liverpool, is a run-down area but it is known as a tight-knit community with a high level of social cohesion. Six high-level security cameras now scan the area and residents want more. When this sort of surveillance is used by a community to keep an eye on its disruptive children there is a radical fracture in bonds of mutual understanding and mutual responsibility.

The essence of what we might call 'old-style' community development is that a resolution of problems is seen as possible within the resources of the people, who might be given new skills or the opportunity to use existing ones to address the resolution of their problems. There is no suggestion that this is straightforward, or that the problems can be dealt with without resources, or that community development is an alternative to other regenerative activity. The key is the nature of the relationship with the community, the process by which power and influence over key decisions are transferred into the community, and the way that structures and skills are developed so that power and influence can be exercised. This is what provides the levelling of status that will draw the community back from the margins. But levelling is not on the regeneration agenda.

Conclusion

The positive portents for an energetic bustle of community development work are deceptive. The work goes on within community councils and projects, through groups and individuals doing important and valuable things, but the idea of community development as a mechanism by which a group of people are given the support and resources to develop and express their potential is not part of any big plan. The sort of approach envisaged in the definition of the Combat Poverty Agency is too open-ended, not neat enough or manageable enough. It would need interventions whose timescale could not be constrained within a two- or three-year tranche of committed funding and ideas. Worse than that, it already seems old-fashioned. The 'modernised' agenda is much more attractive. It is well intentioned and says things that we would like to be true, so that it seems churlish not to join in the hymn of faith. To repeat, 'A modernised community development approach [. . .] links empowerment with building civil society and social capital, and complements, through people's autonomous activities, a range of public service and development initiatives' (CDF, 2002). Now, there is a subject for a hard-headed business-based feasibility study. Visualising this approach is easier than operationalising it. David Westwood, Chief Constable of Humberside, in his former role of Assistant Chief Constable of Merseyside, painted this picture:

> We can imagine trees and green open spaces, well-maintained buildings, opportunities for leisure and entertainment, work opportunities for the skilled people living here and, over all this we want to see people enjoying the amenities of the region free from crime and the fear of crime. (quoted in Rooney and Brown, 1996).

We have here an image of a fresh, vibrant, healthy society whose citizens are bound together in a web of interlinking roles, relationships and responsibilities – a new utopia in which everybody knows their place.

The vision may well be the reality for sectors of the community. There is undoubtedly something of a party going on in Liverpool. The drinks have been subsidised by the statistics of premature death and debility, crime and unemployment, illiteracy and under-education, which keep the indicators of deprivation high enough to pull in the grants that keep the system going. The subsidy also draws in a whole stratum of social managers and entrepreneurs bringing skills that must, presumably, be underdeveloped in the local citizenry. They come and they just love the city and its people, brush up against its edges, give it time, and like the colonial classes elsewhere and in other times either assimilate or move on with an enhanced CV and a bagful of traveller's tales. The image of the city centre says that their work and the regeneration of Liverpool are a real success, with new buildings, traffic systems, bars, cafés and more bars, innovative partnerships, projects and programmes bringing strategic direction at all levels. It is a small leap of faith to conclude that these things tell truths about the quality of life of Liverpool's citizens. But it might be worth taking a couple of hours out to lean against the wall outside the Kwik-Save at the top of Smithdown Road, or plenty of other places around the city. Just watch people moving about their business and speculate about their health, wealth, aspirations and prospects of fulfilling their dreams. The buzz of activity is in the city but it is dislocated from the harsh experiences which are community poverty.

The Eldonians have shown that community development can work, but the Eldonian Village is not typical, and it is extremely difficult to clear away the haze of mystification, bluster and wishful thinking to get an objective measure of just how well similar interventions actually measure up to the objectives they set themselves and just how much they really contribute to the communities whose experiences they invoke. The idea that years of experience have led to a collective wisdom is misplaced. There is not even an economic model in place that can trace how much of the millions of pounds of grant money that are claimed to pour in actually pour out. Nor is there any forum for critical review, independent and insulated from ties of patronage, which takes an interest in the interrelationships between community, social problems and regeneration activity, not as part of the delivery of a prevailing political agenda but to bring a missing integrity to regeneration activity. As it was put in a speech in the old days of pre-history 25 years ago on this very subject:

> There must be provision for activities and proposals of local and central government and other agencies to be critically appraised and their impact on particular areas and groups clearly identified. This will require substantial consultation with and participation of residents throughout the decision-making process [. . .] Funding must be related to progress. Provision should be made to allow for realistic evaluation [. . .] (Mellor, 1976)

References

Anastacio, Jean, et al. (2000), *Reflecting Realities: Participants' Perspectives on Integrated Communities and Sustainable Development*, Bristol: The Policy Press

CDF (Community Development Foundation) (1995), *Working Together Against Poverty: An Information Pack on the Community Development Programme*, Dublin: Department of Social Welfare

— (2002), 'What is Community Development', www.cdf.org.uk

Department of Social Welfare, Dublin (1995), *Working Together Against Poverty*, Dublin: Department of Social Welfare

DETR (Department of the Environment, Transport and the Regions) (1998), *Modernising Local Government*, London: DETR

Forrest, R., and Kearns, A. (1999), *Joined-Up Places? Social Cohesion and Neighbourhood Regeneration*, York: Jospeh Rowntree Foundation

HMSO (1999), *The Stephen Lawrence Inquiry. Report of an Inquiry by Sir William McPherson of Clun*, London: HMSO

Liverpool City Council (2000), *Grant Aid Strategy*, Liverpool: Liverpool City Council

Liverpool Democracy Commission (1999), *Future: The Leading of Liverpool*, Liverpool: Liverpool Democracy Commission, New Local Government Network

Rooney, B., and Brown, M. (1996), *Locked Out: Housing and Young Black People on Merseyside*, Shelter FBHO

Social Exclusion Unit (1998), *Bringing Britain Together – A National Strategy for Neighbourhood Renewal* (Cmd 4045), London: HMSO

— (2000), *National Strategy for Neighbourhood Renewal. Report of PATG*, London: Social Exclusion Unit

Speak, S., and Graham, S. (2000), 'Service Not Included: Social Implications of Private Sector Service Restructuring in Marginalized Communities', *JRF*, Bristol: The Policy Press

Still, M., and Sharp, J. (1997), 'BEON Facing the Future', Exeter: University of Exeter Multimedia Communications Services

12. Futures for Liverpool

Gideon Ben-Tovim

Liverpool in the New Millennium: An Urban Renaissance?

At the beginning of a new century and a new millennium, Liverpool's prospects are more promising now than at any point in the last thirty years. The economic downturn, seen in the decline in the traditional shipping and car industries, has some prospect of being reversed, with the symbolic replacement of the traditional Ford with the more upmarket Jaguar at the new industrial city of Speke/Garston, in contrast to the difficulties faced by the car industry in Birmingham (BMW/Rover) and Dagenham (Ford).

The Port of Liverpool is now enjoying a revival, as the waterfront itself, having been kick-started by the Albert Dock refurbishment, is being transformed with new homes, office blocks and hotels, with plans also being developed for new cultural and leisure facilities and enhanced ferry and cruise-liner facilities. The Liverpool city region is becoming a leading site for call centres, the new factories of the twenty-first century, and there is pioneering work in ICT and biotechnology. The second round of Objective One funding will deliver a further total of £2 billion to Merseyside, including public and private funds matching the European Commission's allocation.

The café and club culture is spawning a host of new restaurants, bars and coffee shops throughout the city centre, and into the suburbs too. There is no let-up in the impact of students on the Liverpool scene, with Liverpool remaining one of the most popular student destinations. New or renovated facilities for educational purposes or for student accommodation are contributing to the construction mini-boom in the city. City living is taking off, thanks to the imaginative, design-conscious conversions of lofts, derelict buildings and redundant office blocks being developed by a group of young entrepreneurs with local connections led by Urban Splash.

There is a talented sector of small creative enterprises, in retail, in the arts, in computer design and e-technology, symbolised by the state-of-the-art new cultural centre established by FACT, the Foundation for Arts and Creative Technology. Liverpool already has one of the country's most profitable retail sectors, with a major new development at Paradise Street under way, while ambitious plans for the complete redesign of the city centre are being developed by Liverpool Vision,

227

Britain's first new Urban Regeneration Company inspired by the Rogers Report *Towards an Urban Renaissance* (Rogers, 1999) and funded by English Partnership, North West Regional Development Agency and Liverpool City Council.

Liverpool City Council is under new management, with a new 'can-do' Chief Executive and a small team of top Executive Directors ambitious to transform the delivery of city council services, working alongside a political leadership which, after a decade of relatively 'hung' administrations, enjoys a clear political majority. There is a consensus of political determination among the leading parties to shake off the old 'high council tax, poor quality of services' reputation, and the 'can't-do culture' of Liverpool City Council.

Liverpool's potential as a major tourist centre is being increasingly acknowledged, with its natural assets in the waterfront, superb architecture, high-quality museums and galleries, extensive parks, celebrated sporting excellence, and a strong international brand image. The new arch in Chinatown, the largest in Europe, built by a team of Chinese craftsmen, indicates the belated acknowledgement of Europe's oldest Chinese community, and perhaps symbolises the ability of Liverpool to begin to play to its competitive strengths. Liverpool John Lennon Airport is being increasingly used for international travel, thanks to the new cheap fares market created by operators such as EasyJet. There has been a growing recognition of the potential benefit of rebranding Liverpool as European City of Culture, which did so much to help transform the image of Glasgow, to help reinvent Liverpool as a premier-league European city, if not a world-class city.

... Or a City in Continuing Decline?

How much of this analysis is simply public relations puff, the routine 'place-boosterism' that is part of current urban competitiveness? What are the prospects of Liverpool recreating itself from a second-class city with a branch economy, an association with crime and squalor immortalised in the 'festival of litter' image of Bill Bryson (1996: 235), and a reputation for second-rate political and managerial leadership, the inheritance left to the city by the Toxteth riots of 1981 and the Militant politics of the mid-1980s? Can Liverpool really become, once again, a leading British city, let alone a leading European or world-class city?

Most critically, can Liverpool climb out from its current levels of significant underperformance? A number of objective measures point relentlessly to the stark reality of Liverpool's relative position as one of the most deprived local authorities in England (MTEC, 1999; Liverpool Vision, 1999; Liverpool First, 1999). The fact that the state of the base economy made Merseyside eligible for a second round of Objective One European funding, on the basis of its level of GDP being less than 75 per cent of the EU average, has to be seen as a sign of continuing failure, rather than an indicator of success.

There has been relatively little significant inward investment into Liverpool, with the decline of traditional industries and relatively few blue chip, footloose multinational companies or chains investing in the city. Unemployment figures of

7 per cent in April 2002 are twice the national average, though real joblessness figures are higher, and 25 per cent of these are long-term unemployed. There are still significant levels of poverty, as seen by the high percentage of households claiming housing or council tax benefit (33%) and the large number of school-children eligible for free school meals (34%), with an estimated 43 per cent of households in poverty or on the margins (Liverpool Partnership Group, 2002).

Educational achievement is well below the national average. In 2002, 39.2 per cent of pupils achieved five or more GCSEs (A–C grade), compared with the national average of 51.6 per cent. Significant numbers of children leave at 16, many without qualifications and disappearing out of official educational records. In 2002, only 35.5 per cent of the local workforce had NVQ Level 3+ qualifications, compared with 42.2 per cent nationally, and at Level 4 the figures were 19 per cent and 23.8 per cent respectively. Nearly 30 per cent of the population of Liverpool have poor basic skills, compared with 24 per cent nationally. Liverpool's education service was nearly 'outsourced' by the government in 1999, as a result of a poor Ofsted inspection of the local education authority and a subsequent damning KPMG consultancy report commissioned by government and Liverpool City Council (Ofsted, 1999; KPMG, 1999).

Levels of ill health are among the highest in Britain, with a standard mortality ratio for 0–75-year-olds at 43 per cent above the national figure, and one of the worst lung cancer rates in the country (Liverpool Health Authority, 2001). Liverpool City Council, despite its claims of modernisation and aspirations for 'best value', was named by the Audit Commission as within the bottom three of all local authorities (Audit Commission, 2000), with serious weaknesses in key service areas, such as social services, street cleaning, housing repairs and benefit services. More recent reports do, however, point to an improvement of Liverpool's position in the civic league table, being designated a 'fair' rather than a 'weak' council, though still neither 'excellent' nor 'good' (Audit Commission, 2002).

Some local areas of the city suffer extreme multiple disadvantages, as do some specific groups, such as members of racial minority groups. Thus Liverpool's British-born Black community is still excluded from city-centre employment, as evidenced by the recent report by South Liverpool Personnel (2000) indicating little improvement in the last decade, with very few city-centre jobs filled by black people. Liverpool City Council's (2000) Equal Opportunities Public Review found little progress had been made within the council's own employment profile, while the city's newest minority, the Somalis, are seriously marginalised from main-stream opportunities, as seen from the Bishop of Liverpool's (2000) *Commission of Inquiry into the Somali Community*. The council is now seeking to redress the balance through a new Somali Umbrella Group and a detailed race equality scheme, but specific practical outcomes are as yet unproven (Liverpool City Council, 2002).

There are substantial pockets of poor housing, derelict land and boarded-up shops, accompanied by a serious problem of demand for social housing (see the CURS (1999) study of Liverpool housing need). House prices are relatively low, with the housing market having virtually collapsed in a large tract of the inner city,

though values are rising in the city centre, the waterfront and the southern suburban areas. There is a lack of in-migration to the city as a whole, and to certain parts
in particular, with insufficient flow of the skilled and professional social strata
needed for dynamic urban innovation.

Population decline is still a serious problem: a 7.7 per cent decline between 1991
and 2001, compared with the national picture of a 2.6 per cent increase – for
Liverpool only a marginal improvement on the 8 per cent population loss between
the early 1980s and the early 1990s. The infrastructure of schools, housing, shops,
parks and roads was built for a population nearly twice the size of Liverpool's
current numbers. It has proved impossible to maintain this infrastructure at
acceptable levels of quality and cost, but the radical restructuring required to re-
engineer the city and its facilities has so far been beyond the grasp of local politicians and civic leaders.

The city's 'public realm' is largely of poor quality, with few pleasant public spaces
or squares apart from the tranquil, but small, Bluecoat Chambers garden. The
main shopping area in the city centre, Church Street, has long been undermined
by low-grade street traders. Liverpool's legacy of fine architecture has not been sustained, with many unsightly modern buildings and empty offices. As a further
visible sign of civic decline and neglect, Liverpool's ring of once resplendent
Victorian parks requires a major transfusion of funds and imaginative restoration.

Liverpool's environmental track-record is poor, with little domestic recycling,
and a late grasp of the wheelie-bin revolution that more far-sighted cities addressed
much earlier, while Liverpool clung to its outmoded black bin-bag culture.
Transport links by road, rail, sea and air provide poor gateways into the city, and
they all need major upgrading. Liverpool's world-renowned Royal Philharmonic
Orchestra has been under serious financial threat for several years; Liverpool's theatres have been in serious decline, symbolised by a long period of closure of the
Liverpool Playhouse; and cinema facilities are limited for a modern city centre.

Objective indicators, then, would suggest that 'city in decline', a nineteenth-
century city gone downhill, seems a more realistic title for Liverpool than the
'renaissance city' to which its leaders now aspire. By comparison, the other major
city in the region, Manchester, seems to continue to race ahead in terms of key economic indicators and image, leaving Liverpool in a weak position to punch its
weight for influence in the increasingly significant northwest region: Liverpool's
failure to have a single major millennium project, consequent on the collapse of
the Discovery Park project at Chavasse Park, and the long-running failure to
develop the Festival Garden site or the King's Dock are perhaps apt symbols of its
continuing tradition as the city of missed opportunities.

Playing the Regeneration Game

On the other hand, Liverpool has been developing a reputation for innovation in
community-based regeneration. There have been pioneering initiatives, such as
the bottom-up recreation of the Eldonian community in their self-generated move

from housing clearance to a reclaimed 'brownfield' site, including the pioneering use of neighbourhood wardens now adopted by the government as key to neighbourhood renewal (Social Exclusion Unit, 2000). Liverpool has led the field in cooperative housing, as in the celebrated Weller Way cooperative. There have been other examples of community enterprise, local exchange and trading schemes, and interesting experiments in the social economy such as the nationally acclaimed work of the Furniture Resource Centre, providing recycled white goods, training and employment opportunities, and support for low-income households.

There is a long-standing and active voluntary sector, with some very experienced and skilful community entrepreneurs, who are now part of a new professional class, regularly rubbing shoulders with civil servants, council officials and the new breed of consultants who have risen to prominence on the back of the regeneration funding maze. The Merseyside 'Pathways' initiative, the public–private voluntary local partnerships established to ensure there was active community involvement in the process of drawing down European regeneration funding, has been of particular significance as a focus for the energies of community activists and the other key players of the regeneration game.

In addition, there is now the added complexity of other initiatives concerned with the regeneration of Liverpool: two Education Action Zones (one in Dingle/Granby/Toxteth, the other Speke–Garston), plus the Excellence in Cities initiative setting up a number of state-of-the-art learning centres; the Health Action Zone, covering Merseyside as a whole; Sure Start initiatives and Healthy Living Centres; the Employment Action Zone, including all of Liverpool; the various Safer Neighbourhood initiatives, together with some housing pilot schemes in neighbourhood management; a Sports Action Zone, covering the more disadvantaged areas around the city centre; and the major New Deal for Communities initiative in the Kensington part of the city.

Does this bewildering array of new regeneration initiatives, when added to the continuation of the Single Regeneration Budget, renewed Objective One funding, and the city-centre company Liverpool Vision, mean that Liverpool really can at last look forward to the end of decline, and to the beginning of renaissance?

The Role of Civic and Political Leadership

Much depends on the ability of Liverpool's political, civic, business and voluntary sector leaders to develop a coherent vision for Liverpool's future, and to find the means to ensure its practical implementation. A crucial ingredient in Liverpool's decline has been the past failure of vision and of strategic action by Liverpool's civic leadership, set within the context of broader structural determinants of local economic decline and national political trends that were antithetical to the city's progress.

During the 1970s, Liverpool developed a reputation for 'Toytown' politics, with uninspiring political leadership bobbing between the Labour Party and the Liberals, and with the city's economic base inhibited, according to some academic commentators, by the 'penny off the rate' budgets of Liberal leader Sir Trevor Jones (Parkinson, 1987). The 1980s were dominated by the excesses of Liverpool's Militant regime. This period saw the 'no cuts in jobs and services' ideology, with the council tax beginning its climb to the unenviable top position in the council tax league table. There was a limited vision of new council houses and leisure centres to be provided at the expense of all other services (including education) and an in-built antagonism to the private sector, to the independent voluntary sector, and to any rapprochement with the then Conservative central government and its local or regional arms (such as the Merseyside Development Corporation).

Even these objectives were deeply flawed by a top-down command-style vision of local governance, 'municipal Stalinism' as the Liverpool Black Caucus (1986: 86) termed it, with a lack of the attention and resources necessary to ensuring sound, community-based management and upkeep for the new housing or leisure resources, many of which had fallen into serious disrepair by the mid- to late 1990s.

The city council was deeply, nearly terminally, wounded by this experience, which was followed by a period of Labour rule, increasingly without an overall majority. However, some signs of civic progress could be identified, such as the City Challenge initiative which began the gradual transformation of the city centre (see Russell, 1994), while a degree of collaboration was achieved with the Merseyside Development Corporation and its successful reclamation of the derelict docklands area. The Local Pathways Partnership initiative began under Objective One, which itself led to one of the significant success stories of this period, the Speke–Garston Development Company (now extended to the Liverpool Land Development Company), which has overseen the extensive growth of a new set of industries in that area, with new private sector investment including several call centres, new leisure facilities, and new educational and training initiatives.

However, most commentators have pointed to the lack of strong political vision and effective managerial leadership of the city council in this period. This was the overwhelming consensus of a survey of 50 of Liverpool's key policy-makers conducted in 1996–97 (Ben-Tovim, 1997). The lack of an overall political majority, allied with a tradition of a strongly partisan local political culture, led to a context in which the city council was seen by its potential local and national partners as an organisation that could not take decisions, and the ones that were taken were not always particularly good ones.

At the same time, there was no powerful business community or alternative civic leadership to push the city forwards as a whole, except perhaps the remarkable double act of former Bishop David Sheppard and former Archbishop Derek Worlock, the city's strongest champions in its most difficult period during the 1980s (see Sheppard and Worlock, 1988: 9). However, in certain areas, such as further and higher education, the housing associations, the business and development sectors, the arts, and the voluntary and community sector, there were significant strands of outward-going and entrepreneurial activity that helped to promote developments in certain sectors of institutional life, both in the city centre and elsewhere.

But progress in disparate strands of Liverpool life, however significant, does not substitute for a coherent overall political vision for the city, or for concerted, strategic partnership action. That does not mean that strategies or partnerships were lacking. On the contrary, Liverpool has been criticised for having too many strategies, too many partnerships, but not enough joined-up implementation, as argued by the Report by the IDEA (1999) into Liverpool's management; while the championing of the city by bishops and vice-chancellors does not make up for a lack of civic leadership.

This takes us back to the current context, in which there is a renewed political and managerial will to take the city forward. There is a clear political majority held by the Liberal Democrats, as a result of their successful attack on the voters' 'high council tax/ poor council services' perception of the previous Labour regime. There is also a renewed managerial team under the Chief Executive, who has radically restructured Liverpool City Council after a successful 'can-do' experience at neighbouring Knowsley Borough Council. Across the council, there is a strong formal commitment to building more strategic and effective partnerships with the complex range of local, sub-regional, regional, national and international players that can influence the city's destiny (Liverpool First, 1999).

But given the complex array of new initiatives, the range of local partnerships, and the scale and diversity of alternative sources of authority and funding that characterise Liverpool, how far will it be possible for there to emerge a single vision, a single partnership and a single implementation mechanism? And how far could such a development hold to an approach that would impact on the most vulnerable and disadvantaged sections of the community as well as acting as a 'booster' for the city's image? How far can the new Liverpool of the twenty-first century serve the interests both of the successful, wealth-creating 'enterprise city' and of the welfare-oriented 'hurt city' (Sheppard and Worlock, 1998)?

A Directly Elected Mayor for Liverpool?

Here, the debate about new forms of local governance, including the idea of a locally elected mayor, could be of particular significance. The concept of a directly elected mayor could have been invented for Liverpool. The government's White Paper *Modern Local Government* (DETR, 1998), followed by the Bill and later Act *Local Leadership, Local Choice* (DETR, 1999), suggest that an elected mayor could help reawaken interest in local government, in a context where active participation in terms of voting has reached extremely low levels: in Liverpool there was a particularly notorious by-election in Melrose ward in 1996 polling a mere 6 per cent of the electorate, with regular average turn-outs in the city of not much more than 20 per cent – a real crisis of legitimacy for city councillors (Ben-Tovim, 1998).

An elected mayor could provide a strong, single voice and champion for the city, working closely with the city's MPs and MEPs. As we have seen, Liverpool has had a weak tradition of civic leadership, a plethora of partnerships with limited implementation and too little joined-up action, and has found it difficult to shake off the post-Militant reputation as a city with a negative political image. An elected mayor could help Liverpool begin to play a more significant role in the region, an opportunity to catch up for the lost years in which Manchester has soared ahead as the success story of the northwest (Ben-Tovim, 1999).

A future vision of Liverpool, then, might have included a cutting-edge form of civic governance with Liverpool as the first major city outside London to choose the route of a directly elected mayor. This was advocated by the independent Liverpool Democracy Commission (1999), which suggested a number of radical reforms, including a elected mayor, in their study *Future – The Leading of Liverpool*. These were, however, rejected by the leadership of the city council, which used the poor public response to its own low-key consultation exercise to legitimise its refusal to hold a formal referendum on the issue. Whatever its potential benefits, there now seems to be no local political will to progress this initiative any further.

... Or an Elected Regional Assembly for the Northwest?

An option more likely to win local political support is for Liverpool to become one of the 'twin capitals' (NWDA, 2000) of a devolved Northwest Region. The northwest already has a Development Agency and an indirectly elected Regional Assembly, made up of councillors from across the region and 'non-local authority' partners, including the trade unions, employers, further and higher education institutions and the like. The Assembly has already set up a Constitutional Convention, which is examining options for regional governance.

Thus pressure is building up for the Assembly's transformation into a directly elected body with enhanced powers, enabling the region to lobby more successfully for regional aid to the northwest and the weighting of mainline services to take account of relevant deprivation factors when considering intervention and support (see Campaign for the English Regions, 2000).

The national government was initially lukewarm on the issue of regional devolution after the relatively weak support for Welsh devolution and the problems of the London mayoral election. But the louder the London-based argument that there is no real 'north/south divide', the stronger has become the pressure for a degree of devolution for the northwest, to enable it to compete more successfully with other regions of Britain. The government's acceptance through the Regional Assemblies (Preparations) Act 2003 of the option for local referendums to establish a regional assembly provides an opportunity for Liverpool to reposition itself at the heart of the new democratic, modernising political agenda, acting as a focal point for economic, social and cultural development and renewal in Liverpool and the surrounding Merseyside region, as well as playing its part in the regeneration of the northwest.

However, this will require Liverpool to develop the skills of building political alliances with the other Merseyside authorities as well as across the northwest. Since the abolition of the Merseyside County Council, the Merseyside authorities have not always presented a strong coherent voice, and rivalry with Manchester has a long history. Mutual mistrust has perhaps been accentuated more recently by the different political colour of the key authorities: all the Merseyside authorities, Manchester and much of Greater Manchester are Labour-led, unlike Liverpool with its Liberal Democrat leadership. In the new Europe of the Regions, Liverpool needs to be part of a strong, unified Merseyside to hold its own within the northwest.

There is a danger that the forging of these bi-partisan alliances could be stymied by the political aspirations of the Liverpool leadership and the antagonism of the other authorities – problems that require resolution by mature, consensual civic leadership rather than the adversarial style of conventional electoral politics. What then are the key challenges facing a coherent, ambitious and non-sectarian political and civic leadership? What is a viable vision for Liverpool, given its strengths, its economic base, its population make-up, its geographical position and its environment? Where might Liverpool be positioned locally, within the Merseyside sub-region, regionally within the northwest as it celebrates its 800th birthday in the year 2007, and also within the national and global contexts?

Liverpool as City of Culture?

There has been a growing recognition within Liverpool that the European Capital of Culture competition has provided an enormous opportunity for the city to reinvent itself, in the same way that Glasgow did with the 'it's miles better' campaign and its success as European City of Culture, and later City of Architecture and Design. Liverpool has many assets that could provide some of the key ingredients for a successful rebranding. It has one of the largest collections of museums and galleries outside London, uniquely established as a department of the National Museums and Galleries, with few of its cultural assets under direct local authority control – a legacy of the abolition of the Merseyside County Council coinciding with the onset of Militant control of Liverpool City Council.

Linked to the museums is the superb set of neo-classical buildings, with St George's Hall at the centre. The city boasts the distinguished Royal Liverpool Philharmonic Orchestra, one of only four world-class provincial orchestras, albeit suffering from long-standing local authority underfunding, with little from the Merseyside authorities outside Liverpool despite their constituents supplying a high proportion of the orchestra's audiences. It has a history of innovative theatre (although suffering a period of decline in the 1990s), and high-quality writing associated with this, from nationally acclaimed authors such as Alan Bleasdale, Ken Campbell, Jimmy McGovern and Willy Russell. Many of these writers were given their first opportunities by the Liverpool theatres in their 1970s heyday, as were celebrated actors such as Pete Postlethwaite, Jonathan Pryce, Kathy Tyson and Julie Walters. And there is of course the whole Beatles connection, as well as the residue of the 1960s/1970s poetry and Merseybeat scene, when Liverpool really seemed to be 'the pool of life'; there are also the strong sporting traditions, particularly football, but also horse racing (the Grand National at Aintree) and golf (notably Royal Birkdale at Southport).

But there is a danger of Liverpool defining itself culturally within a narrow framework of nostalgia, traditionalism and yesterday's successes, rather than looking to the innovative and modern cultural industries more in tune with the new century. This move beyond simplistic and sentimental populism is crucial to the ability of Liverpool to reinvent itself in a sustainable manner.

There are certainly many examples of more modern and experimental cultural activity taking place in Liverpool. The city's superb architectural inheritance makes it a desirable location for the burgeoning local film and TV industry. Liverpool has pioneered the arts-linked use of information and communication technology, as seen in innovative video productions and the moves towards digitalisation demonstrated in the new FACT centre; Liverpool is a real centre of excellence in contemporary visual arts, evidenced in developments at Tate Liverpool, Bluecoat Arts Centre and the Liverpool Biennale; and there is a wealth of musical traditions, pioneering work in dance and design, and a range of talented individuals and groups from Liverpool's ethnic minority communities showcasing their abilities in local festivals.

The Capital of Culture project provides Liverpool with an important opportunity for reinvention if it can reflect and mobilise the talent in the city, and counteract some of the key dimensions of social exclusion, among them exclusion from the cultural world.

The danger is of a backward-looking approach, based on nostalgia, the Beatles and a low-skill bar economy, providing heightened interest for an ephemeral tourist market and an improved consumer lifestyle for the relatively affluent, but contributing little to the real extension of sustainable employment and business opportunities and skills for the local citizens. But a dynamic, forward-looking, inclusive cultural strategy would, if successful, bring enormous benefit for the reinvention of Liverpool.

Towards a High-skill Economic Infrastructure: City of Learning?

The City of Culture could, then, be one important strand of Liverpool's future. But this needs to be linked closely into educational and training developments, as the key to Liverpool's future success, and its transition from a low-skill to a high-skill economy, lies in the transformation of its education system.

As we have seen, Liverpool's overall level of educational attainment falls significantly behind the national average, particularly at school level. Too many people leave school in Liverpool with limited formal educational achievements, with poor basic skills, and at severe risk of perpetuating a cycle of low skills, long-term unemployment, poverty, ill health and vulnerability to crime (see Ofsted, 1999; KPMG, 1999; MTEC, 1999; Liverpool First, 1999). This means that too many of its citizens are locked out of the opportunities emerging from the knowledge-based economy, which limits the ability of the newer electronic industries to achieve a critical mass as a basis for real success in Liverpool and Merseyside. This in turn can make the city less attractive to graduates than other parts of the country, and can encourage businesses to invest elsewhere, or else to recruit from outside the area for skilled staff.

On the other hand, it has become increasingly recognised that education is one of the most significant sectors in the local and regional economy (see FEDA, 1998; NWAOC, 1999). There is a huge student presence in the city, with the two universities, a university college, and a large further education community college, all of which are committed to supporting the city's regeneration, as well as to educating local and mature students in addition to the more conventional student base. Thus a number of flagship education projects, including Blackburne House Women's Centre, the Liverpool Institute of Performing Arts, Liverpool Community College's four new centres, and Liverpool Hope in Everton, have helped bring high-quality buildings back into use, and to regenerate surrounding areas.

It was this perception of the potential significance of the education sector that led to the establishment in the early 1990s of the 'City of Learning' initiative (Ben-Tovim, 1992; DfEE, 1998b) – a sound vision, but one that was in practice difficult to transform into a high level of organisational synergy, perhaps because of the fragmentation and competition of the education sector encouraged by the previous Conservative government.

It is this problem of sectionalism that is crucial to the failure so far of Liverpool to live up to the 'City of Learning' vision. Thus the educational and training landscape is filled by an enormous range of providers, as a result of the competitive ethos introduced by the Conservative governments from 1979 to 1997, the stripping of a number of functions from the local authorities, the creation and then demise of the Training and Enterprise Council, and the fragmentation of funding encouraged by Single Regeneration and European funding. As a result, a huge number of players is involved in every aspect of post-16 education and training, with universities, colleges, the local education authority, private training providers and community organisations all offering courses in an unplanned, market-driven fashion, with scant regard for duplication or gaps, and with no rigorous city-wide overview of quality. And yet there is extensive need in basic skills (Moser, 1999), as well as a range of local and regional skills shortages. It remains to be seen whether the present government's attempts at a more integrated, more inclusive and less competitive system (DfEE, 1998a; 1999a; Kennedy, 1997), the work of new Local Learning and Skills Councils (DfEE, 1999b), and the attempt at local strategic coordination by the Liverpool Lifelong Learning Partnership can really lead to a tightly planned but flexible system of post-16 education and training that can radically improve participation rates, raise standards from basic skills levels upwards, and overcome skills shortages (DfES, 2002).

Schools, in Liverpool's case already divided through the very large voluntary aided sector, have also been encouraged to play the same competitive game, to secure enhanced funding and to guarantee financial survival. The 1999 Ofsted inspection of Liverpool's education service and the KPMG report pointed to an education authority that had failed to provide a stable political decision-making environment, a sufficiently challenging performance management culture, and adequate financial investment in education, through which to secure higher levels of educational achievement within Liverpool schools.

These results have in the past been interpreted locally as a reflection of levels of poverty and unemployment in the city, and also of the divided educational system whereby the majority of comprehensive schools have in fact been de facto secondary modern schools, the voluntary aided sector largely acting as the selective 'grammar school' segment. But clearly an educational 'third way' (Giddens, 1998) needs to acknowledge both the weight of structural and organisational constraints and the possibility of unpromising schools being 'turned around' by high-quality management and teaching.

The Ofsted/KPMG reports led to the wholesale restructuring of the education service, the appointment of a new tier of senior managers and a range of new PFI schools. Again, the jury is out on whether these changes, supported by more generous levels of national funding for education than under previous central governments, together with the Education Action Zones, Excellence in Cities and Sure Start initiatives, as well as the government's literacy and numeracy hours, can make a radical transformation in the levels of educational participation and achievement in the more disadvantaged areas of the city.

This step-change in educational achievement is essential not only to enhance the talent and potential of Liverpool's citizens and hence to strengthen the city's skill base, but also to help attract investment and new talent into the city and to retain people with a high level of skills. This will require the highest level of political commitment, managerial and professional skill, council and city-wide coordination, corporate prioritisation, and inter-agency planning, all of which have in the past proved too difficult to achieve in the face of intractable socio-economic obstacles, as well as institutional autonomy and competition.

From the Social Exclusion of Decline to the Social Inclusion of Regeneration?

It is certainly part of the language of every new social inclusion and regeneration initiative that steps must be taken to encourage people to improve their levels of skills and training in order to improve their own employability and the competitiveness of the city and regions. It is crucial to the strategy of the government, the Northwest Regional Development Agency, the new Objective One programme for Merseyside, and Liverpool's regeneration prospectus, 'Liverpool First' (1999). But whether this will remain simply rhetoric, or be translated into reality, depends crucially on the ability of civic and regional governance to ensure that there is rigorous planned intervention, so that appropriate agencies are enabled to carry out funded, long-term coordinated programmes of action.

There has certainly been a range of local community-based regeneration initiatives across Liverpool, linked particularly to the Objective One programme as well as to the Single Regeneration Budget. There have been a number of one-off developments in education and training, child-care, community safety, health promotion, environmental improvement and business creation. There have been varying levels of community involvement in the programmes of action developed at local level, and in the 'partnerships', restructured into 'clusters' and 'strategic investment areas', which have again had mixed degrees of involvement by the private and public sector.

But there has been relatively little by way of strategic city-wide intervention in the regeneration process as opposed to a reshuffle of localised organisational frameworks – a range of ad hoc, short-term schemes by local community networks or partnerships, who have had to enter into competition with one another to secure funding. Thus the positive strand of community 'empowerment' needs to be set alongside the dangers of 'Balkanisation', the fragmentation of the city into separate fiefdoms with the further isolation of poor neighbourhoods and parochialism, which has meant that a community's problems, such as educational underperformance and skills shortages, have not in practice been dealt with in a holistic manner.

A really successful strategic approach requires more than the rush to short-term funding-induced activity. What is needed is the active implementation of city-wide measures to ensure the coordination of all relevant resources and the active, long-term involvement of the major, mainstream institutions, targeting and redistributing their resources where necessary to reach the most disadvantaged. This approach, however, has at times been rejected by mainstream institutions failing to alter conventional organisational and funding regimes which have under-resourced poorer communities; but also by community activists, in terms of a localist ideology that rejects 'outsiders' in favour of small-scale 'local' groups or agencies that may not be able to deliver a high-quality service or meaningful employment opportunities or, as with education, provide appropriate qualifications and progression routes to higher level skills. Thus an outlook rooted perhaps in an experience of the fickle, self-interested 'parachutism' of big players may also have self-defeating outcomes.

Some local research (e.g., Kyprianou, 1999; Andersen et al., 1999) has also suggested that regeneration programmes may not so far have genuinely engaged a wide cross-section of the community but may have been dominated, particularly in the early stages, by a small number of 'professional' community activists and social entrepreneurs. Some of these activists may have long-standing political histories and connections, and they work alongside a small number of regeneration consultancies dealing with the funding and application maze. There are clear dangers of conflicts of interests, and of the regeneration process being distorted to meet the vested interests of a relatively small group of politically sophisticated and vocal activists, rather than meeting the real, long-term needs of the whole community, particularly the socially excluded. Again, research has suggested that public and private agencies may pay lip-service to community involvement, while continuing to pursue their own competitive and protectionist institutional agendas, particularly where the Black community is involved (Ben-Tovim et al., 1998).

Here the outcome of the government's more recent initiatives such as New Deal for Communities and the Neighbourhood Renewal Fund will be of particular interest, with Liverpool piloting new developments and receiving considerable levels of new funding (Social Exclusion Unit, 2000). The rhetoric of the government, echoing that of the city council, is to talk about the virtues of the Liverpool programme as being based on real community involvement, and genuine partnership between the community and other players.

It is crucial that those leading and monitoring the initiatives, at council, community and government level, ensure that this partnership involvement is broadly based, and that long-term, high-quality initiatives in education, training, employment and quality of life are developed that are not dominated by parochialism or vested interests.

Council and government officials, as well as the political players involved, need to have the courage, sophistication and vision to judge the success of these regeneration initiatives, not by a naïve suspension of judgement before a forceful 'community' voice, or by party political expediency, or by the professionally easy route of ensuring short-term tick-box outputs, but by the sustainable outcomes secured with equity for all the different strands of the local community.

The New Deal for Communities is particularly significant because of its potential for a more holistic and long-term approach to social exclusion than has been possible by means of the other initiatives. A major problem of the activities of the new Labour government since its election in 1997 has been the plethora of disjointed, departmentalised 'zone' style initiatives taken in the fields of education, employment, health, childcare, community safety and sports, the 'initiative-itis' described by the Social Exclusion Unit (1998: 38). These small-scale actions have been widely welcomed in themselves, but they have also been seen to compound further the complexity of the range of different local authority directorates, central government departments and quangos, with their unique ways of working and funding regimes, along with additional uncoordinated sources of funding such as the National Lottery. The government has itself acknowledged the need to create 'joined-up' ways of thinking and acting to secure real progress in overcoming social exclusion (see Social Exclusion Unit, 1998; 2000), and therefore it is essential that the New Deal for Communities is seen not as another new and separate initiative but as the test-bed for the coordination of the various new programmes, leading to a clear set of policies and forms of intervention that can be replicated across the city.

Joined-up Initiatives to Improve the Quality of Life

The outline of what such a 'joined-up' strategy could look like has already been developed through many of the disparate regeneration activities in Liverpool in recent years, in particular through the work of the Liverpool Partnership Group/ Liverpool First Board, which has brought together all of the city's key public sector agencies and has produced a comprehensive strategic framework and action plan under the aegis of the *New Commitment to Regeneration* (Liverpool First, 1999).

Part of the vision for Liverpool's future has to encompass the gradual improvement in the quality of life in Liverpool's most disadvantaged local areas. There have been piecemeal improvements in the quality of housing in some of the worst estates, through Estate Action, Housing Action Trust, Estate Renewal Challenge Fund, and partnerships between the city council, tenants and housing associations in enabling stock transfer to new housing companies. This process is likely to continue through the Housing Market Renewal Initiative, requiring these partnerships to be strengthened to deal in a strategic, coordinated way with the real problems of lack of demand for social housing, and the need for high levels of expenditure in both council and housing association stock, to recreate viable, mixed-tenure communities.

This will require difficult decisions to be taken over renewal, rehabilitation and demolition, necessitating genuine community involvement, firm non-competitive professional advice by council officers and housing associations and non-sectarian political leadership, to ensure that community need and rational planning are not overcome by professional and political self-interest. But it is essential to learn from the failures of the past that physical improvement has to be complemented by a range of other interventions.

Pockets of experience in Liverpool have shown that imaginative, joined-up thinking and action can link housing improvement with training and job creation in the various processes involved (community engagement, project management, house building, community warden schemes), though sharply targeted approaches are needed to ensure that ethnic minorities get a fair share of available opportunities. Environmental programmes, to deal with litter, dog fouling, graffiti, dumping and derelict sites, recycling and waste management, and energy conservation are, in some cases, being coordinated with new housing programmes, and antisocial behaviour projects, as with the pioneering neighbourhood management work of the 'Include' partnership. Again, these can be used to raise skills and create jobs or community-based businesses, as can initiatives to improve security within the home, or by alley-gating and CCTV schemes.

Again, health promotion and improvement programmes, with local health and fitness centres and primary care developments, provide further opportunities for employment and training initiatives as well as contributing to improved quality of life. Through the Sure Start initiative, and other sources of funding, schemes are being developed to improve early years provision, and to link social services, health provision, education and libraries. The aim is to provide a comprehensive package of intervention and support for families with young children, improving access to vital services, raising levels of awareness of parents and improving the health and educational potential of young children; possibilities are also opened up for parents to enhance their own education and skills, and therefore facilitate access to sustainable, high-quality employment. Educational initiatives such as Education Action Zones and Excellence in Cities, breakfast and after-school clubs, summer schools, learning support units, mentoring programmes and heightened IT facilities are being used to provide extra support for students at risk of educational failure, exclusion or underachievement.

But there is a limit to the impact of small-scale, pepper-potting local initiatives on the life-chances of Liverpool's citizens, even if they become more integrated by some form of neighbourhood management (Social Exclusion Unit, 1998). Where interventions are clearly of benefit, they need to be spread across the city as quickly as possible, not simply remaining the preserve of a few pilot areas. Sustainable regeneration will only occur if extra sources of moneys are integrated with mainstream funding that is bent and shaped to meet the needs of the more disadvantaged areas and groups; and if regeneration forms of working, community-focused and partnership-based, become built into normal service delivery.

This means that a clear commitment is required by mainstream institutions not to retreat to their bunkers when they have dealt with the regeneration add-on, but to move to a new culture and style of working that put the holistic needs of local communities and individual citizens before the sectional interests and traditional routines and mechanisms for resource distribution of autonomous organisations or departments. This returns us to the need for city-wide, strategic leadership, to keep hold of the broader vision necessary to knit together the plethora of uncoordinated local and ad hoc programmes that are beginning to make small-scale impact, but are incapable on their own, without the coherent targeting of effort together with the combining of resources at a level that will enable their redistribution, of making the most of the new opportunities to transform the fortunes of the city.

Linking the 'Hurt' City and the 'Enterprise' City for Liverpool's Renewal

It is possible, then, on the basis of the success of some of the disparate regeneration activity taking place across Liverpool, to envisage the gradual improvement in the quality of life in Liverpool's more disadvantaged localities. This can emerge through the strategic coordination of the work of the city's main agencies, a more corporate style of working on the part of the city council itself, the integration of mainstream and regeneration funding which links local, regional and central government activities into a coherent whole, and the rolling out of the government's national programmes and policies to combat poverty and social exclusion and to support the move of poorer families from dependency on welfare benefits into education, training and the labour market.

All this will require a focused, ambitious civic leadership, supported perhaps by a strengthened northwest with its own directly elected Regional Assembly. The crucial role of this leadership will be to increase confidence in the city's ability to deliver in terms of the key services of education, health, housing and environmental improvement, community safety, transport and planning, many of which are dependent on successful partnership working with key local, regional and national agencies.

If the civic leadership can create the appropriate climate of internal and external confidence, and can deliver (directly or by partnership mechanisms) services that enhance the skills of local residents and secure the quality of life that external investors (including the government) are seeking, then further business and employment opportunities will be created for residents in the more disadvantaged parts of the city, in addition to the opportunities emerging from the regeneration initiatives themselves. This is not to suggest that there will be an automatic trickle-down of benefit. Robust mechanisms to link new investment with local people, including targeted approaches to reach out to minority groups and to improve the educational and skills levels of the more disadvantaged citizens, are essential. Otherwise there are dangers that Liverpool's rising values and mini-boom in construction, flat development and the leisure industry will lead to short-term speculative growth, resulting in the further polarisation of Liverpool as a dual city, with patterns of working-class and minority group exclusion exacerbated rather than diminished.

But the metamorphosis of Ford into Jaguar within a transformed Speke–Garston indicates the possibility of reinvention and renewal that lies ahead for Liverpool in the new millennium. The decline in Liverpool's population and its limited heavy industrial presence can be turned into positive assets, with the possibility of making Liverpool a gracious city with superb parks and attractive open spaces, matching the unrivalled architecture of much of the city. The City of Culture vision, linked to the City of Learning theme, with a 'wired-up city' sub-text, could provide both a significant rebranding of the city, and a pointer to Liverpool repositioning itself at the heart of the new twenty-first century knowledge-based cultural and electronic industries. The compact and relatively unspoilt city centre has the prospect of major investment and transformation through the Liverpool Vision partnership of central, regional and local government and the private sector, making it an attractive mix of living, retail, office, educational and leisure quarters. Finally, the innovative and articulate voluntary, community and social economy sectors, reflecting the resilience, wit and creativity of Liverpudlians, provide the possibility of a vibrant social infrastructure that can help ensure that the city's urban renaissance is truly inclusive of all its citizens, including the most disadvantaged.

Of course national policies and global trends will have an enormous impact on Liverpool's prospects, particularly given the very significant levels of unemployment and poverty that are so deep-seated in the city. But it has become increasingly recognised that cities do have the capacity to affect their own destinies, and to overcome some of the more intractable socio-economic problems through clear, committed and imaginative political leadership, solid city-wide partnerships and high-quality civic management (see Nystrom, 1999; Rogers, 1999).

There are signs that Liverpool is beginning to reverse its historic decline. Parts of the city are booming; a focused managerial team has taken radical steps to reduce council costs and to improve services; a clear political majority has facilitated council decision making; there is a return of civic ambition as seen in the Capital of Culture project; and additional central government and European Union funding is gradually making some impact on the still heavy legacy of poverty and unemployment. But improvements are still fragile and reversible. Continuing underperformance on a range of key indicators remains deep-seated and the social exclusion of working-class and minority communities persists.

Liverpool, with all of its natural assets – a stunning waterfront, superb architecture,

beautiful parks, prestigious and innovative cultural traditions, an influential educational infrastructure with the potential to create a truly knowledge-based local
economy, an uncluttered, potentially spacious and attractive city centre, easy access
to the pleasant environment of the northwest, a strong voluntary sector and an inventive, diverse and enduring people – has the potential to achieve an outstanding quality
of life for all: whether its civic leadership can deliver remains to be seen.

References

Anderson, H., Munck, R., et al. (1999), *Neighbourhood Images in Liverpool: 'It's All Down to the People'*, York: Joseph Rowntree Foundation

Audit Commission (2000), *Comparative Figures for Local Authority Services 1998–1999*, London: Audit Commission

Audit Commission (2002), *Comprehensive Performance Assessment of Local Authorities 2002*, London: Audit Commission

Ben-Tovim, G. S. (1992), 'Liverpool – A City of Learning for the '90s', *Municipal Review*, 729 (July)

— (1997), 'Liverpool Renewed – Visions for a 21st Century City', unpublished paper, Department of Sociology, University of Liverpool

— (1998), 'Local Democracy and the Local State', in *It's Our Party – Democratic Problems in Local Government*, London: Local Government Management Board

— (1999), 'A Quiet Revolution', *New Local Government Network News* (Sept–Oct)

Ben-Tovim, G. S., Brown, M., Kyprianou, P., and Rooney, B. (1998), 'Poverty, Race and Partnership – A Study of the Third European Anti-Poverty Programme in Liverpool', in M. Lavalette et al. (eds), *Anti-Racism and Social Welfare*, Aldershot: Ashgate

Bishop of Liverpool (2000), *Report of Commission of Inquiry into the Somali Community in Liverpool*, Merseyside Broad-based Organisation

Bryson, Bill (1996), *Notes from a Small Island*, London: Black Swan

Campaign for the English Regions (2000), *Democratic Regions Newsletter*, 1(1)

CURS (Centre for Urban and Regional Studies) (1999), *Measuring the Sustainability of Neighbourhoods in Liverpool*, Birmingham: CURS, University of Birmingham

DETR (Department for the Environment, Transport and the Regions) (1998), *Modern Local Government – In Touch with the People* (Cm 4014), London: The Stationery Office

— (1999), *Local Leadership, Local Choice*, London: DETR

DfEE (Department of Education and Employment) (1998a), *The Learning Age – A Renaissance for a New Britain* (Cm 3790), London: The Stationery Office

— (1998b), *Learning Towns, Learning Cities*, London: DfEE

— (1999a), *Learning to Succeed – A New Framework for Post-16 Learning* (Cm 4392), London: The Stationery Office

— (1999b), *Learning and Skills Council Prospectus*, London: DfEE

DfES (Department for Education and Skills) (2002), *Success for All*, London: DfES

FEDA (Further Education Development Agency) (1998), *Further Education –
    Aspects of Economic Development*, London: FEDA

Giddens, A. (1998), *The Third Way*, Cambridge: Polity Press

IDEA (Local Government Improvement and Development Agency) (1999),
    Report: Liverpool City Council, London: IDEA

Kennedy, H. (1997), *Learning Works – Widening Participation in Further Education*,
    London: Further Education Funding Council

KPMG (1999), *Liverpool Education Service Consultancy Project*, London: DfEE

Kyprianou, P. (1999), *Community Participation and Partnership – A Review of
    Community Participation in the Liverpool Objective One Partnerships*, Liverpool:
    Liverpool Euro Community Network

Liverpool Black Caucus (1986), *The Racial Politics of Militant – The Black
    Community's Struggle for Participation in Local Politics 1980–1986*, ed. G. Ben-
    Tovim, London: Runnymede Trust

Liverpool City Council (2000), *A Challenge to Change – Report of the Equal
    Opportunities Public Review*, Liverpool: Liverpool City Council

— (2002), *Race Equality Scheme and Race Equality Action Plan 2002–2005*,
    Liverpool: Liverpool City Council

Liverpool Democracy Commission (1999), *Future – The Leading of Liverpool*,
    Liverpool: New Local Government Network

Liverpool First (1999), *The Prospectus – Liverpool Partnership Group*, Liverpool:
    Liverpool City Council

Liverpool Health Authority (2001), *Liverpool's Health 2001*, Liverpool: LHA

Liverpool Partnership Group (2002), *Liverpool First Workbook 2002–2005*,
    Liverpool: Liverpool City Council

Liverpool Vision (1999), *City Centre Vision – Baseline Study*, Liverpool: Building
    Design Partnership et al.

— (2000), *Liverpool Vision Regeneration Strategy – Outline Draft Strategy*,
    Liverpool: Skidmore, Owings & Merill et al.

MTEC (1999), *Merseyside Labour Market Assessment*, Liverpool: Merseyside
    Economic Forum

Moser, C. (1999), *Improving Literacy and Numeracy – A Fresh Start*, London:
    DfEE

NWAOC (1999), *Further Education – A Region-wide Resource for Learning, Training
    and Development*, Warrington: NWDA/AOC

NWDA (2000), *England's North West – A Strategy towards 2020*, Warrington:
    Northwest Development Agency

Nystrom, L. (1999), *City and Culture – Cultural Processes and Urban Sustainability*,
    Stockholm: Swedish Urban Environment Council

Ofsted (1999), *Inspection of Liverpool Local Education Authority*, London: Office of
    Her Majesty's Chief Inspector of Schools/Audit Commission

Parkinson, M. (1987), *City on the Brink*, Bristol: Policy Press

Rogers, Lord (1999), *Towards an Urban Renaissance – Final Report of the Urban
    Task Force*, London: DETR

Russell, H. (1994), *Liverpool City Challenge – Evaluation Report*, Liverpool: European Institute of Urban Affairs, Liverpool John Moores University

Sheppard, D., and Worlock, D. (1988), *Better Together*, London: Hodder & Stoughton

— (1998), *With Hope in our Hearts*, London: Hodder & Stoughton

Social Exclusion Unit (1998), *Bringing Britain Together – A National Strategy for Neighbourhood Renewal* (Cmd 4045), London: HMSO

— (2000), *National Strategy for Neighbourhood Renewal – A Framework for Consultation*, London: Cabinet Office

South Liverpool Personnel (2000), *Just Where do Black People Work in Liverpool City Centre?*, Liverpool: South Liverpool Personnel

Index

248   *Reinventing the City?*

capitalism
    disorganised 57, 59
    and urban deprivation 191–2
car industry 227, 243
car use (private) 31, 162
Caradog Jones Survey 123
Cardiff 39, 129
Caribbean Community Centre, Liverpool
    132
Castells, Manuel 2, 3, 13
Catholic Church 132
Census 1991 125
Census 2001 3, 27, 54, 70
central governance 84
central government
    and regeneration 60–1, 64–5, 76–7
    strengthening of 60–1
    see also Conservative governments;
        Labour governments
Chaplin, E. 195, 196
Charles Wootton College, Liverpool 130–1
Chester 70
Chicago school 191
Child Poverty Action Group 145
childcare services 114–15, 117, 119, 131
children
    disadvantaged 144–57
    lack of discipline 114
    lack of local services for 115–16, 117–18
    out-of-control 166–7
    women's responsibility for looking after
        114–16, 117–18, 119
Chinatown, Liverpool 122, 124, 125, **127**,
    128, 132–5, **134**, 138–41, 228
Chinese Arch, Chinatown 124, 133, 228
Chinese community 122, 123, 124–5, 126,
    128, 132–5, 136, 137–41
cities
    analysis 191–2
    anthropomorphication 87
    colonial 39
    divided 23, 27–30
    ecological perspective 191
    global 1–5, 7, 23, 36–42, 49
    heterogeneity 28
    homogeneity 7, 26–7
    interconnectedness 6–7
    political economy approach to 191
    post-colonial 4
    post-Fordist 82, 83–7, 90–1
    post-industrial 4, 5
    postmodern 1–5, 15, 30

privatised 23, 30–3
reinvention 24–5
representation in images 194–207, **199**,
    201, 203, 206, 208
spatial polarisation 192
text as 13–14, 15
citizenship, education for 148, 157
Citizenship Advisory Group 148
City Action Teams 60
city centres
    contracts with inner cities 26
    regeneration 66–7
City Challenge 62, 63, 66, 104, 211, 232
'City of Learning' initiative 237, 243
City of Liverpool Handbook 1930 48
'city living' 227
    see also 'loft living'; 'urban living'
civic engagement 16
civic leadership 231–3, 238, 242–3, 244
civil society 16–17, 60, 61, 86–7
closed-circuit television (CCTV) cameras
    31–2
Cochrane, A. 89
Cockburn, T. 154
Coles, B. 144
colonial mode of production 37, 38, 39
Combat Poverty Agency, Ireland 212, 224
Commonwealth 45, 48
communitarianism 16, 17
communities 178–9, 182–4, 231
    Balkanisation 239
    of Dingle 205–6
    fractured 28
    fragmented 184, 186, 223
    gated 32
    intolerant/closed 16
    and older people 162–4, 165–7, 170–1
    participation 98–100, 101–3, 105
    self-help 182–3, 190
    of Speke 200
    and young people 186
community consultations 15–17, 187
community development 5, 211–25, 238–9
    accountability 221–2
    defining 212–13
    funding 211–12, 214, 217, 222, 225
Community Development Foundation
    (CDF) 213, 223
Community Development Projects 57–8,
    177
Community Empowerment Fund 211–12,
    214